BR MOTIVE POWER ALLOCATIONS 1959-1968

I: BR STANDARDS & AUSTERITIES

BR
MOTIVE POWER
ALLOCATIONS
1959-1968

I:
BR STANDARDS
& AUSTERITIES

PAUL TEAL

LONDON

IAN ALLAN LTD

Half title:
WD 2-8-0 No 90044 stands off duty at York MPD on 23 October 1965. *E. F. Bentley*

Previous page:
'Britannia' class 4-6-0 No 70050 *Firth of Clyde* is seen under the coaling plant at Leeds Holbeck MPD. *J. S. Whiteley*

Front cover:
No 75021 seen inside Wrexham shed in July 1965. *G. N. Kneale*

Back cover, top:
No 92223 at Patricroft in 1967. *J. R. Carter*

Back cover, bottom:
No 90155 at Darlington on 26 June 1964. *Dr D. P. Williams*

Right:
BR Standard Class 9 2-10-0 No 92066 (52H) surrounded by ash and clinker, at Tyne Dock MPD 19 May 1964. No 92066 was one of 10 Class 9s fitted with Westinghouse air compressors for working the Tyne Dock-Consett iron ore traffic. They were mounted on the right-hand side and can be seen in the photograph just above the centre driving wheels. *P. H. Groom*

Contents

First published 1985

ISBN 0 7110 1540 6

Published by Ian Allan Ltd, Shepperton, Surrey; and printed by Ian Allan Printing Ltd at their works at Coombelands in Runnymede, England.

Preface

The concept behind researching this project was to formulate a definitive list that would – through a system of locomotive allocations and important stock data – form a comprehensive record of British Railways motive power stock through the transitional years of the 1960s.

Its purpose, to inform the railway enthusiast of BR's changing traffic pattern and to alleviate the often exacting task of tracing engine allocations for the period under review.

This volume examines the BR Standard and WD Austerity locomotives numbered between 70000-92250, and records – where applicable – all locomotive names, allocations, re-allocations, depot code changes, dates of introduction and withdrawal from January 1959 to August 1968, the end of steam operation on BR.

Further summaries include, annual class stock and totals, the demise of each class in chronological order and surveys of BR's regional locomotive distribution and withdrawal programmes.

A key to all depots, depot codes and depot code changes, has been provided together with a selection of maps showing their respective locations. For enhanced readability and to reduce the need for cross-referencing, all engine allocations have been set out in full.

I would like to thank the many friends who helped with the preparation of this work, in particular, my long-standing friend John Corkingdale, his freely given help in times of need was most appreciated.

This book is dedicated to my parents Gordon Teal and Brenda Teal, for without their invaluable support I doubt this book would ever have reached completion.

Paul Teal
Walsall

Introduction to the Series

On 1 January 1959 British Railways possessed some 17,383 main line locomotives allocated to 326 motive power depots throughout the system.

By the end of December 1968 the number of locomotives had dwindled to a mere 4,704 stabled at 103 depots.

Of these figures it is perhaps interesting to note that of the locomotives remaining on 31 December 1968 4,205 were introduced after 1 January 1959. Therefore, during the last decade of steam operation, British Railways transition to diesel and electrics had resulted in the wholesale withdrawal of some 16,865 locomotives – 16,122 of which were steam.

This series sets out to record the allocation of these locomotives from 1 January 1959 to 31 December 1968.

For convenience, I have adopted the proven method of segregating the locomotives into a numbered series, ie:

Ex GWR locomotives numbered between 1000-9799
Ex SR locomotives numbered between 30021-35030
Ex LMSR locomotives numbered between 40001-58850
Ex LNER locomotives numbered between 60001-69936
BR locomotives numbered between 70000-92250
BR locomotives numbered between D1-15236

It is from this list that the allocated history of some 21,500 locomotives – either extant or in the course of introduction through the 1959 to 1968 period – will be recorded.

However, while every effort has been made to ensure accuracy, and the list is, I believe, definitive, with the number of locomotives surveyed, certain differences will inevitably arise, consequently, should any reader wish to contact me regarding corrections or omissions, I would gladly welcome their communication.

Below:
WD 2-10-0 No 90770 on shed at Motherwell (66B), 21 April 1961. *M. J. G. Howarth*

Explanatory notes about contents

The MPD list

As the course of this volume spans many years, the need to avoid confusion with BR's occasional re-organisation of certain depot codes has necessitated the formulation of a MPD coding system that could be utilised throughout the period under review.

The resulting list is a modified compilation of those depots extant from 1959 to 1968.

All transfers and code changes – whether boundary, Regional or general reshuffle – are listed *from the date the new code came into effect*. However, although each main line depot has been dealt with in situ, sub sheds, stabling and signing on points have not been included for locomotives attached to these locations were as a rule the responsibility of the parent depot from which they were allocated.

The map section: Depot locations

The location of each depot can be found under its respective code group. Code groupings are those at January 1959.

Locomotive allocations

Against each locomotive is shown the code and name of its home shed as at 1 January 1959. Its subsequent history of movements, if any, continues thereafter recording all changes affecting its allocation until final withdrawal.

Locomotives introduced after 1 January 1959 ie the Class 9 2–10–0s, commence from the date of introduction and continue as mentioned above.

Below:
BR Standard Class 6 4-6-2 No 72006 *Clan Mackenzie* (12A) at Patricroft MPD 15 May 1964. The 'Clan' class became extinct with No 72006 when it was withdrawn at Kingmoor in May 1966.
J. R. Carter

British Railways locomotive depots & depot codes 1959–1968

London Midland Region

	11/60	LMW	Western AC Lines
	1/65	ML	Midland Lines
	4/66	WL	Western Lines
	4/66	**D01**	**London Division**
		1A	Willesden
		1B	Camden
		1C	Watford
		1D	Devons Road (Bow) – 1J 9/63
	9/63	1D	Marylebone
		1E	Bletchley
2A	9/63	1F	Rugby
2F	9/63	1G	Woodford Halse
2E	9/63	1H	Northampton
1D	9/63	1J	Devons Road (Bow)
	4/66	**DO2**	**Birmingham Division**
		2A	Rugby – 1F 9/63
84E	9/63	2A	Tyseley
		2B	Nuneaton – 5E 9/63
84B	9/63	2B	Oxley
84F	9/63	2C	Stourbridge Junction
		2D	Coventry
84C	9/63	2D	Banbury
		2E	Northampton – 1H 9/63
21A	9/63	2E	Saltley
		2F	Woodford Halse – 1G 9/63
21B	9/63	2F	Bescot
21F	9/63	2G	Walsall (Ryecroft)
21E	9/63	2H	Monument Lane
21D	9/63	2J	Aston
21C	9/63	2K	Bushbury

84D	9/63	2L	Leamington Spa
84H	9/63	2M	Wellington (Salop)
84G	9/63	2P	Kidderminster
		3A	Bescot – 21B 6/60
		3B	Bushbury – 21C 6/60
		3C	Walsall (Ryecroft) – 21F 6/60
		3D	Aston – 21D 6/60
		3E	Monument Lane – 21E 6/60
	4/66	**DO5**	**Stoke Division**
		5A	Crewe North
	5/65	5A	Crewe Diesel Depot
		5B	Crewe South
		5C	Stafford
		5D	Stoke
		5E	Alsager
2B	9/63	5E	Nuneaton
		5F	Uttoxeter
		6A	Chester (Midland)
		6B	Mold Junction
		6C	Birkenhead – 8H 9/63
89B	9/63	6C	Croes Newydd
		6D	Chester (Northgate)
89A	9/63	6D	Shrewsbury
		6E	Chester (West)
89D	9/63	6E	Oswestry
		6F	Bidston
89C	9/63	6F	Machynlleth
		6G	Llandudno Junction

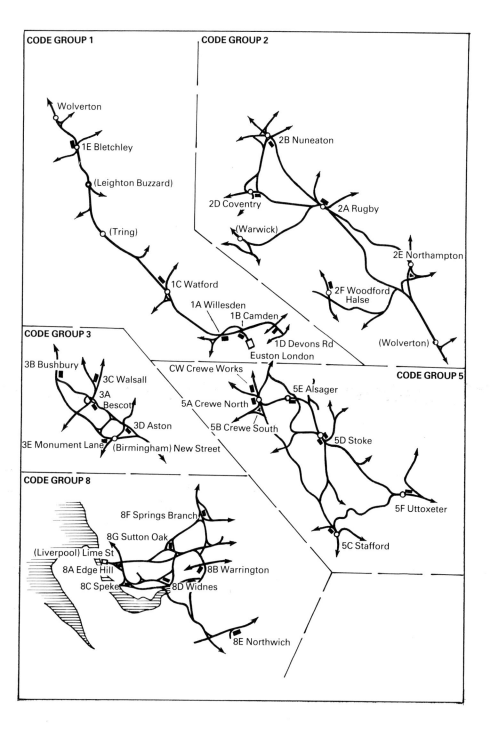

CODE GROUP 1

Wolverton

1E Bletchley

(Leighton Buzzard)

(Tring)

1C Watford

1A Willesden

1B Camden

1D Devons Rd

Euston London

CODE GROUP 2

2B Nuneaton

2D Coventry

(Warwick)

2A Rugby

2E Northampton

2F Woodford Halse

(Wolverton)

CODE GROUP 3

3B Bushbury

3C Walsall

3A Bescot

3D Aston

3E Monument Lane

(Birmingham) New Street

CW Crewe Works

5A Crewe North

5B Crewe South

5E Alsager

5D Stoke

CODE GROUP 5

5F Uttoxeter

5C Stafford

CODE GROUP 8

8F Springs Branch

8G Sutton Oak

(Liverpool) Lime St

8A Edge Hill

8C Speke

8D Widnes

8B Warrington

8E Northwich

9

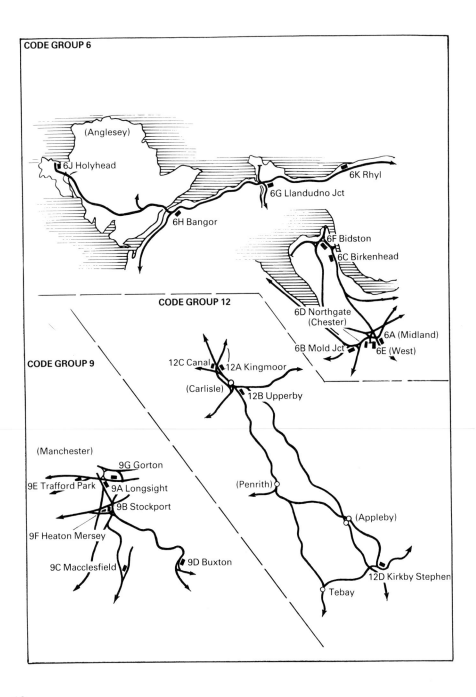

CODE GROUP 6

(Anglesey)

6J Holyhead

6K Rhyl

6G Llandudno Jct

6H Bangor

6F Bidston

6C Birkenhead

CODE GROUP 12

6D Northgate
(Chester)

6A (Midland)

6B Mold Jct

6E (West)

CODE GROUP 9

12C Canal

12A Kingmoor

(Carlisle)

12B Upperby

(Manchester)

9G Gorton

9E Trafford Park

9A Longsight

9B Stockport

(Penrith)

(Appleby)

9F Heaton Mersey

9C Macclesfield

9D Buxton

12D Kirkby Stephen

Tebay

10

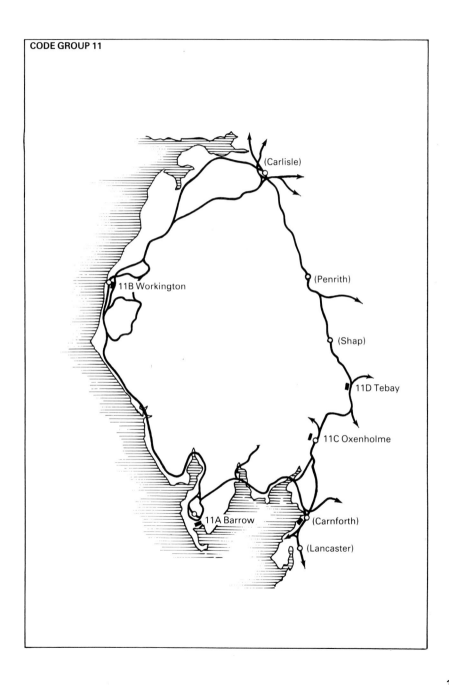

(Carlisle)

(Penrith)

11B Workington

(Shap)

11D Tebay

11C Oxenholme

11A Barrow

(Carnforth)

(Lancaster)

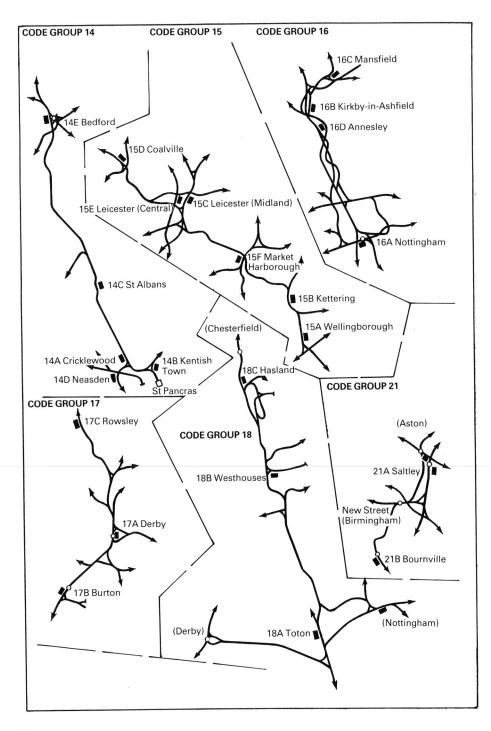

CODE GROUP 14   CODE GROUP 15   CODE GROUP 16

16C Mansfield

16B Kirkby-in-Ashfield

14E Bedford

16D Annesley

15D Coalville

15C Leicester (Midland)

15E Leicester (Central)

16A Nottingham

15F Market Harborough

14C St Albans

15B Kettering

(Chesterfield)

15A Wellingborough

14A Cricklewood

14B Kentish Town

18C Hasland

14D Neasden

St Pancras

CODE GROUP 21

CODE GROUP 17

17C Rowsley

(Aston)

CODE GROUP 18

21A Saltley

18B Westhouses

New Street (Birmingham)

17A Derby

21B Bournville

17B Burton

(Derby)

18A Toton

(Nottingham)

		6H	Bangor	24G	9/63	10G	Skipton
		6J	Holyhead	24D	9/63	10H	Lower Darwen
		6K	Rhyl	24J	9/63	10J	Lancaster (Green Ayre)
	6/68	**DO8**	**Liverpool Division**			11A	Barrow – 12E 6/60
		8A	Edge Hill			11B	Workington – 12F 6/60
		8B	Warrington (Dallam)			11C	Oxenholme – 12G 6/60
		8C	Speke Junction			11D	Tebay – 12H 6/60
		8D	Widnes			12A	Carlisle (Kingmoor)
		8E	Northwich		1/68	12A	Carlisle Diesel Depot
		8F	Springs Branch (Wigan)			12B	Carlisle (Upperby)
		8G	Sutton Oak			12C	Carlisle (Canal)
	7/60	8H	Allerton – 8J 9/63	12E	9/63	12C	Barrow
6C	9/63	8H	Birkenhead			12D	Kirkby Stephen
8H	9/63	8J	Allerton	12F	9/63	12D	Workington
27A	9/63	8K	Bank Hall	11A	6/60	12E	Barrow – 12C 9/63
27B	9/63	8L	Aintree	12H	9/63	12E	Tebay
27C	9/63	8M	Southport	11B	6/60	12F	Workington – 12D 9/63
27D	9/63	8P	Wigan (Central)	11C	6/60	12G	Oxenholme
27E	9/63	8R	Walton-on-the-Hill	11D	6/60	12H	Tebay – 12E 9/63
	6/68	**D09**	**Manchester Division**		1/65	**D14**	**London (Midland) Division**
		9A	Longsight (Manchester)			14A	Cricklewood – 14B 9/63
		9B	Stockport (Edgeley)		9/63	14A	Cricklewood East
		9C	Macclesfield			14B	Kentish Town
	9/63	9C	Reddish	14A	9/63	14B	Cricklewood West
		9D	Buxton – 9L 9/63			14C	St. Albans
26A	9/63	9D	Newton Heath	14E	9/63	14C	Bedford
		9E	Trafford Park			14D	Neasden
		9F	Heaton Mersey	14E	9/63	14E	Bedford – 14C 9/63
		9G	Gorton				
26F	9/63	9H	Patricroft				
26B	9/63	9J	Agecroft		1/65	**D15**	**Leicester Division**
26C	9/63	9K	Bolton			15A	Wellingborough – 15B 9/63
9D	9/63	9L	Buxton	15C	9/63	15A	Leicester (Midland)
26D	9/63	9M	Bury			15B	Kettering – 15C 9/63
26E	9/63	9P	Lees (Oldham)	15A	9/63	15B	Wellingborough
	6/68	**D10**	**Preston Division**				
24L	9/63	10A	Carnforth				
24E	9/63	10B	Blackpool				
24F	9/63	10C	Fleetwood				
24C	9/63	10D	Lostock Hall				
24A	9/63	10E	Accrington				
24B	9/63	10F	Rose Grove				

		15C	Leicester (Midland) – 15A 9/63
15B	9/63	15C	Kettering
		15D	Coalville – 15E 9/63
15E	9/63	15D	Leicester (Central)
		15E	Leicester (Central) – 15D 9/63
15D	9/63	15E	Coalville
		15F	Market Harborough
	1/65	**D16**	**Nottingham Division**
		16A	Nottingham – 16D 9/63
18A	9/63	16A	Toton (Stapleford & Sandiacre)
		16B	Kirkby-in-Ashfield – 16E 9/63
16D	9/63	16B	Annesley
40E	1/66	16B	Colwick
		16C	Mansfield
17A	9/63	16C	Derby
		16D	Annesley – 16B 9/63
16A	9/63	16D	Nottingham
16B	9/63	16E	Kirkby-in-Ashfield
17B	9/63	16F	Burton
18B	9/63	16G	Westhouses
18C	9/63	16H	Hasland
17C	9/63	16J	Rowsley
		17A	Derby – 16C 9/63
		17B	Burton – 16F 9/63
		17C	Rowsley – 16J 9/63
		18A	Toton (Stapleford & Sandiacre) – 16A 9/63
		18B	Westhouses – 16G 9/63
		18C	Hasland – 16H 9/63
		21A	Saltley – 2E 9/63
		21B	Bournville

3A	6/60	21B	Bescot – 2F 9/63
3B	6/60	21C	Bushbury – 2K 9/63
3D	6/60	21D	Aston – 2J 9/63
3E	6/60	21E	Monument Lane – 2H 9/63
3C	6/60	21F	Walsall (Ryecroft) – 2G 9/63
		24A	Accrington – 10E 9/63
		24B	Rose Grove – 10F 9/63
		24C	Lostock Hall – 10D 9/63
		24D	Lower Darwen – 10H 9/63
		24E	Blackpool – 10B 9/63
		24F	Fleetwood – 10C 9/63
		24G	Skipton – 10G 9/63
		24H	Hellifield
		24J	Lancaster (Green Ayre) – 10J 9/63
		24K	Preston
		24L	Carnforth – 10A 9/63
		26A	Newton Heath – 9D 9/63
		26B	Agecroft – 9J 9/63
		26C	Bolton – 9K 9/63
		26D	Bury – 9M 9/63
		26E	Lees (Oldham) – 9P 9/63
		26F	Patricroft – 9H 9/63
		27A	Bank Hall – 8K 9/63
		27B	Aintree – 8L 9/63
		27C	Southport – 8M 9/63
		27D	Wigan (Central) – 8P 9/63
		27E	Walton-on-the-Hill – 8R 9/63
		27F	Brunswick (Liverpool)

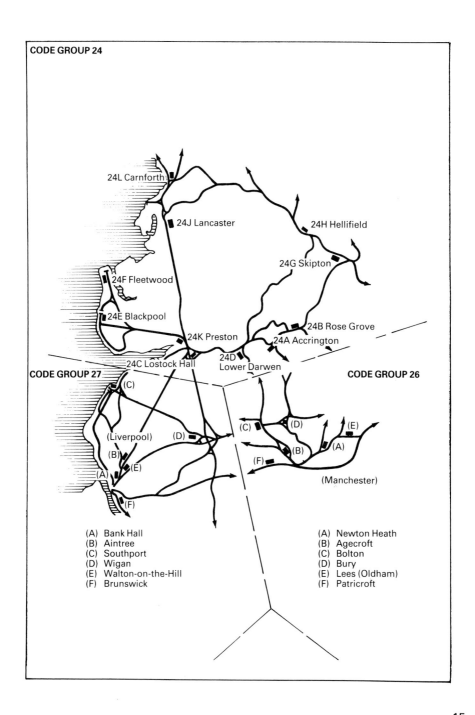

CODE GROUP 24

24L Carnforth

24J Lancaster

24H Hellifield

24G Skipton

24F Fleetwood

24E Blackpool

24B Rose Grove

24K Preston

24A Accrington

24D
Lower Darwen

24C Lostock Hall

CODE GROUP 27

CODE GROUP 26

(C)

(C)

(D)

(E)

(Liverpool)

(D)

(B)

(B)

(A)

(F)

(A)

(E)

(Manchester)

(F)

(A) Bank Hall
(B) Aintree
(C) Southport
(D) Wigan
(E) Walton-on-the-Hill
(F) Brunswick

(A) Newton Heath
(B) Agecroft
(C) Bolton
(D) Bury
(E) Lees (Oldham)
(F) Patricroft

15

Eastern Region

Code	Name			Code	Name
30A	Stratford			34F	Grantham
30B	Hertford East	FP	1/61	34G	Finsbury Park
30C	Bishops Stortford				
30E	Colchester			36A	Doncaster
30F	Parkeston			36C	Frodingham
				36E	Retford
31A	Cambridge			40A	Lincoln
31B	March			40B	Immingham
31C	Kings Lynn			40E	Colwick – 16B
31D	South Lynn				1/66
31E	Bury St Edmunds			40F	Boston
31F	Spital Bridge				
	(Peterborough)			41A	Sheffield
32A	Norwich (Thorpe)				(Darnall) – 41B
32B	Ipswich				5/64
32C	Lowestoft Central		5/64	41A	Tinsley
32D	Yarmouth South				(Sheffield)
	Town			41B	Sheffield
32E	Yarmouth				(Grimesthorpe)
	Vauxhall	41A	5/64	41B	Sheffield
32F	Yarmouth Beach				(Darnall)
32G	Melton Constable			41C	Millhouses
			10/63	41C	Wath
33A	Plaistow			41D	Canklow
33B	Tilbury			41E	Staveley (Barrow
33C	Shoeburyness				Hill)
				41F	Mexborough
34A	Kings Cross			41G	Barnsley
34B	Hornsey			41H	Staveley (GC)
34C	Hatfield			41J	Langwith
34D	Hitchin		2/66	41J	Shirebrook West
34E	New England			41K	Tuxford

North Eastern Region

		Code	Name	Code	Name
		50A	York – 55B 12/67	51A	Darlington
		50B	Leeds (Neville	51C	West Hartlepool
			Hill) – 55H 1/60	51E	Stockton
53A	1/60	50B	Hull (Dairycoates)	51F	West Auckland
		50C	Selby	51G	Haverton Hill
53B	1/60	50C	Hull (Botanic	51J	Northallerton
			Gardens)	51L	Thornaby
		50D	Starbeck		
53E	1/60	50D	Goole	52A	Gateshead
		50E	Scarborough	52B	Heaton
		50F	Malton	52C	Blaydon
		50G	Whitby	52D	Tweedmouth

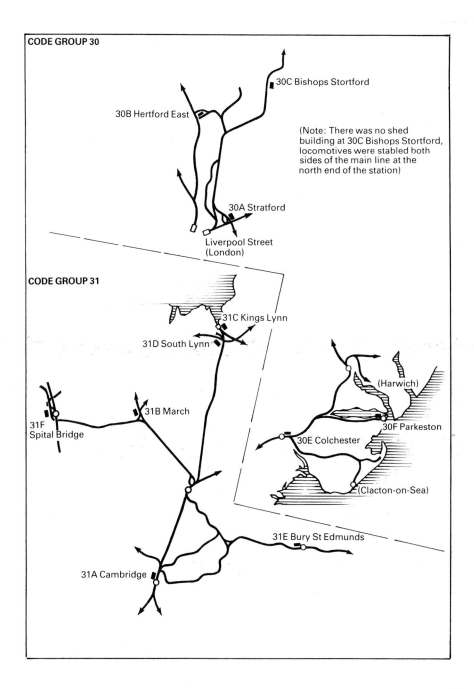

CODE GROUP 30

30C Bishops Stortford

30B Hertford East

(Note: There was no shed
building at 30C Bishops Stortford,
locomotives were stabled both
sides of the main line at the
north end of the station)

30A Stratford

Liverpool Street
(London)

CODE GROUP 31

31C Kings Lynn

31D South Lynn

(Harwich)

31B March

31F
Spital Bridge

30F Parkeston

30E Colchester

(Clacton-on-Sea)

31E Bury St Edmunds

31A Cambridge

17

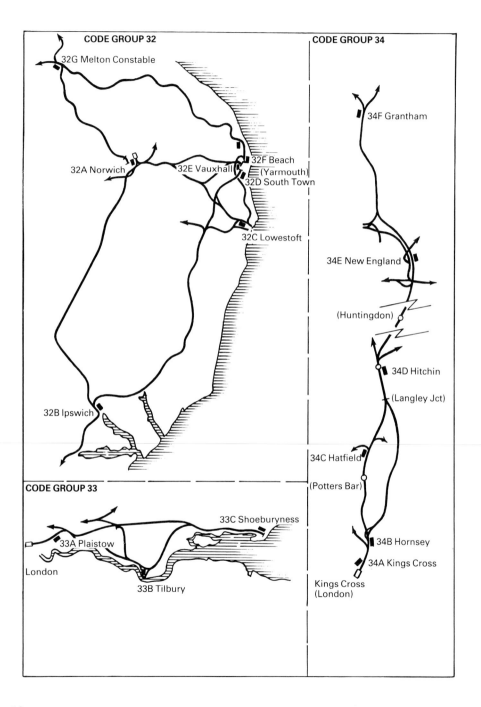

CODE GROUP 32

32G Melton Constable

32A Norwich

32E Vauxhall

32F Beach
(Yarmouth)

32D South Town

32C Lowestoft

32B Ipswich

CODE GROUP 33

33C Shoeburyness

33A Plaistow

London

33B Tilbury

CODE GROUP 34

34F Grantham

34E New England

(Huntingdon)

34D Hitchin

(Langley Jct)

34C Hatfield

(Potters Bar)

34B Hornsey

34A Kings Cross

Kings Cross
(London)

18

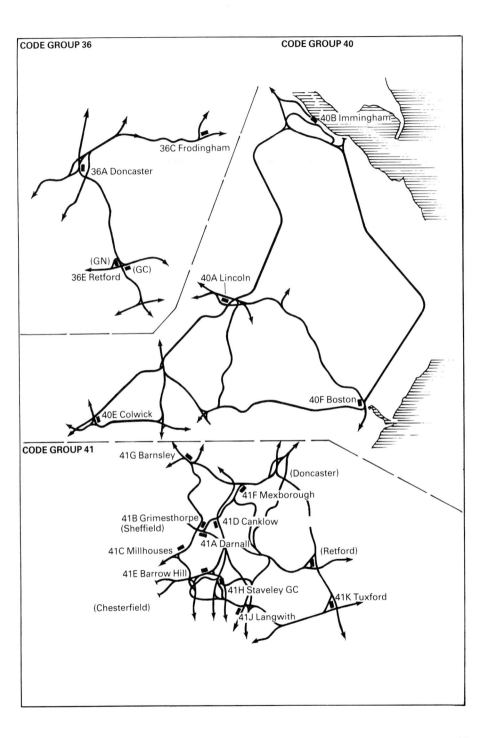

CODE GROUP 36

CODE GROUP 40

36C Frodingham

36A Doncaster

(GN)
36E Retford (GC)

40B Immingham

40A Lincoln

40E Colwick

40F Boston

CODE GROUP 41

41G Barnsley

(Doncaster)

41F Mexborough

41B Grimesthorpe
(Sheffield)

41D Canklow

41C Millhouses

41A Darnall

(Retford)

41E Barrow Hill

41H Staveley GC

(Chesterfield)

41K Tuxford

41J Langwith

19

		52E	Percy Main			55D	Royston	
		52F	North & South Blyth			55E	Normanton	
		52G	Sunderland			55F	Bradford (Manningham)	
		52H	Tyne Dock	56G	12/67	55F	Bradford (Hammerton Street)	
		52J	Borough Gardens					
		52K	Consett			55G	Huddersfield	
		53A	Hull (Dairycoates) – 50B 1/60		12/67	55G	Knottingley	
				50B	1/60	55H	Leeds (Neville Hill)	
		53B	Hull (Botanic Gardens) – 50C 1/60					
						56A	Wakefield	
		53D	Bridlington			56B	Ardsley	
		53E	Goole – 50D 1/60			56C	Copley Hill	
						56D	Mirfield	
						56E	Sowerby Bridge	
		55A	Leeds (Holbeck)			56F	Low Moor	
		55B	Stourton			56G	Bradford (Hammerton Street) – 55F 12/67	
50A	12/67	55B	York					
		55C	Farnley					
HM	12/67	55C	Healey Mills					

Scottish Region

		60A	Inverness			64A	St Margarets (Edinburgh)	
		60B	Aviemore					
		60C	Helmsdale			64B	Haymarket	
		60D	Wick			64C	Dalry Road	
		60E	Forres			64D	Carstairs – 66E 5/60	
		61A	Kittybrewster			64E	Polmont – 65K 5/60	
		61B	Aberdeen (Ferryhill)			64F	Bathgate	
		61C	Keith			64G	Hawick	
					11/59	64H	Leith Central	
		62A	Thornton					
		62B	Dundee (Tay Bridge)			65A	Eastfield (Glasgow)	
		62C	Dunfermline			65B	St Rollox	
						65C	Parkhead	
		63A	Perth			65D	Dawsholm	
		63B	Stirling – 65J 5/60			65E	Kipps	
65J	5/60	63B	Fort William			65F	Grangemouth	
		63C	Forfar			65G	Yoker	
63D	11/59	63C	Oban			65H	Helensburgh	
		63D	Oban – 63C 11/59			65I	Balloch	

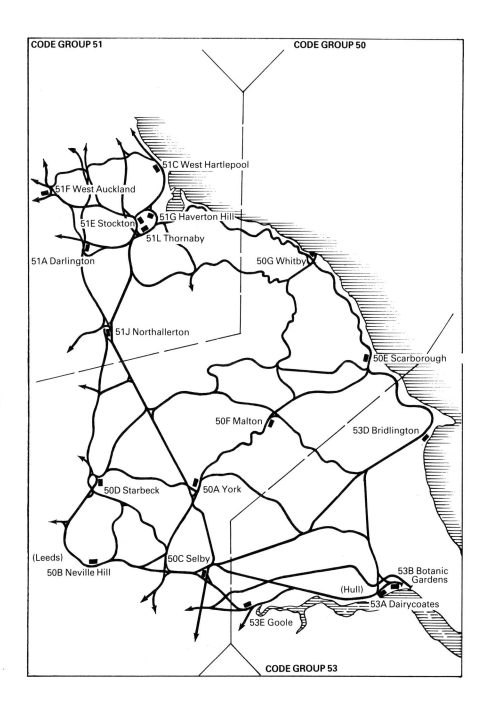

CODE GROUP 51

CODE GROUP 50

51C West Hartlepool

51F West Auckland

51E Stockton

51G Haverton Hill

51L Thornaby

51A Darlington

50G Whitby

51J Northallerton

50E Scarborough

50F Malton

53D Bridlington

50D Starbeck

50A York

(Leeds)

50B Neville Hill

50C Selby

53B Botanic Gardens

(Hull)

53A Dairycoates

53E Goole

CODE GROUP 53

21

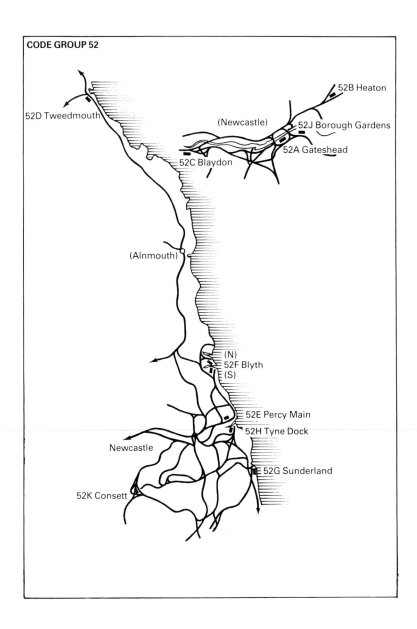

CODE GROUP 52

52D Tweedmouth

52B Heaton

(Newcastle)

52J Borough Gardens

52A Gateshead

52C Blaydon

(Alnmouth)

(N)
52F Blyth
(S)

52E Percy Main

52H Tyne Dock

Newcastle

52G Sunderland

52K Consett

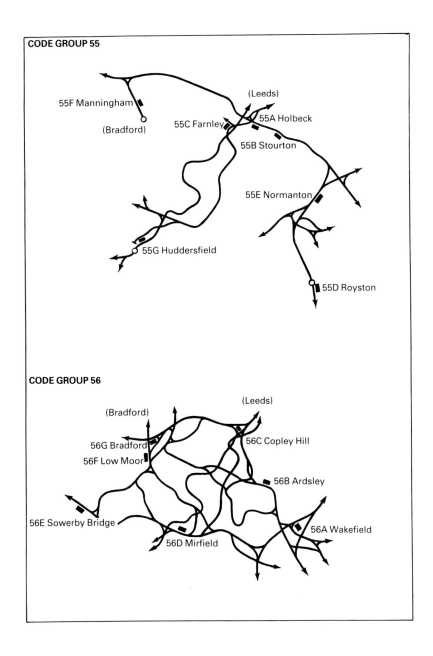

CODE GROUP 55

55F Manningham

(Bradford)

(Leeds)

55C Farnley

55A Holbeck

55B Stourton

55E Normanton

55G Huddersfield

55D Royston

CODE GROUP 56

(Bradford)

(Leeds)

56G Bradford

56C Copley Hill

56F Low Moor

56B Ardsley

56E Sowerby Bridge

56A Wakefield

56D Mirfield

		65J	Fort William – 63B 5/60			67A	Corkerhill (Glasgow)
63B	5/60	65J	Stirling			67B	Hurlford
64E	5/60	65K	Polmont			67C	Ayr
						67D	Ardrossan
				68B	7/62	67E	Dumfries
		66A	Polmadie (Glasgow)	/68C	7/62	67F	Stranraer
		66B	Motherwell			68B	Dumfries – 67E 7/62
		66C	Hamilton				
		66D	Greenock (Ladyburn)			68C	Stranraer – 67F 7/62
64D	5/60	66E	Carstairs			68D	Beattock – 66F 7/62
68D	7/62	66F	Beattock				

Southern Region

		70A	Nine Elms			72C	Yeovil Town – 83E 9/63
		70B	Feltham				
		70C	Guildford			72E	Barnstaple Junction – 83F 9/63
		70D	Basingstoke				
71A	9/63	70D	Eastleigh				
		70E	Reading South			72F	Wadebridge – 84E 9/63
72B	12/62	70E	Salisbury				
		70F	Fratton				
71B	9/63	70F	Bournemouth Central			73A	Stewarts Lane – 75D 6/62
71G	9/63	70G	Weymouth			73B	Bricklayers Arms
		70H	Ryde (IoW)			73C	Hither Green
71I	9/63	70I	Southampton Docks		6/63	73D	Gillingham (Kent)
						73D	St Leonards
						73E	Faversham
		71A	Eastleigh – 70D 9/63			73F	Ashford (Kent)
						73G	Ramsgate
		71B	Bournemouth Central – 70F 9/63			73H	Dover
						73J	Tonbridge
		71G	Weymouth – 70G 9/63				
						75A	Brighton
		71H	Yeovil Pen Mill			75B	Redhill
		71I	Southampton Docks – 70I 9/63			75C	Norward Junction
					7/66	75C	Selhurst
		72A	Exmouth Junction – 83D 9/63	73A	6/62	75D	Horsham
						75D	Stewarts Lane
		72B	Salisbury – 70E 12/62			75E	Three Bridges
						75F	Tunbridge Wells West

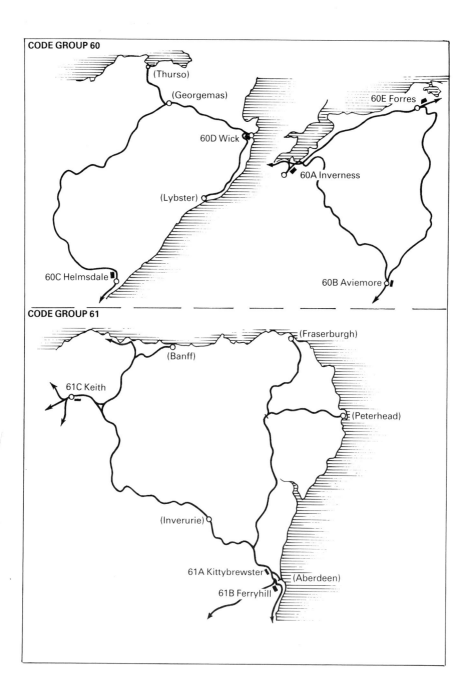

CODE GROUP 60

(Thurso)

(Georgemas)

60E Forres

60D Wick

60A Inverness

(Lybster)

60C Helmsdale

60B Aviemore

CODE GROUP 61

(Fraserburgh)

(Banff)

61C Keith

E (Peterhead)

(Inverurie)

61A Kittybrewster

(Aberdeen)

61B Ferryhill

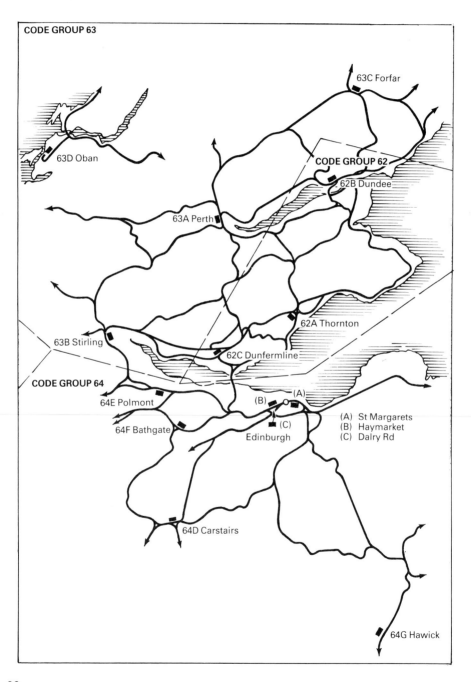

CODE GROUP 63

63C Forfar

63D Oban

CODE GROUP 62

62B Dundee

63A Perth

62A Thornton

63B Stirling

62C Dunfermline

CODE GROUP 64

64E Polmont

(A)
(B)

(C)
Edinburgh

(A) St Margarets
(B) Haymarket
(C) Dalry Rd

64F Bathgate

64D Carstairs

64G Hawick

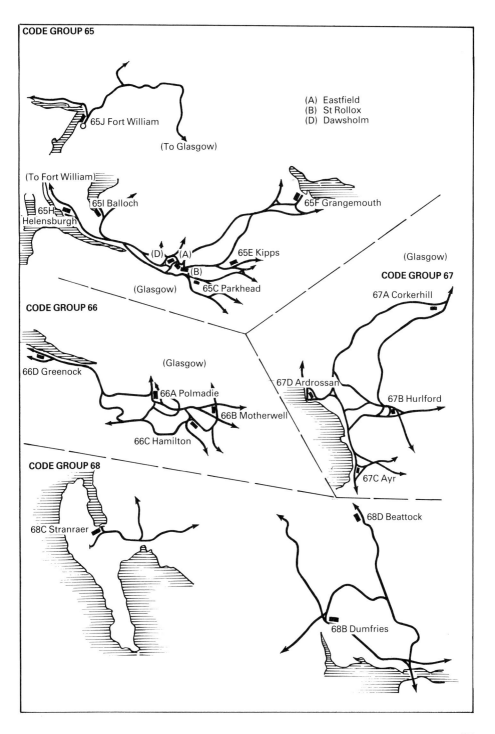

CODE GROUP 65

65J Fort William

(To Glasgow)

(A) Eastfield
(B) St Rollox
(D) Dawsholm

(To Fort William)

65I Balloch

65H Helensburgh

65F Grangemouth

(D) (A)

(B)

65E Kipps

65C Parkhead

(Glasgow)

(Glasgow)

CODE GROUP 67

67A Corkerhill

CODE GROUP 66

66D Greenock

(Glasgow)

66A Polmadie

67D Ardrossan

67B Hurlford

66B Motherwell

66C Hamilton

CODE GROUP 68

67C Ayr

68C Stranraer

68D Beattock

68B Dumfries

27

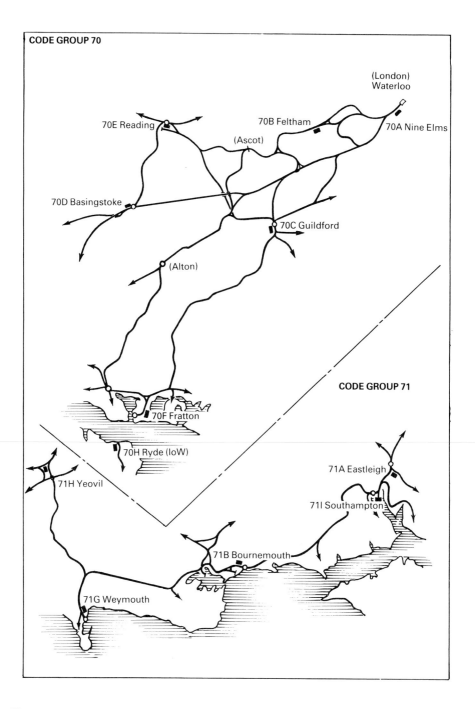

CODE GROUP 70

(London)
Waterloo

70E Reading

70B Feltham

70A Nine Elms

(Ascot)

70D Basingstoke

70C Guildford

(Alton)

CODE GROUP 71

70F Fratton

70H Ryde (IoW)

71A Eastleigh

71H Yeovil

71I Southampton

71B Bournemouth

71G Weymouth

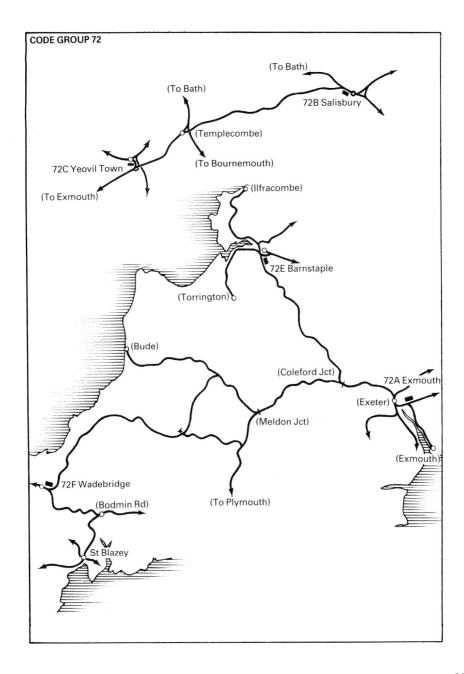

CODE GROUP 72

(To Bath)

(To Bath)

72B Salisbury

(Templecombe)

72C Yeovil Town

(To Bournemouth)

(To Exmouth)

(Ilfracombe)

72E Barnstaple

(Torrington)

(Bude)

(Coleford Jct)

72A Exmouth

(Exeter)

(Meldon Jct)

(Exmouth)

72F Wadebridge

(Bodmin Rd)

(To Plymouth)

St Blazey

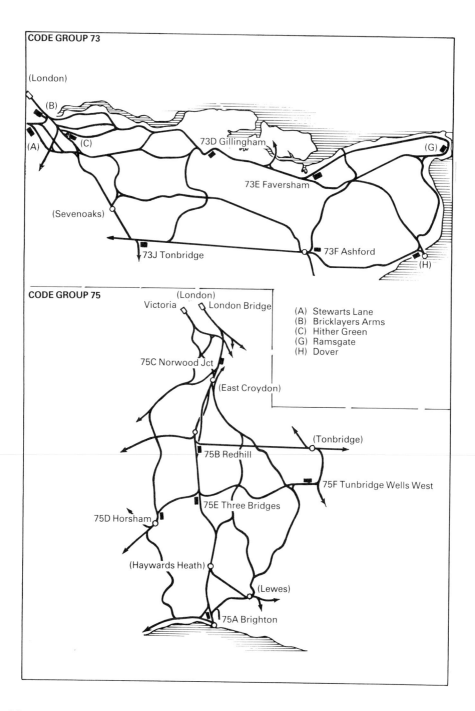

CODE GROUP 73

(London)

(B)

(A)   (C)

73D Gillingham

(G)

73E Faversham

(Sevenoaks)

73J Tonbridge

73F Ashford

(H)

CODE GROUP 75

(London)
Victoria   London Bridge

75C Norwood Jct

(East Croydon)

(A) Stewarts Lane
(B) Bricklayers Arms
(C) Hither Green
(G) Ramsgate
(H) Dover

(Tonbridge)

75B Redhill

75F Tunbridge Wells West

75E Three Bridges

75D Horsham

(Haywards Heath)

(Lewes)

75A Brighton

30

Western Region

		81A	Old Oak Common			84E	Tyseley – 2A 9/63
		81B	Slough	72F	9/63	84E	Wadebridge
		81C	Southall			84F	Stourbridge
		81D	Reading				Junction – 2C
		81E	Didcot				9/63
		81F	Oxford			84G	Shrewsbury –
							89A 1/61
		82A	Bristol (Bath	85D	1/61	84G	Kidderminster –
			Road)				2P 9/63
		82B	St Phillip's Marsh			84H	Wellington
			(Bristol)				(Salop) – 2M 9/63
		82C	Swindon			84J	Croes Newydd –
		82D	Westbury – 83C				89B 1/61
			10/63			84K	Wrexham
		82E	Bristol (Barrow				(Rhosddu)
			Road)			85A	Worcester
		82F	Bath (Green Park)			85B	Gloucester
		82G	Templecombe				(Horton Road)
						85C	Hereford – 86C
		83A	Newton Abbot				1/61
		83B	Taunton	85E	1/61	85C	Gloucester
		83C	Exeter				(Barnwood)
82D	10/63	83C	Westbury			85D	Kidderminster –
		83D	Laira (Plymouth)				84G 1/61
			– 84A 9/63	85F	1/61	85D	Bromsgrove
72A	9/63	83D	Exmouth			85E	Gloucester
			Junction				(Barnwood) – 85C
		83E	St Blazey – 84B				1/61
			9/63			85F	Bromsgrove –
72C	9/63	83E	Yeovil Town				85D 1/61
		83F	Truro – 84C 9/63				
72E	9/63	83F	Barnstaple			86A	Newport (Ebbw
			Junction				Junction) – 86B
		83G	Penzance – 84D				9/63
			9/63	88A	9/63	86A	Cardiff (Canton)
82G	10/63	83G	Templecombe			86B	Newport (Pill)
		83H	Plymouth (Friary)	86A	9/63	86B	Newport (Ebbw
							Junction)
		84A	Wolverhampton			86C	Cardiff (Canton) –
			(Stafford Road)				88A 10/60
83D	9/63	84A	Laira (Plymouth)	85C	1/61	86C	Hereford
		84B	Oxley – 2B 9/63			86D	Llantrisant – 88G
83E	9/63	84B	St Blazey				10/60
		84C	Banbury – 2D			86E	Severn Tunnel
			9/63				Junction
83F	9/63	84C	Truro			86F	Tondu – 88H
		84D	Leamington Spa				10/60
			– 2L 9/63	86H	10/60	86F	Aberbeeg
83G	9/63	84D	Penzance			86G	Pontypool Road

31

		86H	Aberbeeg – 86F 10/60	86J	10/60	88J	Aberdare
		86J	Aberdare – 88J 10/60	89B	10/60	88K	Brecon
		86K	Tredegar	CED	3/62	88L	Cardiff East Dock – 88A 9/63
					3/62	88M	Cardiff (Cathays)
		87A	Neath			89A	Oswestry – 89D 1/61
		87B	Duffryn Yard				
	3/64	87B	Margam	84G	1/61	89A	Shrewsbury – 6D 9/63
		87C	Danygraig				
		87D	Swansea East Dock			89B	Brecon – 88K 10/60
		87E	Landore	84J	1/61	89B	Croes Newydd – 6C 9/63
		87F	Llanelly				
		87G	Carmarthen			89C	Machynlleth – 6F 9/63
		87H	Neyland				
	10/63	87H	Whitland	89A	1/61	89D	Oswestry – 6E 9/63
		87J	Goodwick (Fishguard)				
		87K	Swansea (Paxton Street)			CW	Crewe Works
						HW	Horwich Works
		88A	Cardiff (Radyr) – 88B 10/60			RW	St Rollox Works
86C	10/60	88A	Cardiff (Canton) – 86A 9/63			WW	Wolverton Works
88L	9/63	88A	Cardiff East Dock			DW	Derby Works
		88B	Cardiff East Dock – CED 10/60			AW	Ashford Works
88A	10/60	88B	Cardiff (Radyr)			RTS	Rugby Testing Station
		88C	Barry	88B	10/60	STS	Swindon Testing Station
		88D	Merthyr				
	11/64	88D	Rhymney	88B	10/60	CED	Cardiff East Dock – 88L 3/62
		88E	Abercynon			DG	Danygraig
		88F	Treherbert			FP	Finsbury Park
86D	10/60	88G	Llantrisant			HM	Healey Miles
86F	10/60	88H	Tondu			NCB	National Coal Board

Abbreviations used

SB	Stationary Boiler
OL	On Loan
S	Stored
R	Reinstated
Wdn	Withdrawn

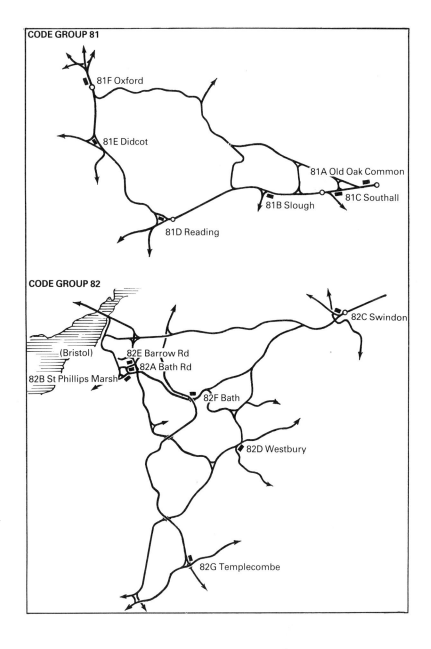

CODE GROUP 81

81F Oxford

81E Didcot

81A Old Oak Common

81C Southall

81B Slough

81D Reading

CODE GROUP 82

82C Swindon

(Bristol)

82E Barrow Rd

82A Bath Rd

82B St Phillips Marsh

82F Bath

82D Westbury

82G Templecombe

33

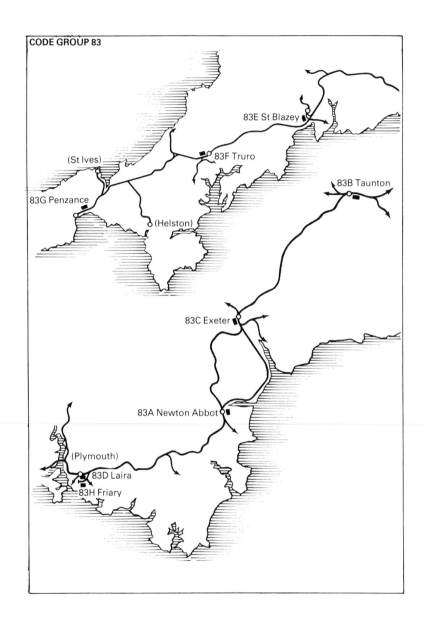

CODE GROUP 83

83E St Blazey

(St Ives)

83F Truro

83B Taunton

83G Penzance

(Helston)

83C Exeter

83A Newton Abbot

(Plymouth)

83D Laira

83H Friary

34

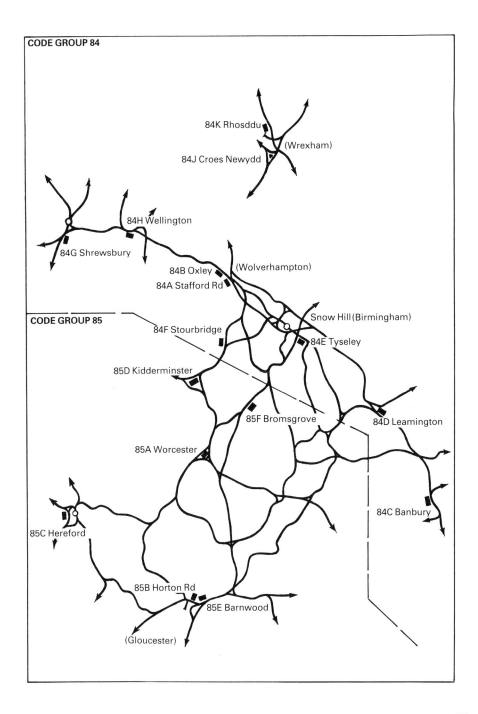

CODE GROUP 84

84K Rhosddu
(Wrexham)
84J Croes Newydd

84H Wellington
84G Shrewsbury
84B Oxley
84A Stafford Rd
(Wolverhampton)
Snow Hill (Birmingham)

CODE GROUP 85
84F Stourbridge
84E Tyseley

85D Kidderminster
85F Bromsgrove
84D Leamington
85A Worcester

84C Banbury
85C Hereford

85B Horton Rd
85E Barnwood
(Gloucester)

35

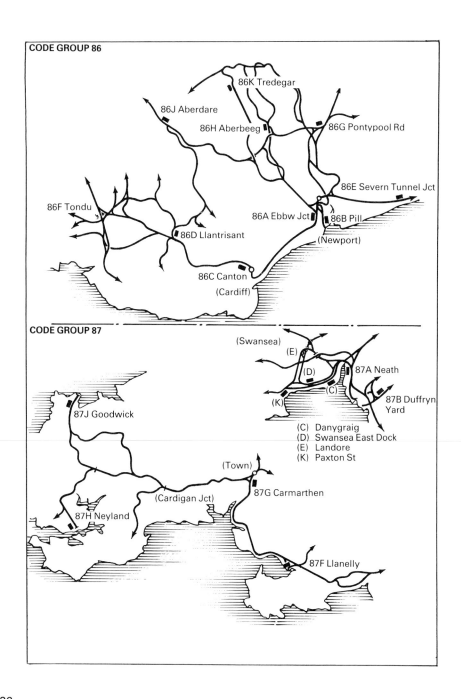

CODE GROUP 86

86K Tredegar

86J Aberdare

86H Aberbeeg

86G Pontypool Rd

86E Severn Tunnel Jct

86F Tondu

86A Ebbw Jct

86B Pill

(Newport)

86D Llantrisant

86C Canton

(Cardiff)

CODE GROUP 87

(Swansea)

(E)

(D)

87A Neath

(C)

87B Duffryn Yard

(K)

87J Goodwick

(C) Danygraig
(D) Swansea East Dock
(E) Landore
(K) Paxton St

(Town)

(Cardigan Jct)

87G Carmarthen

87H Neyland

87F Llanelly

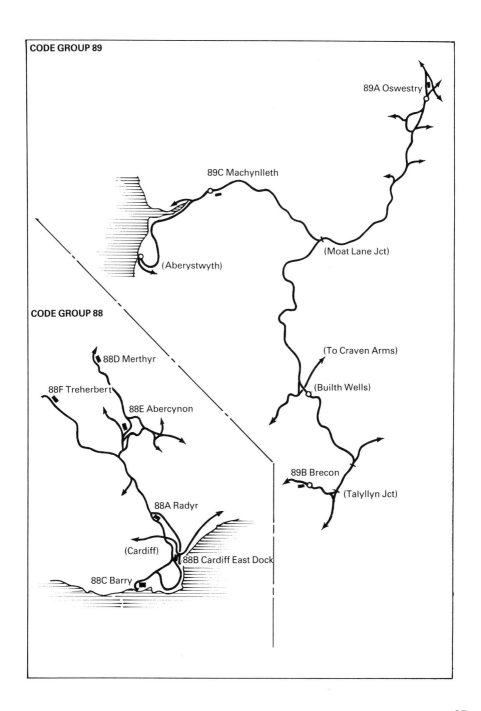

CODE GROUP 89

89A Oswestry

89C Machynlleth

(Moat Lane Jct)

(Aberystwyth)

CODE GROUP 88

(To Craven Arms)

(Builth Wells)

88D Merthyr

88F Treherbert

88E Abercynon

89B Brecon

(Talyllyn Jct)

88A Radyr

(Cardiff)

88B Cardiff East Dock

88C Barry

37

Regional locomotive distribution 1 January 1959

	WR	ER	ScR	SR	NER	LMR		Class Total
4-6-2 Cl 8:	–	–	–	–	–	1	:	1
4-6-2 Cl 7:	12	22	3	–	3	15	:	55
4-6-2 Cl 6:	–	–	5	–	–	5	:	10
4-6-0 Cl 5:	27	15	48	27	17	38	:	172
4-6-0 Cl 4:	17	–	–	12	–	51	:	80
2-6-0 Cl 4:	–	5	35	37	6	32	:	115
2-6-0 Cl 3:	–	–	10	–	10	–	:	20
2-6-0 Cl 2:	10	6	10	–	6	33	:	65
2-6-4T Cl 4:	–	28	46	23	5	53	:	155
2-6-2T Cl 3:	20	–	–	14	4	7	:	45
2-6-2T Cl 2:	–	–	–	10	1	19	:	30
2-8-0 Cl 8:	45	230	60	–	224	174	:	733
2-10-0 Cl 8:	–	–	24	–	–	1	:	25
2-10-0 Cl 9	39	55	–	–	10	129	:	233
Regional total	170	361	241	123	286	558	:	1,739

BR Std Cl 9 2-10-0 Nos 92203-92220 still to be delivered.

Below:
'Britannias' at Patricroft MPD 10 July 1966 Nos 70010 *Owen Glendower* (12A) and 70023 *Venus* (5B) await their next duties *P. Hawkins*

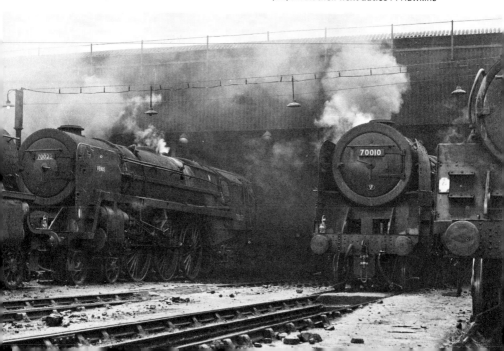

British Railways locomotive allocations 1959-1968

BR Standard Class 7 4-6-2 'Britannia'

Introduced: 1951
Purpose: Mixed traffic
Power classification: 7P6F
Tractive effort: 32,150 lb

Locomotive Names

70000	Britannia	70027	Rising Star
70001	Lord Hurcomb	70028	Royal Star
70002	Geoffrey Chaucer	70029	Shooting Star
70003	John Bunyan	70030	William Wordsworth
70004	William Shakespeare	70031	Byron
70005	John Milton	70032	Tennyson
70006	Robert Burns	70033	Charles Dickens
70007	Coeur-de-Lion	70034	Thomas Hardy
70008	Black Prince	70035	Rudyard Kipling
70009	Alfred the Great	70036	Boadicea
70010	Owen Glendower	70037	Hereward the Wake
70011	Hotspur	70038	Robin Hood
70012	John of Gaunt	70039	Sir Christopher Wren
70013	Oliver Cromwell	70040	Clive of India
70014	Iron Duke	70041	Sir John Moore
70015	Apollo	70042	Lord Roberts
70016	Ariel	70043	Lord Kitchener
70017	Arrow	70044	Earl Haig
70018	Flying Dutchman	70045	Lord Rowallan
70019	Lightning	70046	Anzac
70020	Mercury	70048	The Territorial Army 1908-1958
70021	Morning Star	70049	Solway Firth
70022	Tornado	70050	Firth of Clyde
70023	Venus	70051	Firth of Forth
70024	Vulcan	70052	Firth of Tay
70025	Western Star	70053	Moray Firth
70026	Polar Star	70054	Dornoch Firth

Stock analysis 1959-1968

1.1.59	(55)	70000-54
1.1.60	(55)	70000-54
1.1.61	(55)	70000-54
1.1.62	(55)	70000-54
1.1.63	(55)	70000-54
1.1.64	(55)	70000-54
1.1.65	(55)	70000-54
1.1.66	(53)	70000-06/08-42/44-54
1.1.67	(41)	70002-06/08-16/20-29/31-35/38-42/45-49/51-53
1.1.68	(1)	70013

Locomotive depot allocations
1959-1968

70000	30A	Stratford		3/63	1A	Willesden
2/59	32A	Norwich		12/63	2J	Aston
6/61	31B	March		10/64	12A	Kingmoor: *Wdn 7/67*
3/63	1A	Willesden		**70006**	32A	Norwich
5/63	5A	Crewe North		11/61	31B	March
5/65	5B	Crewe South		12/63	12A	Kingmoor: *Wdn 5/67*
3/66	9D	Newton Heath: *Wdn 5/66*		**70007**	32A	Norwich
				11/61	31B	March
70001	30A	Stratford		12/63	12A	Kingmoor: *Wdn 6/65*
2/59	32A	Norwich		**70008**	32A	Norwich
9/61	31B	March		9/61	31B	March
3/63	1A	Willesden		12/63	12A	Kingmoor: *Wdn 1/67*
12/63	2J	Aston		**70009**	32A	Norwich
10/64	12A	Kingmoor: *Wdn 9/66*		9/61	31B	March
70002	30A	Stratford		12/63	12A	Kingmoor: *Wdn 1/67*
1/59	32D	Yarmouth South Town		**70010**	32A	Norwich
2/59	32A	Norwich		11/61	31B	March
6/61	31B	March		3/63	1A	Willesden
12/63	12A	Kingmoor: *Wdn 1/67*		1/65	5A	Crewe North
70003	30A	Stratford		5/65	5B	Crewe South
2/59	32A	Norwich		6/65	12A	Kingmoor: *Wdn 9/67*
7/61	31B	March		**70011**	32A	Norwich
12/63	12A	Kingmoor: *Wdn 3/67*		9/61	31B	March
70004	9E	Trafford Park		12/63	12A	Kingmoor
12/60	1A	Willesden		2/65	12B	Upperby
2/62	21D	Aston		12/66	12A	Kingmoor: *Wdn 12/67*
4/62	1A	Willesden		**70012**	32A	Norwich
5/63	12C	Carlisle (Canal)		1/59	32D	Yarmouth South Town
6/63	12A	Kingmoor		2/59	32A	Norwich
7/63	1A	Willesden		9/61	31B	March
1/65	5A	Crewe North		3/63	1A	Willesden
5/65	9B	Stockport (Edgeley)		1/65	5A	Crewe North
6/67	12A	Kingmoor: *Wdn 12/67*		5/65	5B	Crewe South
70005	30A	Stratford		2/66	6G	Llandudno Junction
2/59	32A	Norwich		4/66	5B	Crewe South
9/61	31B	March		8/66	12A	Kingmoor: *Wdn 12/67*

70013	32D	Yarmouth South Town	5/65	5B	Crewe South
2/59	32A	Norwich	3/66	12B	Upperby
9/61	31B	March	12/66	12A	Kingmoor: *Wdn 12/66*
12/63	12A	Kingmoor	**70019**	86C	Cardiff (Canton): 88A
2/65	12B	Upperby			10/60
12/66	12A	Kingmoor	9/61	12A	Kingmoor
1/68	10A	Carnforth: *Wdn 8/68*	6/62	9A	Longsight
70014	9E	Trafford Park	9/62	5A	Crewe North
12/60	26A	Newton Heath	5/63	21D	Aston: 2J 9/63
9/61	14D	Neasden	9/63	5A	Crewe North
6/62	16D	Annesley	5/65	5B	Crewe South
9/62	1A	Willesden	7/65	12B	Upperby: *Wdn 3/66*
12/62	6G	Llandudno Junction	**70020**	86C	Cardiff (Canton): 88A
5/63	1A	Willesden			10/60
1/65	5A	Crewe North	9/61	12A	Kingmoor
5/65	5B	Crewe South	6/62	9A	Longsight
2/66	6G	Llandudno Junction	9/62	5A	Crewe North
4/66	5B	Crewe South	1/63	12C	Carlisle (Canal)
8/66	12A	Kingmoor: *Wdn 12/67*	5/63	1A	Willesden
70015	9E	Trafford Park	1/65	5A	Crewe North
12/60	26A	Newton Heath	5/65	5B	Crewe South
9/61	14D	Neasden	7/65	12B	Upperby
6/62	16D	Annesley	12/66	12A	Kingmoor: *Wdn 1/67*
9/62	1A	Willesden	**70021**	9E	Trafford Park
12/62	6G	Llandudno Junction	3/62	1A	Willesden
9/63	5A	Crewe North	1/65	5A	Crewe North
5/65	9B	Stockport (Edgeley)	5/65	5B	Crewe South
6/67	12A	Kingmoor: *Wdn 8/67*	7/65	9D	Newton Heath
70016	86C	Cardiff (Canton): 88A	5/66	9B	Stockport (Edgeley)
		10/60	6/67	12A	Kingmoor: *Wdn 12/67*
9/61	12C	Carlisle (Canal)	**70022**	86C	Cardiff (Canton): 88A
5/62	9A	Longsight			10/60
9/62	5A	Crewe North	9/61	12A	Kingmoor
12/62	6G	Llandudno Junction	6/62	9A	Longsight
3/63	6J	Holyhead	9/62	21D	Aston
5/63	21D	Aston: 2J 9/63	10/62	2A	Rugby
10/64	12A	Kingmoor: *Wdn 8/67*	2/63	21D	Aston: 2J 9/63
70017	9E	Trafford Park	10/64	12A	Kingmoor
12/60	1A	Willesden	11/64	12B	Upperby
9/61	21D	Aston	12/66	12A	Kingmoor: *Wdn 12/67*
10/62	2A	Rugby	**70023**	86C	Cardiff (Canton): 88A
2/63	21D	Aston			10/60
5/63	6G	Llandudno Junction	9/61	12A	Kingmoor
9/63	5A	Crewe North	6/62	9A	Longsight
5/65	5B	Crewe South	9/62	21D	Aston
7/65	9D	Newton Heath	10/62	2A	Rugby
5/66	12A	Kingmoor: *Wdn 9/66*	2/63	21D	Aston: 2J 9/63
70018	86C	Cardiff (Canton): 88A	9/63	5A	Crewe North
		10/60	9/64	6J	Holyhead
9/61	12C	Carlisle (Canal)	2/65	5A	Crewe North
5/62	9A	Longsight	5/65	5B	Crewe South
9/62	5A	Crewe North	2/66	6G	Llandudno Junction

4/66	5B	Crewe South
9/66	12A	Kingmoor: *Wdn 12/67*
70024	86C	Cardiff (Canton): 88A
		10/60
9/61	21D	Aston
10/62	2A	Rugby
2/63	21D	Aston
4/63	1A	Willesden
11/63	5A	Crewe North
9/64	6J	Holyhead
2/65	5A	Crewe North
5/65	5B	Crewe South
2/66	6G	Llandudno Junction
4/66	5B	Crewe South
8/66	12B	Upperby
12/66	12A	Kingmoor: *Wdn 12/67*
70025	86C	Cardiff (Canton): 88A
		10/60
9/61	21D	Aston
5/63	5A	Crewe North
5/65	5B	Crewe South
2/66	6G	Llandudno Junction
4/66	5B	Crewe South
9/66	12A	Kingmoor: *Wdn 12/67*
70026	86C	Cardiff (Canton): 88A
		10/60
9/61	21D	Aston
4/63	6J	Holyhead
5/65	9B	Stockport (Edgeley):
		Wdn 167
70027	86C	Cardiff (Canton): 88A
		10/60
9/61	21D	Aston
5/63	6J	Holyhead
2/65	5A	Crewe North
5/65	5B	Crewe South
2/66	6G	Llandudno Junction
4/66	5B	Crewe South
9/66	12A	Kingmoor: *Wdn 6/67*
70028	86C	Cardiff (Canton): 88A
		10/60
9/61	21D	Aston
3/62	9A	Longsight
6/62	21D	Aston
7/62	9A	Longsight
9/62	21D	Aston
5/63	1A	Willesden
9/63	5A	Crewe North
5/65	5B	Crewe South
2/66	6G	Llandudno Junction
4/66	5B	Crewe South
9/66	12A	Kingmoor: *Wdn 9/67*

70029	86C	Cardiff (Canton): 88A
		10/60
9/61	21D	Aston: 2J 9/63
10/64	12A	Kingmoor
11/64	12B	Upperby
12/66	12A	Kingmoor: *Wdn 10/67*
70030	32A	Norwich
6/61	31B	March
7/63	5A	Crewe North
5/65	5B	Crewe South
7/65	12B	Upperby: *Wdn 6/66*
70031	9A	Longsight
4/60	9E	Trafford Park
9/60	9A	Longsight
9/61	21D	Aston
4/63	1A	Willesden
1/65	5A	Crewe North
5/65	5B	Crewe South
7/65	12B	Upperby
12/66	12A	Kingmoor: *Wdn 11/67*
70032	9A	Longsight
2/60	9E	Trafford Park
1/61	1A	Willesden
10/64	12A	Kingmoor
11/64	12B	Upperby
12/66	12A	Kingmoor: *Wdn 9/67*
70033	9A	Longsight
2/60	9E	Trafford Park
1/61	1A	Willesden
12/62	6G	Llandudno Junction
3/63	6J	Holyhead
5/63	1A	Willesden
9/63	5A	Crewe North
5/65	5B	Crewe South
6/65	12A	Kingmoor: *Wdn 7/67*
70034	32D	Yarmouth South Town
2/59	32A	Norwich
6/61	31B	March
3/63	1A	Willesden
6/64	5A	Crewe North
5/65	5B	Crewe South
7/65	9D	Newton Heath
5/66	12A	Kingmoor: *Wdn 5/67*
70035	32D	Yarmouth South Town
2/59	32A	Norwich
10/61	40B	Immingham
6/63	31B	March
12/63	12A	Kingmoor: *Wdn 12/67*
70036	30A	Stratford
2/59	32A	Norwich
11/60	31B	March
9/61	40B	Immingham

12/63	12B	Upperby
2/64	12A	Kingmoor: *Wdn 10/66*
70037	30A	Stratford
2/59	32A	Norwich
11/60	31B	March
9/61	40B	Immingham
12/63	12B	Upperby
1/64	12A	Kingmoor: *Wdn 11/66*
70038	30A	Stratford
2/59	32A	Norwich
11/60	31B	March
10/61	40B	Immingham
12/63	12B	Upperby
1/64	12A	Kingmoor: *Wdn 8/67*
70039	30A	Stratford
2/59	32A	Norwich
12/60	40B	Immingham
12/63	12B	Upperby
2/64	12A	Kingmoor: *Wdn 9/67*
70040	30A	Stratford
2/59	32A	Norwich
12/60	40B	Immingham
12/63	12B	Upperby
2/64	12A	Kingmoor: *Wdn 4/67*
70041	30A	Stratford
2/59	32A	Norwich
12/60	40B	Immingham
12/63	12B	Upperby
1/64	12A	Kingmoor: *Wdn 4/67*
70042	9E	Trafford Park
12/60	1A	Willesden
5/63	5A	Crewe North
5/65	5B	Crewe South
6/65	6J	Holyhead
12/65	12A	Kingmoor: *Wdn 5/67*
70043	9A	Longsight
9/61	21D	Aston
3/62	9A	Longsight
6/62	21D	Aston
4/63	1A	Willesden
6/64	5A	Crewe North
5/65	5B	Crewe South: *Wdn 8/65*
70044	55A	Holbeck
8/62	5A	Crewe North
5/65	5B	Crewe South
7/65	9D	Newton Heath
5/66	9B	Stockport: *Wdn 10/66*
70045	6J	Holyhead
10/59	6A	Chester (Midland)
11/59	5A	Crewe North
12/59	1B	Camden
1/60	26A	Newton Heath

9/61	14D	Neasden
6/62	21D	Aston
12/62	6J	Holyhead
6/65	2B	Oxley
9/65	2D	Banbury
1/66	12A	Kingmoor: *Wdn 12/67*
70046	6J	Holyhead
11/59	5A	Crewe North
2/60	9A	Longsight
9/61	12A	Kingmoor
10/61	1A	Willesden
4/62	21D	Aston
12/62	6J	Holyhead
2/65	5A	Crewe North
5/65	5B	Crewe South
6/65	6J	Holyhead
9/65	2D	Banbury
1/66	12A	Kingmoor: *Wdn 7/67*
70047	6J	Holyhead
11/59	5A	Crewe North
8/60	6J	Holyhead
6/61	1A	Willesden
9/61	12A	Kingmoor
10/61	1A	Willesden
3/62	21D	Aston: 2J 9/63
12/63	1A	Willesden
1/64	6J	Holyhead
6/65	2B	Oxley
9/65	2D	Banbury
1/66	12A	Kingmoor: *Wdn 7/67*
70048	6J	Holyhead
11/59	5A	Crewe North
12/59	1B	Camden
1/60	26A	Newton Heath
9/61	14D	Neasden
6/62	16D	Annesley
9/62	1A	Willesden
12/62	6J	Holyhead
4/63	21D	Aston 2J 9/63
10/64	12A	Kingmoor
11/64	12B	Upperby
12/66	12A	Kingmoor: *Wdn 5/67*
70049	6J	Holyhead
10/59	6A	Chester (Midland)
11/59	5A	Crewe North
12/59	1B	Camden
1/60	5A	Crewe North
2/60	26A	Newton Heath
9/61	14D	Neasden
6/62	16D	Annesley
9/62	1A	Willesden
12/62	6J	Holyhead

5/63	21D	Aston 2J 9/63
11/63	5A	Crewe North
3/64	1A	Willesden
10/64	12A	Kingmoor
11/64	12B	Upperby
12/66	12A	Kingmoor: *Wdn 12/67*
70050	66A	Polmadie
3/62	67A	Corkerhill
10/62	5A	Crewe North
12/62	6J	Holyhead
1/63	5A	Crewe North
5/65	5B	Crewe South
9/65	2D	Banbury
1/66	12A	Kingmoor: *Wdn 8/66*
70051	66A	Polmadie
3/62	67A	Corkerhill
10/62	5A	Crewe North
12/62	6J	Holyhead
1/63	5A	Crewe North
5/65	5B	Crewe South
9/65	2D	Banbury
1/66	12A	Kingmoor: *Wdn 12/67*
70052	66A	Polmadie
3/62	67A	Corkerhill
10/62	5A	Crewe North
5/65	5B	Crewe South
9/65	2D	Banbury
1/66	12A	Kingmoor: *Wdn 3/67*
70053	55A	Holbeck
8/62	5A	Crewe North
6/64	6J	Holyhead
6/65	2B	Oxley
9/65	2D	Banbury
1/66	12A	Kingmoor: *Wdn 4/67*
70054	55A	Holbeck
8/62	5A	Crewe North
3/64	1A	Willesden
?64	5A	Crewe North
5/65	5B	Crewe South
9/65	2D	Banbury
1/66	12A	Kingmoor: *Wdn 11/66*

Demise of the BR Standard Class 7 4-6-2s

Withdrawals

6/65: 70007
8/65: 70043
3/66: 70019
5/66: 70000
6/66: 70030
8/66: 70050
9/66: 70001/17
10/66: 70036/44
11/66: 70037/54
12/66: 70018
1/67: 70002/08/09/20/26
3/67: 70003/52
4/67: 70040/41/53
5/67: 70006/34/42/48
6/67: 700027

7/67: 70005/33/46/47
8/67: 70015/16/38
9/67: 70010/28/32/39
10/67: 70029
11/67: 70031
12/67: 70004/11/12/14/21/22/23/24/25/
35/45/49/51
8/68: 70013

Below:
BR Standard Class 7 4-6-2 No 70007 *Coeur-de-Lion* (31B) at March MPD 25 May 1963. Inroads into the 'Britannia' class commenced in June 1965 with No 70007 (12A) and was followed by No 70043 (5B) in August, a further 11 went in 1966 and 41 (40 off Carlisle Kingmoor) in 1967. No 70013 *Oliver Cromwell* (10A) survived to the end of steam on BR in August 1968 and has since been preserved.
N. E. Preedy

Above:
The 'Britannia' depot. BR Standard Class 7 4-6-2
Nos 70024 *Vulcan* (12A) and 70025 *Western Star*
(12A) at Carlisle Kingmoor May 1967. *B. Lister*

Below:
BR Standard Class 7 4-6-2 No 70026 *Polar Star* (6J)
under repair at Llandudno MPD December 1964.
N. Kneale

45

Above:
BR Standard Class 8 4-6-2 No 71000 *Duke of Gloucester* on the ashpit at Crewe North MPD 25 September 1955. This prototype Standard Class 8 Pacific based at Crewe North was withdrawn in November 1962, it was purchased for preservation in 1974 after spending 12 years in open storage – seven at Barry docks. *D. McGarry*

Below:
BR Standard Class 6 4-6-2 No 72003 *Clan Fraser* (66A) at Polmadie MPD 18 May 1959. No 72003 together with its sister engines Nos 72000/01/02/04 all (66A), were withdrawn from the Scottish Region en masse in December 1962 and following a period of storage at Polmadie, Parkhead and Darlington, finally succumbed to the torch early in 1964. *C. W. Woodhead*

BR Standard Class 8P 4-6-2
'71XXX'

Introduced: 1954
Purpose: Express passenger
Power classification: 8P
Tractive effort: 39,080lb

Locomotive Name
71000   *Duke of Gloucester*

Stock analysis 1959-1962
1/1/59-1/1/62 (1): 71000

Locomotive depot allocations 1959-1962
71000   5A Crewe North: *Wdn 11/62*

BR Standard Class 6 4-6-2
'Clan'

Introduced: 1952
Purpose: Mixed traffic
Power classification: 6P5F
Tractive effort: 27,520lb

Locomotive names
72000   *Clan Buchanan*
72001   *Clan Cameron*
72002   *Clan Campbell*
72003   *Clan Fraser*
72004   *Clan MacDonald*
72005   *Clan MacGregor*
72006   *Clan MacKenzie*
72007   *Clan MacKintosh*
72008   *Clan MacLeod*
72009   *Clan Stewart*

Stock analysis 1959-1966
1/1/59   (10):   72000-09
1/1/60   (10):   72000-09
1/1/61   (10):   72000-09
1/1/62   (10):   72000-09
1/1/63   (5):   72005-09
1/1/64   (5):   72005-09
1/1/65   (5):   72005-09
1/1/66   (2):   72006/08

Locomotive depot allocations 1959-1966

72000	66A	Polmadie
12/59	64A	St Margarets
3/60	66A	Polmadie: *Wdn 12/62*
72001	66A	Polmadie
11/59	64B	Haymarket
3/60	66A	Polmadie: *Wdn 12/62*
72002	66A	Polmadie
11/59	64B	Haymarket
3/60	66A	Polmadie: *Wdn 12/62*
72003	66A	Polmadie
11/59	64A	St Margarets
3/60	66A	Polmadie: *Wdn 12/62*
72004	66A	Polmadie
11/59	64A	St Margarets
3/60	66A	Polmadie: *Wdn 12/62*
72005	12A	Kingmoor: *Wdn 4/65*
72006	12A	Kingmoor: *Wdn 5/66*
72007	12A	Kingmoor: *Wdn 12/65*
72008	12A	Kingmoor: *Wdn 4/66*
72009	12A	Kingmoor: *Wdn 8/65*

Demise of the BR Standard Class 6 4-6-2s
Withdrawals
12/62:   72000/01/02/03/04
 4/65:   72005
 8/65:   72009
12/65:   72007
 4/66:   72008
 5/66:   72006

BR Standard Class 5 4-6-0 '73XXX'

Introduced: 1951
Purpose: Mixed Traffic
Power classification: 5MT
Tractive effort: 26,120lb

Number series: 73000-73124, 73155-73171
Number series: 73125-73154: Fitted with Caprotti valve gear

Locomotive names

73080	*Merlin*	73110	*The Red Knight*
73081	*Excalibur*	73111	*King Uther*
73082	*Camelot*	73112	*Morgan le Fay*
73083	*Pendragon*	73113	*Lyonnesse*
73084	*Tintagel*	73114	*Etarre*
73085	*Melisande*	73115	*King Pellinore*
73086	*The Green Knight*	73116	*Iseult*
73087	*Linette*	73117	*Vivien*
73088	*Joyous Gard*	73118	*King Leodegrance*
73089	*Maid of Astolat*	73119	*Elaine*

Stock analysis 1959-1968

1/1/59 (172): 73000-99,73100-71
1/1/60 (172): 73000-99, 73100-71
1/1/61 (172): 73000-99, 73100-71
1/1/62 (172): 73000-99, 73100-71
1/1/63 (172): 73000-99, 73100-71
1/1/64 (172): 73000-99, 73100-71
1/1/65 (157): 73000-11/13-16/18-23/25/26/28-45/48-51/53-57/59/60/62-73/75/77-79, 73100-08/10-15/17-60/62/63/65-71
1/1/66 (115): 73000/02/04-07/09-11/13/14/16/18-20/22/25/26/28/29/33-35/37/39/40/43/ 45/48/50/53/55/57/59/60/63-67/69-73/78-83/85-89/92-99,73100-02/05/07/ 08/10/13-15/ 17-21/25-46/49-51/53-60/69-71
1/1/67 (76): 73000/02/04/06/10/11/14/18-20/22/25/26/29/33-35/37/39/40/43/45/48/50/ 53/59/60/64-67/69-71/73/79/85/92-94/96/97, 73100/10/13/15/17-19/25-44/46/55-60
1/1/68 (23): 73000/10/33-35/40/50/53/67/69, 73125/26/28/31-36/38/42/43/57

Locomotive depot allocations
1959-1968

73000	41B	Grimesthorpe		10/66	9H	Patricroft: *Wdn 3/68*
1/61	41D	Canklow		**73001**	82C	Swindon
1/62	17A	Derby		1/64	82E	Bristol (Barrow Rd)
9/62	2F	Woodford Halse: 1G		1/65	85B	Gloucester (Horton Rd)
		9/63		2/65	82F	Bath (Green Park): *Wdn*
1/65	2B	Oxley				*12/65*
4/65	6D	Shrewsbury		**73002**	41D	Canklow
4/66	9J	Agecroft		1/60	41C	Millhouses

48

4/61	41D	Canklow
11/62	71A	Eastleigh
9/63	70G	Weymouth: *Wdn 3/67*
73003	82E	Bristol (Barrow Rd)
3/63	89A	Shrewsbury: 6D 9/63
9/63	82E	Bristol (Barrow Rd)
6/65	81F	Oxford: *Wdn 12/65*
73004	41C	Millhouses
2/60	6A	Chester (Midland)
5/60	1A	Willesden
3/64	1E	Bletchley
1/65	5E	Nuneaton
6/65	6C	Croes Newydd
4/66	9K	Bolton: *Wdn 10/67*
73005	63A	Perth
1/63	67A	Corkerhill: *Wdn 6/66*
73006	63A	Perth
1/63	67A	Corkerhill
7/64	9H	Patricroft: *Wdn 3/67*
73007	63A	Perth
6/64	65F	Grangemouth
10/65	65J	Stirling: *Wdn 3/66*
73008	63A	Perth
7/64	61B	Aberdeen: *Wdn 9/65*
73009	63A	Perth
1/63	67A	Corkerhill: *Wdn 7/66*
73010	55A	Holbeck
9/59	15E	Leicester (Central)
6/60	14D	Neasden
6/62	2F	Woodford Halse: 1G 9/63
1/65	2B	Oxley
4/65	9H	Patricroft: *Wdn 6/68*
73011	41C	Millhouses
2/60	6J	Holyhead
2/63	6G	Llandudno Junction
11/63	1G	Woodford Halse
1/65	2B	Oxley
4/65	9H	Patricroft: *Wdn 11/67*
73012	82C	Swindon
1/64	87F	Llanelly
6/64	82E	Bristol (Barrow Rd): *Wdn 11/64*
73013	6E	Chester (West)
9/59	6A	Chester (Midland)
5/60	1A	Willesden
3/64	1E	Bletchley
1/65	2B	Oxley
6/65	2D	Banbury
4/66	9K	Bolton: *Wdn 5/66*
73014	6E	Chester (West)
4/60	6A	Chester (Midland)

5/60	1A	Willesden
3/64	1E	Bletchley
2/65	2B	Oxley
6/65	2D	Banbury
4/66	9K	Bolton: *Wdn 7/67*
73015	82E	Bristol (Barrow Rd)
6/65	82F	Bath (Green Park): *Wdn 8/65*
73016	41C	Millhouses
1/62	41D	Canklow
11/62	71A	Eastleigh: 70D 9/63
12/63	70B	Feltham
11/64	70A	Nine Elms
10/65	70B	Feltham
11/65	70G	Weymouth: *Wdn 12/66*
73017	71G	Weymouth: 70G 9/63: *Wdn 10/64*
73018	71G	Weymouth: 70G 9/63
4/67	70C	Guildford: *Wdn 7/67*
73019	82F	Bath (Green Park)
7/60	82E	Bristol (Barrow Road)
10/60	82F	Bath (Green Park)
4/62	85C	Gloucester (Barnwood)
4/64	85B	Gloucester (Horton Road)
11/64	2B	Oxley
4/66	9K	Bolton: *Wdn 1/67*
73020	71G	Weymouth: 70G 9/63
4/67	70C	Guildford: *Wdn 7/67*
73021	6E	Chester (West)
4/59	86C	Cardiff (Canton)
4/60	84G	Shrewsbury
5/60	87F	Llanelly
7/62	82E	Bristol (Barrow Road)
9/62	85C	Gloucester (Barnwood)
4/64	85B	Gloucester (Horton Road)
6/65	81F	Oxford: *Wdn 8/65*
73022	71G	Weymouth: 70G 9/63
9/64	70D	Eastleigh
5/65	70C	Guildford
6/66	70A	Nine Elms: *Wdn 4/67*
73023	6E	Chester (West)
4/59	86C	Cardiff (Canton)
5/60	87F	Llanelly
6/64	82F	Bath (Green Park)
9/64	81F	Oxford: *Wdn 8/65*
73024	6E	Chester (West)
4/59	86C	Cardiff (Canton)
4/60	84G	Shrewsbury: 89A 1/61
7/62	82E	Bristol (Barrow Rd)
10/62	85C	Gloucester (Barnwood)

3/63	89A	Shrewsbury: 6D 9/63
9/63	87F	Llanelly
6/64	82E	Bristol (Barrow Rd)
9/64	81F	Oxford: Wdn 11/64
73025	6E	Chester (West)
4/59	84G	Shrewsbury: 89A 1/61
	89A	Shrewsbury: 6D 9/63
1/65	2B	Oxley
3/65	6D	Shrewsbury
4/66	9J	Agecroft
10/66	9H	Patricroft: Wdn 10/67
73026	6E	Chester (West)
4/59	84G	Shrewsbury: 89A 1/61
	89A	Shrewsbury: 6D 9/63
10/64	2L	Leamington Spa
6/65	2A	Tyseley
4/66	9K	Bolton: Wdn 4/67
73027	82C	Swindon: Wdn 2/64
73028	82F	Bath (Green Park)
7/60	82E	Bristol (Barrow Rd)
10/60	82F	Bath (Green Park)
5/61	82E	Bristol (Barrow Rd)
11/63	82C	Swindon
1/64	85C	Gloucester (B'Wood)
4/64	85B	Gloucester (H'ton Rd)
11/64	2B	Oxley
4/66	9K	Bolton: Wdn 12/66
73029	71G	Weymouth: 70G 9/63
8/64	70D	Eastleigh
5/65	70C	Guildford
6/66	70A	Nine Elms: Wdn 7/67
73030	26F	Patricroft: 9H 9/63
10/63	83D	Exmouth Junction
9/64	82E	Bristol (Barrow Rd)
1/65	82F	Bath (Green Park)
2/65	82E	Bristol (Barrow Rd)
6/65	81F	Oxford: Wdn 8/65
73031		Rugby Testing Station
11/61	82F	Bath (Green Park)
4/62	85C	Gloucester (B'Wood)
4/64	85B	Gloucester (H'ton Rd)
6/65	81F	Oxford: Wdn 9/65
73032	6C	Birkenhead
5/60	1A	Willesden
10/60	14D	Neasden
6/62	2F	Woodford Halse: 1G 9/63
8/64	5E	Nuneaton
5/65	6C	Croes Newydd: Wdn 8/65
73033	6E	Chester (West)
9/59	6A	Chester (Midland)

5/60	1A	Willesden
7/62	6A	Chester (Midland)
8/62	1A	Willesden
3/64	1E	Bletchley
1/65	2B	Oxley
3/65	5E	Nuneaton
7/65	9H	Patricroft: Wdn 1/68
73034	84G	Shrewsbury: 89A 1/61
	89A	Shrewsbury: 6D 9/63
4/66	9J	Agecroft
10/66	9H	Patricroft: Wdn 3/68
73035	84G	Shrewsbury: 89A 1/61
	89A	Shrewsbury: 6D 9/63
7/65	9H	Patricroft: Wdn 1/68
73036	84G	Shrewsbury: 89A 1/61
	89A	Shrewsbury: 6D 9/63
	6D	Shrewsbury: Wdn 9/65
73037	84G	Shrewsbury: 89A 1/61
4/62	87F	Llanelly
6/64	82E	Bristol (Barrow Rd)
9/64	81F	Oxford
4/65	70D	Eastleigh
5/65	70C	Guildford
6/66	70A	Nine Elms: Wdn 7/67
73038	6E	Chester (West)
4/60	6A	Chester (Midland)
11/62	6G	Llandudno Junction
11/63	1A	Willesden
3/64	1E	Bletchley
1/65	2B	Oxley
3/65	5E	Nuneaton
7/65	6D	Shrewsbury: Wdn 9/65
73039	6C	Birkenhead
5/60	1A	Willesden
3/64	1E	Bletchley
1/65	5E	Nuneaton
7/65	9H	Patricroft: Wdn 9/67
73040	6A	Chester (Midland)
11/63	1A	Willesden
3/64	1E	Bletchley
1/65	5E	Nuneaton
7/65	6C	Croes Newydd
4/66	9K	Bolton
4/68	9H	Patricroft: Wdn 5/68
73041	73A	Stewarts Lane
5/59	70A	Nine Elms
11/59	71G	Weymouth
2/61	71A	Eastleigh
4/61	71G	Weymouth: 70G 9/63
8/64	70D	Eastleigh
5/65	70C	Guildford: Wdn 6/65
73042	73A	Stewarts Lane

5/59	70A	Nine Elms
11/59	71G	Weymouth
2/61	71A	Eastleigh
4/61	71G	Weymouth: 70G 9/63
	70G	Weymouth: *Wdn 8/65*
73043	41B	Grimesthorp
4/61	41D	Canklow
11/62	71A	Eastleigh: 70D 9/63
12/63	70B	Feltham
8/64	70D	Eastleigh
5/65	70C	Guildford
6/66	70A	Nine Elms: *Wdn 7/67*
73044	26F	Patricroft: 9H 9/63
10/63	83D	Exmouth Junction
1/65	81F	Oxford: *Wdn 3/65*
73045	55A	Holbeck
9/59	15E	Leicester (Central)
6/60	14D	Neasden
6/62	2F	Woodford Halse: 1G 9/63
6/64	6D	Shrewsbury
9/64	5E	Nuneaton
5/65	6C	Croes Newydd
7/65	9H	Patricroft: *Wdn 8/67*
73046	41C	Millhouses
4/61	41D	Canklow
11/62	70A	Nine Elms: *Wdn 9/64*
73047	82F	Bath (Green Park)
7/64	6D	Shrewsbury: *Wdn 12/64*
73048	41C	Millhouses
2/60	6A	Chester (Midland)
11/63	1A	Willesden
3/64	1E	Bletchley
1/65	5E	Nuneaton
6/65	2D	Banbury
4/66	9K	Bolton: *Wdn 10/67*
73049	82F	Bath (Green Park)
4/60	84G	Shrewsbury: 89A 1/61
6/62	82E	Bristol (Barrow Rd)
7/62	82F	Bath (Green Park)
9/64	81F	Oxford: *Wdn 3/65*
73050	82F	Bath (Green Park)
8/62	85C	Gloucester (B wood)
11/62	82F	Bath (Green Park)
3/64	87F	Llanelly
4/64	6D	Shrewsbury
4/66	9J	Agecroft
10/66	9H	Patricroft: *Wdn 6/68*
73051	82F	Bath (Green Park): *Wdn 8/65*
73052	82F	Bath (Green Park): *Wdn 12/64*
73053	55A	Holbeck
9/59	15E	Leicester (Central)
6/60	14D	Neasden
6/62	2F	Woodford Halse
5/63	14A	Cricklewood
7/63	14E	Bedford
8/63	2F	Woodford Halse: 1G 9/63
7/64	6D	Shrewsbury
7/65	9H	Patricroft: *Wdn 3/68*
73054	82E	Bristol (Barrow Rd)
4/61	82F	Bath (Green Park): *Wdn 8/65*
73055	66A	Polmadie: *Wdn 5/66*
73056	66A	Polmadie
7/64	61B	Aberdeen: *Wdn 6/65*
73057	66A	Polmadie
6/64	67A	Corkerhill: *Wdn 3/66*
73058	66A	Polmadie
7/64	61B	Aberdeen: *Wdn 11/64*
73059	66A	Polmadie: *Wdn 5/67*
73060	66A	Polmadie: *Wdn 5/67*
73061	66A	Polmadie: *Wdn 12/64*
73062	66A	Polmadie: *Wdn 6/65*
73063	66A	Polmadie: *Wdn 6/66*
73064	66A	Polmadie: *Wdn 5/67*
73065	41C	Millhouses
1/62	41D	Canklow
11/62	71A	Eastleigh: 70D 9/63
12/63	70B	Feltham
11/64	70A	Nine Elms
5/65	70C	Guildford
6/66	70A	Nine Elms: *Wdn 7/67*
73066	55A	Holbeck
9/59	15E	Leicester (Central)
6/60	14D	Neasden
6/62	15E	Leicester (Central)
1/63	2F	Woodford Halse
5/63	14A	Cricklewood: 14B 9/63
10/64	2L	Leamington Spa
6/65	2A	Tyseley
4/66	9K	Bolton: *Wdn 4/67*
73067	41C	Millhouses
2/60	6J	Holyhead
2/63	6A	Chester (Midland)
11/63	1A	Willesden
3/64	1E	Bletchley
1/65	2B	Oxley
4/65	6D	Shrewsbury
4/66	9J	Agecroft
10/66	9H	Patricroft: *Wdn 3/68*
73068	82E	Bristol (Barrow Rd)

9/62	85C	Gloucester (Barnwood)		4/61	71G	Weymouth: 70G 9/63
4/64	82F	Bath (Green Park)			70G	Weymouth: *Wdn 12/66*
1/65	85B	Gloucester (Horton Road)		**73081**	73A	Stewarts Lane
4/65	82F	Bath (Green Park): *Wdn 12/65*		5/59	70A	Nine Elms
				5/65	70C	Guildford: *Wdn 7/66*
73069	55A	Holbeck		**73082**	73A	Stewarts Lane
9/59	15E	Leicester (Central)		5/59	70A	Nine Elms
6/60	14D	Neasden		5/65	70C	Guildford: *Wdn 6/66*
6/62	15E	Leicester (Central)		**73083**	73A	Stewarts Lane
2/63	2F	Woodford Halse		5/59	70A	Nine Elms
5/63	14A	Cricklewood: 14B 9/63		8/64	70B	Feltham
10/64	2L	Leamington Spa		11/64	70G	Weymouth: *Wdn 9/66*
6/65	2A	Tyseley		**73084**	73A	Stewarts Lane
4/66	9K	Bolton		5/59	70A	Nine Elms
4/68	9H	Patricroft		10/65	70B	Feltham
7/68	10A	Carnforth: *Wdn 8/68*		11/65	70D	Eastleigh: *Wdn 12/65*
73070	6A	Chester (Midland)		**73085**	73A	Stewarts Lane
11/63	1A	Willesden		5/59	70A	Nine Elms
3/64	1E	Bletchley		10/65	70B	Feltham
6/64	6D	Shrewsbury		11/65	70D	Eastleigh
4/66	9K	Bolton: *Wdn 4/67*		6/66	70A	Nine Elms: *Wdn 7/67*
73071	6A	Chester (Midland)		**73086**	73A	Stewarts Lane
5/63	14A	Cricklewood		5/59	70A	Nine Elms: *Wdn 10/66*
7/63	14E	Bedford		**73087**	70A	Nine Elms
8/63	2F	Woodford Halse: 1G 9/63		5/59	82F	Bath (Green Park)
1/65	2B	Oxley		4/60	70A	Nine Elms
4/65	6D	Shrewsbury		6/60	82F	Bath (Green Park)
7/65	9H	Patricroft: *Wdn 9/67*		6/61	70A	Nine Elms
73072	66A	Polmadie: *Wdn 10/66*		8/64	70B	Feltham
73073	41C	Millhouses		9/64	70D	Eastleigh
2/60	6J	Holyhead		5/65	70C	Guildford: *Wdn 10/66*
2/63	6G	Llandudno Junction		**73088**	70A	Nine Elms
11/63	1G	Woodford Halse		10/65	70C	Guildford: *Wdn 10/66*
7/64	5E	Nuneaton		**73089**	70A	Nine Elms
7/65	9H	Patricroft: *Wdn 11/67*		9/64	70D	Eastleigh
73074	41B	Grimesthorpe		10/65	70C	Guildford: *Wdn 9/66*
4/61	41D	Canklow		**73090**	84G	Shrewsbury: 89A 1/61
11/62	70A	Nine Elms: *Wdn 9/64*			89A	Shrewsbury: 6D 9/63
73075	66A	Polmadie: *Wdn 12/65*		1/65	2B	Oxley
73076	66A	Polmadie: *Wdn 7/64*		3/65	6D	Shrewsbury: *Wdn 10/65*
73077	65A	Eastfield		**73091**	84G	Shrewsbury: 89A 1/61
1/63	67A	Corkerhill: *Wdn 1/65*		9/61	85C	Gloucester (Barnwood)
73078	65A	Eastfield		4/64	85B	Gloucester: *Wdn 5/65*
1/66	66E	Carstairs: *Wdn 7/66*		**73092**	84G	Shrewsbury: 89A 1/61
73079	67A	Corkerhill		9/61	85C	Gloucester (Barnwood)
4/67	66A	Polmadie: *Wdn 5/67*		4/64	85B	Gloucester (Horton Rd)
73080	73A	Stewarts Lane		7/64	82F	Bath (Green Park)
5/59	70A	Nine Elms		4/65	70D	Eastleigh
11/59	71G	Weymouth		10/65	70C	Guildford: *Wdn 7/67*
2/61	71A	Eastleigh		**73093**	84G	Shrewsbury: 89A 1/61
				9/61	85C	Gloucester (Barnwood)
				4/64	85B	Gloucester (Horton Rd)

2/65	82F	Bath (Green Park)
4/65	70D	Eastleigh
10/65	70C	Guildford: *Wdn 7/67*
73094	84G	Shrewsbury: 89A 1/61
9/61	82E	Bristol (Barrow Rd)
11/61	85C	Gloucester (Barnwood)
4/64	85B	Gloucester (Horton Rd)
5/64	6D	Shrewsbury
7/65	9H	Patricroft: *Wdn 5/67*
73095	84G	Shrewsbury: 89A 1/61
	89A	Shrewsbury: 6D 9/63
8/65	6C	Croes Newydd
4/66	9J	Agecroft: *Wdn 8/66*
73096	84G	Shrewsbury: 89A 1/61
7/62	85C	Gloucester (Barnwood)
4/64	85B	Gloucester (Horton Rd)
11/64	2B	Oxley
3/65	5E	Nuneaton
6/65	6C	Croes Newydd
7/65	9H	Patricroft: *Wdn 11/67*
73097	84G	Shrewsbury: 89A 1/61
	89A	Shrewsbury: 6D 9/63
7/65	9H	Patricroft: *Wdn 5/67*
73098	66A	Polmadie: *Wdn 3/66*
73099	66A	Polmadie
7/60	66C	Hamilton
9/61	66A	Polmadie: *Wdn 10/66*
73100	67A	Corkerhill: *Wdn 1/67*
73101	67A	Corkerhill: *Wdn 8/66*
73102	67A	Corkerhill: *Wdn 12/66*
73103	67A	Corkerhill: *Wdn 10/65*
73104	67A	Corkerhill: *Wdn 10/65*
73105	65A	Eastfield
12/64	65F	Grangemouth
10/65	65J	Stirling
6/66	67A	Corkerhill: *Wdn 9/66*
73106	63A	Perth
6/64	67A	Corkerhill: *Wdn 6/65*
73107	63A	Perth
6/64	66B	Motherwell: *Wdn 9/66*
73108	65A	Eastfield
1/66	66E	Carstairs: *Wdn 12/66*
73109	65A	Eastfield: *Wdn 10/64*
73110	70A	Nine Elms
8/64	70D	Eastleigh
10/65	70C	Guildford: *Wdn 1/67*
73111	70A	Nine Elms
8/64	70D	Eastleigh: *Wdn 10/65*
73112	70A	Nine Elms
8/64	70D	Eastleigh
9/64	70A	Nine Elms: *Wdn 6/65*
73113	70A	Nine Elms

8/64	70D	Eastleigh
10/65	70G	Weymouth: *Wdn 1/67*
73114	70A	Nine Elms
8/64	70D	Eastleigh
10/65	70G	Weymouth: *Wdn 6/66*
73115	70A	Nine Elms
8/64	70D	Eastleigh
6/66	70A	Nine Elms
10/66	70C	Guildford: *Wdn 3/67*
73116	70A	Nine Elms
5/59	82F	Bath (Green Park)
4/60	70A	Nine Elms
8/64	70D	Eastleigh: *Wdn 11/64*
73117	70A	Nine Elms
8/64	70D	Eastleigh
6/66	70A	Nine Elms
10/66	70C	Guildford: *Wdn 3/67*
73118	70A	Nine Elms
8/64	70D	Eastleigh
6/66	70A	Nine Elms
10/66	70C	Guildford: *Wdn 7/67*
73119	70A	Nine Elms
8/64	70D	Eastleigh: *Wdn 3/67*
73120	63A	Perth
1/63	67A	Corkerhill: *Wdn 12/66*
73121	67A	Corkerhill: *Wdn 1/66*
73122	67A	Corkerhill: *Wdn 9/65*
73123	67A	Corkerhill: *Wdn 5/65*
73124	67A	Corkerhill: *Wdn 12/65*
73125	26F	Patricroft: 9H 9/63
	9H	Patricroft: *Wdn 6/68*
73126	26F	Patricroft: 9H 9/63
	9H	Patricroft: *Wdn 4/68*
73127	26F	Patricroft: 9H 9/63
	9H	Patricroft: *Wdn 11/67*
73128	26F	Patricroft: 9H 9/63
2/64	16J	Rowsley
4/64	9H	Patricroft: *Wdn 5/68*
73129	26F	Patricroft: 9H 9/63
	9H	Patricroft: *Wdn 12/67*
73130	26F	Patricroft: 9H 9/63
	9H	Patricroft: *Wdn 1/67*
73131	26F	Patricroft: 9H 9/63
	9H	Patricroft: *Wdn 1/68*
73132	26F	Patricroft: 9H 9/63
	9H	Patricroft: *Wdn 3/68*
73133	26F	Patricroft: 9H 9/63
	9H	Patricroft: *Wdn 6/68*
73134	26F	Patricroft: 9H 9/63
	9H	Patricroft: *Wdn 6/68*
73135	15C	Leicester (Midland)
1/59	17A	Derby

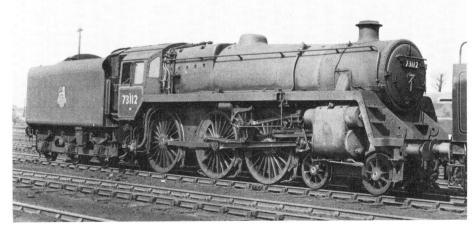

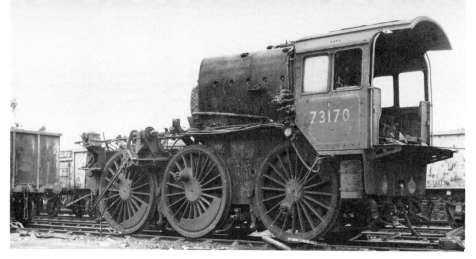

Above left:
BR Standard Class 5 4-6-0 No 73112 (70A) later *Morgan le Fay*, at Eastleigh MPD 9 May 1959. No 73112 was one of 20 Southern based Class 5s to receive names formerly carried by Urie 'King Arthur's. No 73116 *Iseult* (70D) was the first of these named engines to be taken out of service in November 1964. Nos 73085 *Melisande* (70A) and 73118 *King Leodegrance* (70C) survived to the end of steam on the Southern in July 1967.
R. A. Panting

Centre left:
BR Standard Class 5 4-6-0 No 73158 (14A) at Cricklewood MPD 1 July 1962. *J. A. Fleming*

Bottom left:
BR Standard Class 5 4-6-0 No 73150 (65B) fitted with Caprotti valve gear, at St Rollox MPD 17 May 1964. *P. H. Groom*

Above:
Last days. BR Standard Class 5 4-6-0 No 73170 withdrawn off Eastleigh in June 1966 being cut up at Weymouth goods station by Cashmore's of Newport January 1967. *N. J. Cape*

Below:
A group of youngsters pay their last respects to BR Standard Class 5 Nos 73065 (70A) and 73093 (70C) at Basingstoke MPD 7 July 1967. Two days before steam closure on the Southern.
R. I. D. Hoyle

11/59	17C	Rowsley: 16J 9/63
4/64	16C	Derby
9/64	9H	Patricroft: *Wdn 3/68*
73136	15C	Leicester (Midland)
1/59	17A	Derby
11/59	17C	Rowsley: 16J 9/63
5/64	9H	Patricroft: *Wdn 3/68*
73137	15C	Leicester (Midland)
1/59	17A	Derby
11/59	17C	Rowsley
5/62	15C	Leicester (Midland)
6/62	17C	Rowsley: 16J 9/63
6/64	9H	Patricroft: *Wdn 6/67*
73138	15C	Leicester (Midland)
1/59	17A	Derby
11/59	17C	Rowsley: 16J 9/63
5/64	9H	Patricroft: *Wdn 468*
73139	15C	Leicester (Midland)
1/59	17A	Derby
11/59	17C	Rowsley: 16J 9/63
6/64	9H	Patricroft: *Wdn 5/67*
73140	17A	Derby
11/59	17C	Rowsley
9/61	17A	Derby
2/62	17C	Rowsley: 16J 9/63
5/64	9H	Patricroft: *Wdn 10/67*
73141	15C	Leicester (Midland)
1/59	17A	Derby
11/59	17C	Rowsley: 16J 9/63
5/64	9H	Patricroft: *Wdn 7/67*
73142	15C	Leicester (Midland)
1/59	17A	Derby
11/59	17C	Rowsley: 16J 9/63
4/64	16C	Derby
5/64	9H	Patricroft: *Wdn 4/68*
73143	16A	Nottingham
1/59	17A	Derby
11/59	17C	Rowsley: 16J 9/63
2/64	9H	Patricroft: *Wdn 6/68*
73144	16A	Nottingham
1/59	17A	Derby
11/59	17C	Rowsley
9/61	17A	Derby
2/62	17C	Rowsley: 16J 9/63
4/64	16C	Derby
5/64	9H	Patricroft: *Wdn 8/67*
73145	65B	St Rollox
1/66	65A	Eastfield
9/66	67C	Ayr: *Wdn 9/66*
73146	65B	St Rollox
1/66	65A	Eastfield
11/66	66B	Motherwell: *Wdn 5/67*
73147	65B	St Rollox: *Wdn 8/65*
73148	65B	St Rollox: *Wdn 9/65*
73149	65B	St Rollox
11/66	65J	Stirling: *Wdn 12/66*
73150	65B	St Rollox
11/66	65J	Stirling: *Wdn 12/66*
73151	65B	St Rollox: *Wdn 8/66*
73152	65B	St Rollox: *Wdn 12/65*
73153	65B	St Rollox
11/66	65J	Stirling: *Wdn 12/66*
73154	65B	St Rollox
12/65	65J	Stirling
6/66	66B	Motherwell: *Wdn 12/66*
73155	41C	Millhouses
1/62	41D	Canklow
11/62	71A	Eastleigh: 70D 9/63
12/63	70B	Feltham
11/64	70D	Eastleigh
4/67	70C	Guildford: *Wdn 7/67*
73156	34E	New England
1/59	41B	Grimesthorpe
8/60	17A	Derby
9/60	14D	Neasden
6/62	15E	Leicester (Central)
3/63	2F	Woodford Halse
5/63	14A	Cricklewood: 14B 9/63
10/64	2L	Leamington Spa
6/65	2A	Tyseley
4/66	9K	Bolton: *Wdn 11/67*
73157	14D	Neasden
2/59	17A	Derby
6/60	14D	Neasden
6/62	14A	Cricklewood
5/63	6A	Chester (Midland)
11/63	1G	Woodford Halse
1/65	2B	Oxley
4/65	9H	Patricroft: *Wdn 5/68*
73158	41A	Darnall
1/59	14D	Neasden
2/59	17A	Derby
6/60	14D	Neasden
6/62	14A	Cricklewood
7/63	14E	Bedford
8/63	14A	Cricklewood: 14B 9/63
4/64	9H	Patricroft: *Wdn 10/67*
73159	14D	Neasden
2/59	17A	Derby
6/60	14D	Neasden
6/62	15E	Leicester (Central)
1/63	2F	Woodford Halse: 1G 9/63
9/64	5E	Nuneaton

7/65	9H	Patricroft: *Wdn 10/67*
73160	55E	Normanton
4/64	1E	Bletchley
1/65	2B	Oxley
4/65	9H	Patricroft: *Wdn 11/67*
73161	55E	Normanton
6/62	55H	Neville Hill
6/63	56A	Wakefield
9/63	83D	Exmouth Jct: *Wdn 12/64*
73162	55G	Huddersfield
6/61	55H	Neville Hill
6/63	56A	Wakefield
9/63	83D	Exmouth Jct
1/65	81F	Oxford: *Wdn 5/65*
73163	55G	Huddersfield
8/64	56A	Wakefield
11/64	2B	Oxley
4/65	9H	Patricroft: *Wdn 11/65*
73164	55G	Huddersfield
9/63	82F	Bath (Green Park)
11/63	82E	Bristol (Barrow Rd)
9/64	81F	Oxford: *Wdn 12/64*
73165	55G	Huddersfield
8/64	56A	Wakefield
11/64	2B	Oxley
4/65	9H	Patricroft: *Wdn 9/65*
73166	55G	Huddersfield
4/59	55A	Holbeck
9/60	55G	Huddersfield
4/62	55A	Holbeck
9/62	55D	Royston
6/63	26F	Patricroft: 9H 9/63
10/63	83D	Exmouth Jct
9/64	83E	Yeovil Town
6/65	81F	Oxford: *Wdn 12/65*
73167	55E	Normanton
2/59	50E	Scarborough
6/59	55E	Normanton
6/63	55A	Holbeck
9/63	70B	Feltham
8/64	6D	Shrewsbury: *Wdn 8/65*
73168	55A	Holbeck
2/59	50E	Scarborough
6/59	55A	Holbeck
10/61	55H	Neville Hill
6/63	56A	Wakefield
9/63	70B	Feltham
11/64	70D	Eastleigh: *Wdn 12/65*
73169	55A	Holbeck
2/59	50E	Scarborough
6/59	55A	Holbeck
6/61	55H	Neville Hill
6/63	56A	Wakefield
9/63	70B	Feltham
11/64	70D	Eastleigh: *Wdn 10/66*
73170	55A	Holbeck
2/59	50E	Scarborough
6/59	55A	Holbeck
9/62	55D	Royston
9/63	70B	Feltham
11/64	70D	Eastleigh: *Wdn 6/66*
73171	55A	Holbeck
9/62	55D	Royston
9/63	70B	Feltham
11/64	70D	Eastleigh: *Wdn 10/66*

Demise of the BR Standard Class 5 4-6-0s

Withdrawals

2/64: 73027
7/64: 73076
9/64: 73046/74
10/64: 73017, 73109
11/64: 73012/24/58, 73116
12/64: 73047/52/61, 73161/64
1/65: 73077
3/65: 73044/49
5/65: 73091, 73123/62
6/65: 73041/56/62, 73106/12
8/65: 73015/21/23/30/32/42/51/54, 73147/67
9/65: 73008/31/36/38, 73122/48/65
10/65: 73090, 73103/04/11
11/65: 73163
12/65: 73001/03/68/75/84, 73124/52/66/68
1/66: 73121
3/66: 73007/57/98
5/66: 73013/55
6/66: 73005/63/82, 73114/70
7/66: 73009/78/81
8/66: 73095, 73101/51
9/66: 73083/89, 73105/07/45
10/66: 73072/86/87/88/99, 73169/71
12/66: 73016/28/80, 73102/08/20/49/50/53/54
1/67: 73019, 73100/10/13/30
3/67: 73002/06, 73115/17/19
4/67: 73022/26/66/70
5/67: 73059/60/64/79/94/97, 73139/46
6/67: 73137
7/67: 73014/18/20/29/37/43/65/85/92/93, 73118/41/55

8/67: 73045, 73144
9/67: 73039/71
10/67: 73004/25/48, 73140/58/59
11/67: 73011/73/96, 73127/56/60
12/67: 73129
1/68: 73033/35, 73131

3/68: 73000/34/53/67, 73132/35/36
4/68: 73126/38/42
5/68: 73040, 73128/57
6/68: 73010/50, 73125/33/34/43
8/68: 73069

BR Standard Class 4 4-6-0
'75XXX'

Introduced: 1951
Purpose: Mixed Traffic
Power classification: 4MT
Tractive effort: 25,100lb

Stock analysis 1959-1968

1.1.59 (80): 75000-79
1.1.60 (80): 75000-79
1.1.61 (80): 75000-79
1.1.62 (80): 75000-79
1.1.63 (80): 75000-79
1.1.64 (80): 75000-79
1.1.65 (78): 75000/02-66/68-79
1.1.66 (67): 75002/04/06/09-21/23/24/26/27/29-37/39-66/68-71/74-79
1.1.67 (46): 75002/04/06/09/10/12/13/15-21/24/26/27/29/30/32-35/37/39-43/46-48/52/
              55/58-62/64/68/71/74-77
1.1.68 (10): 75009/19-21/27/32/34/41/48/62

Locomotive depot allocations
1959-1968

75000	82C	Swindon		12/66	6C	Croes Newydd
8/59	84E	Tyseley		6/67	5D	Stoke: *Wdn 8/67*
2/61	81F	Oxford		**75003**	85A	Worcester
7/62	82E	Bristol (Barrow Rd)		7/60	84E	Tyseley: 2A 9/63
9/62	84D	Leamington: 2L 9/63		10/63	83E	Yeovil Town
9/63	83E	Yeovil Town		6/65	85A	Worcester: *Wdn 10/65*
6/65	85A	Worcester: *Wdn 12/65*		**75004**	82E	Bristol (Barrow Rd)
75001	81F	Oxford		11/61	82G	Templecombe
3/63	82E	Bristol (Barrow Rd)		5/62	82F	Bath (Green Park)
9/63	83E	Yeovil Town: *Wdn 12/64*		10/62	89C	Machynlleth: 6F 9/63
				1/66	6D	Shrewsbury: *Wdn 3/67*
75002	82C	Swindon		**75005**	6E	Chester (West)
1/60	85E	Gloucester (Bwd): 85C 1/61		4/59	84E	Tyseley
				7/60	85A	Worcester
9/61	82G	Templecombe		1/64	85B	Gloucester (H'ton Rd)
6/62	82E	Bristol (Barrow Rd)		3/64	83D	Exmouth Jct
9/62	89C	Machynlleth: 6F 9/63		4/65	83E	Yeovil Town

6/65	85A	Worcester: *Wdn 11/65*
75006	6E	Chester (West)
4/59	84E	Tyseley
9/62	89C	Machynlleth
3/63	89B	Croes Newydd: 6C 9/63
11/64	5D	Stoke
7/65	2A	Tyseley
11/65	6D	Shrewsbury
3/67	6C	Croes Newydd
6/67	5D	Stoke: *Wdn 8/67*
75007	81F	Oxford
3/63	82G	Templecombe: 83G 10/63
9/64	83E	Yeovil Town: *Wdn 3/65*
75008	81F	Oxford
7/64	83G	Templecombe
9/64	83D	Exmouth Jct
6/65	85A	Worcester: *Wdn 12/65*
75009	85E	Gloucester (Bwd): 85C 1/61
9/61	82G	Templecombe
11/62	89C	Machynlleth
3/63	89B	Croes Newydd: 6C 9/63
2/66	6G	Llandudno Jct
6/66	6F	Machynlleth
12/66	6D	Shrewsbury
3/67	6C	Croes Newydd
5/67	10D	Lostock Hall
6/67	10A	Carnforth: *Wdn 8/68*
75010	6G	Llandudno Jct
10/62	2B	Nuneaton
3/63	6A	Chester (Midland)
3/66	6C	Croes Newydd
5/67	10D	Lostock Hall
6/67	10A	Carnforth: *Wdn 10/67*
75011	6G	Llandudno Jct
10/62	2B	Nuneaton
5/63	17A	Derby: 16C 9/63
11/63	8F	Springs Branch
3/65	10G	Skipton: *Wdn 11/66*
75012	6G	Llandudno Jct
10/62	2B	Nuneaton
3/63	6A	Chester (Midland)
1/66	6F	Machynlleth
3/66	6C	Croes Newydd
3/66	6D	Shrewsbury: *Wdn 1/67*
75013	6G	Llandudno Jct
9/59	6A	Chester (Midland)
4/60	6B	Mold Junction
4/62	1E	Bletchley
6/65	6F	Machynlleth
12/66	6D	Shrewsbury
3/67	6C	Croes Newydd
5/67	5D	Stoke: *Wdn 8/67*
75014	6A	Chester (Midland)
6/59	6G	Llandudno Jct
9/59	6A	Chester (Midland)
4/60	6B	Mold Junction
4/62	1E	Bletchley
5/63	5D	Stoke
6/64	2A	Tyseley
9/64	6D	Shrewsbury: *Wdn 12/66*
75015	27C	Southport: 8M 9/63
12/63	8L	Aintree
4/64	8F	Springs Branch
3/65	10G	Skipton
2/67	10A	Carnforth: *Wdn 12/67*
75016	27C	Southport
5/63	2B	Nuneaton: 5E 9/63
6/65	6D	Shrewsbury
3/67	6C	Croes Newydd
6/67	16B	Colwick: (SB): *Wdn 7/67*
75017	27C	Southport: 8M 9/63
12/63	8F	Springs Branch
3/65	10G	Skipton: *Wdn 1/67*
75018	27C	Southport
5/63	2B	Nuneaton
6/63	6H	Bangor
9/63	5D	Stoke
4/66	5E	Nuneaton
6/66	5D	Stoke: *Wdn 6/67*
75019	27C	Southport: 8M 9/63
12/63	8F	Springs Branch
3/65	10G	Skipton
1/67	10A	Carnforth
4/67	12E	Tebay
1/68	10A	Carnforth: *Wdn 8/68*
75020	6E	Chester (West)
4/59	84E	Tyseley
6/59	89C	Machynlleth
3/63	89B	Croes Newydd: 6C 9/63
1/65	5D	Stoke
1/66	6D	Shrewsbury
3/67	8L	Aintree
6/67	10A	Carnforth: *Wdn 8/68*
75021	82E	Bristol (Barrow Rd)
10/60	81F	Oxford
5/62	89C	Machnylleth
3/63	89B	Croes Newydd: 6C 9/63
3/66	6D	Shrewsbury
7/66	6C	Croes Newydd
4/67	10A	Carnforth: *Wdn 2/68*
75022	82E	Bristol (Barrow Rd)
9/61	81F	Oxford

59

4/64	83D	Exmouth Jct
1/65	82E	Bristol (Barrow Rd)
2/65	83D	Exmouth Jct
6/65	85A	Worcester: *Wdn 12/65*
75023	85E	Gloucester (Bwd): 85C 1/61
9/61	82G	Templecombe
9/62	89C	Machynlleth
3/63	89B	Croes Newydd: 6C 9/63
1/65	5D	Stoke: *Wdn 1/66*
75024	81F	Oxford
3/59	82C	Swindon
8/59	84E	Tyseley
11/62	89C	Machynlleth
3/63	89B	Croes Newydd: 6C 9/63
6/65	6J	Holyhead
7/66	6F	Machnylleth
12/66	5D	Stoke
5/67	12E	Tebay: *Wdn 11/67*
75025	85A	Worcester
8/60	89C	Machnylleth
11/60	85A	Worcester
1/64	85B	Gloucester (H'ton Rd)
3/64	83D	Exmouth Jct
6/65	85A	Worcester: *Wdn 12/65*
75026	6E	Chester (West)
4/59	84E	Tyseley
6/59	89C	Machynlleth
3/63	89B	Croes Newydd: 6C 9/63
2/65	8K	Bank Hall
10/66	8L	Aintree
11/66	10G	Skipton
4/67	10A	Carnforth
4/67	12E	Tebay: *Wdn 12/67*
75027	81F	Oxford
2/59	82C	Swindon
2/60	82G	Templecombe
11/62	89C	Machynlleth
3/63	89B	Croes Newydd: 6C 9/63
2/65	8K	Bank Hall
10/66	8L	Aintree
11/66	10G	Skipton
1/67	10A	Carnforth
4/67	12E	Tebay
1/68	10A	Carnforth: *Wdn 8/68*
75028	6E	Chester (West)
6/59	6K	Rhyl
9/59	6E	Chester (West)
4/60	11B	Workington: 12F 6/60
6/60	6B	Mold Jct
6/61	6K	Rhyl
9/61	6B	Mold Jct
4/62	1E	Bletchley
6/65	6F	Machynlleth: *Wdn 12/65*
75029	27C	Southport
1/59	81F	Oxford
2/59	82C	Swindon
11/60	81F	Oxford
1/61	84E	Tyseley
11/62	89C	Machynlleth
3/63	89B	Croes Newydd: 6C 9/63
6/65	6G	Llandudno Jct
9/66	6D	Shrewsbury
3/67	6C	Croes Newydd
6/67	5D	Stoke: *Wdn 8/67*
75030	1E	Bletchley
11/59	6D	Chester (Northgate)
1/60	1A	Willesden
1/63	2B	Nuneaton: 5E 9/63
9/63	5D	Stoke
5/67	12E	Tebay: *Wdn 12/67*
75031	6A	Chester (Midland)
6/59	6G	Llandudno Jct
9/59	6A	Chester (Midland)
4/60	6B	Mold Junction
6/61	6L	Rhyl
9/61	1A	Willesden
12/62	21D	Aston: 2J 9/63
9/63	5D	Stoke: *Wdn 2/66*
75032	6G	Llandudno Jct
9/59	6A	Chester (Midland)
6/62	6G	Llandudno Jct
10/62	2B	Nuneaton
5/63	27C	Southport
7/63	27A	Bank Hall: 8K 9/63
2/66	5D	Stoke
5/67	12E	Tebay
1/68	10A	Carnforth: *Wdn 2/68*
75033	6A	Chester (Midland)
6/59	6K	Rhyl
9/59	6E	Chester (West)
4/60	11B	Workington: 12F 6/60
6/60	6B	Mold Junction
4/62	6K	Rhyl
9/62	6G	Llandudno Jct
10/62	2B	Nuneaton
5/63	27C	Southport
7/63	27A	Bank Hall: 8K 9/63
4/66	9F	Heaton Mersey
4/66	6A	Chester (Midland)
5/66	6C	Croes Newydd
1/67	6D	Shrewsbury
3/67	6C	Croes Newydd

4/67	10A	Carnforth: *Wdn 12/67*
75034	6A	Chester (Midland)
6/61	6K	Rhyl
9/61	6B	Mold Junction
4/62	6K	Rhyl
9/62	6G	Llandudno Jct
10/62	2B	Nuneaton
12/62	21D	Aston: 2J 9/63
9/63	5D	Stoke
6/67	10A	Carnforth: *Wdn 2/68*
75035	6A	Chester (Midland)
6/62	6K	Rhyl
9/62	6G	Llandudno Jct
10/62	2B	Nuneaton
6/63	6H	Bangor
12/64	5E	Nuneaton
6/66	5D	Stoke
5/67	12E	Tebay: *Wdn 7/67*
75036	1E	Bletchley
6/61	6G	Llandudno Jct
10/62	2B	Nuneaton
6/63	6H	Bangor
7/63	2B	Nuneaton: 5E 9/63
9/63	5D	Stoke: *Wdn 6/66*
75037	1E	Bletchley
12/62	21D	Aston: 2J 9/63
9/63	5D	Stoke
5/67	12E	Tebay: *Wdn 12/67*
75038	1E	Bletchley
10/64	6D	Shrewsbury: *Wdn 12/65*
75039	6A	Chester (Midland)
3/62	1E	Bletchley
5/63	17A	Derby: 16C 9/63
11/63	8F	Springs Branch
3/65	10G	Skipton
1/67	10A	Carnforth
4/67	12E	Tebay: *Wdn 9/67*
75040	14E	Bedford
1/60	17A	Derby
2/60	15C	Leicester (Midland)
9/62	17A	Derby: 16C 9/63
10/63	5D	Stoke
6/67	10A	Carnforth: *Wdn 10/67*
75041	14E	Bedford
1/60	15C	Leicester (Midland)
9/62	17A	Derby: 16C 9/63
11/63	8F	Springs Branch
3/65	10G	Skipton
4/67	10A	Carnforth: *Wdn 1/68*
75042	14E	Bedford
4/59	15C	Leicester (Midland)
9/62	17A	Derby: 16C 9/63
11/63	8F	Springs Branch
3/65	10G	Skipton
4/67	10A	Carnforth: *Wdn 11/67*
75043	14E	Bedford
1/60	15C	Leicester (Midland)
9/62	17A	Derby: 16C 9/63
11/63	8R	Walton-on-the-Hill
12/63	8L	Aintree
6/67	10A	Carnforth: *Wdn 12/67*
75044	14E	Bedford
1/60	16A	Nottingham
2/60	15C	Leicester (Midland)
9/62	17A	Derby: 16C 9/63
11/63	8F	Springs Branch
3/65	10G	Skipton: *Wdn 3/66*
75045	27A	Bank Hall
5/63	2B	Nuneaton: 5E 9/63
	5E	Nuneaton: *Wdn 4/66*
75046	27A	Bank Hall: 8K 9/63
4/66	9F	Heaton Mersey
4/66	6A	Chester (Midland)
5/66	6C	Croes Newydd
5/67	5D	Stoke: *Wdn 8/67*
75047	27A	Bank Hall: 8K 9/63
2/66	5D	Stoke
3/66	6C	Croes Newydd
7/66	6F	Machynlleth
12/66	6C	Croes Newydd
1/67	6D	Shrewsbury
3/67	6C	Croes Newydd
6/67	5D	Stoke: *Wdn 8/67*
75048	27A	Bank Hall: 8K 9/63
4/66	6A	Chester (Midland)
5/66	6C	Croes Newydd
5/67	10D	Lostock Hall
6/67	10A	Carnforth: *Wdn 8/68*
75049	27A	Bank Hall: 8K 9/63
	8K	Bank Hall: *Wdn 10/66*
75050	6A	Chester (Midland)
6/62	6H	Bangor
9/62	6G	Llandudno Jct
10/62	2B	Nuneaton
5/63	27A	Bank Hall: 8K 9/63
2/66	5D	Stoke
3/66	5E	Nuneaton
6/66	5D	Stoke: *Wdn 11/66*
75051	6A	Chester (Midland)
6/62	1E	Bletchley
5/63	17A	Derby: 16C 9/63
11/63	8F	Springs Branch
3/65	10G	Skipton: *Wdn 10/66*
75052	1E	Bletchley

12/59	6D	Chester (Northgate)
1/60	1A	Willesden
1/63	2B	Nuneaton: 5E 9/63
6/65	6J	Holyhead
7/66	6F	Machynlleth
12/66	6C	Croes Newydd
6/67	5D	Stoke: *Wdn 8/67*
75053	6A	Chester (Midland)
6/60	6K	Rhyl
9/60	6B	Mold Junction
4/62	1E	Bletchley
12/62	21D	Aston: 2J 9/63
9/63	5D	Stoke
9/64	6D	Shrewsbury: *Wdn 9/66*
75054	6A	Chester (Midland)
6/60	6K	Rhyl
9/60	6B	Mold Junction
4/62	1E	Bletchley
1/65	5D	Stoke: *Wdn 8/66*
75055	14E	Bedford
1/60	16A	Nottingham
2/60	15C	Leicester (Midland)
1/61	16A	Nottingham
2/62	15C	Leicester (Midland)
9/62	17A	Derby
5/63	1E	Bletchley
9/64	6D	Shrewsbury
10/64	1E	Bletchley
6/65	6F	Machynlleth
12/66	6D	Shrewsbury
3/67	6C	Croes Newydd
5/67	5D	Stoke: *Wdn 5/67*
75056	16A	Nottingham
9/62	17A	Derby
5/63	1E	Bletchley
9/63	5D	Stoke: *Wdn 6/66*
75057	15C	Leicester (Midland)
9/62	17A	Derby: 16C 9/63
11/63	8F	Spring Branch
3/65	10G	Skipton: *Wdn 2/66*
75058	15C	Leicester (Midland)
9/62	17A	Derby: 16C 9/63
1/64	8F	Springs Branch
3/65	10G	Skipton
4/67	10A	Carnforth: *Wdn 12/67*
75059	15C	Leicester (Midland)
9/62	17A	Derby: 16C 9/63
11/63	8F	Springs Branch
3/65	10G	Skipton
4/67	10A	Carnforth: *Wdn 7/67*
75060	15C	Leicester (Midland)
9/62	17A	Derby: 16C 9/63

11/63	8R	Walton-on-the-Hill
12/63	8L	Aintree
6/65	8A	Edge Hill
4/66	9F	Heaton Mersey
4/66	6A	Chester (Midland)
5/66	6C	Croes Newydd: *Wdn 4/67*
75061	15C	Leicester (Midland)
9/62	17A	Derby: 16C 9/63
11/63	8R	Walton-on-the-Hill
12/63	8L	Aintree: *Wdn 2/67*
75062	16A	Nottingham
9/62	17A	Derby: 16C 9/63
10/63	5D	Stoke
5/67	10D	Lostock Hall
6/67	10A	Carnforth: *Wdn 2/68*
75063	16A	Nottingham
9/62	17A	Derby
5/63	2B	Nuneaton: 5E 9/63
9/64	6D	Shrewsbury: *Wdn 5/66*
75064	16A	Nottingham
9/62	17A	Derby: 16C 9/63
11/63	8R	Walton-on-the-Hill
12/63	8L	Aintree: *Wdn 5/67*
75065	73H	Dover
5/59	71B	Bournemouth
8/61	71A	Eastleigh
11/62	70D	Basingstoke
3/63	71A	Eastleigh: 70D 9/63
	70D	Eastleigh: *Wdn 9/66*
75066	73H	Dover
5/59	71B	Bournemouth
7/61	71A	Eastleigh
11/62	70D	Basingstoke
3/63	71A	Eastleigh: 70D 9/63
	70D	Eastleigh: *Wdn 2/66*
75067	73H	Dover
5/59	71B	Bournemouth
8/61	71A	Eastleigh
11/62	75A	Brighton
4/63	75D	Stewarts Lane
9/63	75C	Norward Jct
12/63	70D	Eastleigh: *Wdn 10/64*
75068	73H	Dover
5/59	71B	Bournemouth
5/61	71A	Eastleigh
11/62	75A	Brighton
4/63	75D	Stewarts Lane
9/63	75C	Norward Jct
12/63	70D	Eastleigh: *Wdn 7/67*
75069	73H	Dover
5/59	71B	Bournemouth

Above:
BR Standard Class 4 4-6-0 No 75075 (75E) sporting a double chimney at Three Bridges MPD 28 April 1962. *I. G. Holt*

Below:
BR Standard Class 4 4-6-0 Nos 75058 (10G) in a cloud of steam and 75015 (10G) at Skipton MPD 16 October 1965. *E. F. Bentley*

Above:
**BR Standard Class 4 4-6-0 No 75060 (6C) rubs
shoulders with sister engine No 75010 (6C) outside
their home shed Croes Newydd 1966.** *A. Wynn*

Below:
**Awaiting its next banking turn. BR Standard Class
4 4-6-0 No 75037 (12E) at Tebay MPD a few days
before closure 30 December 1967.** *J. M. Boyes*

11/59	73A	Stewarts Lane: 75D 6/62	**75074**	70D	Basingstoke
8/63	70A	Nine Elms	1/59	73A	Stewarts Lane: 75D 6/62
5/65	70D	Eastleigh: *Wdn 9/66*	7/63	75C	Norward Jct
75070	71A	Eastleigh	12/63	70D	Eastleigh
1/59	73A	Stewarts Lane	8/64	70A	Nine Elms
2/59	75A	Brighton	5/65	70D	Eastleigh: *Wdn 7/67*
1/60	75E	Three Bridges	**75075**	70D	Basingstoke
10/62	75D	Stewarts Lane	1/59	75E	Three Bridges
8/63	70A	Nine Elms	10/62	75D	Stewarts Lane
5/65	70D	Eastleigh: *Wdn 9/66*	7/63	75C	Norward Jct
75071	82F	Bath (Green Park)	12/63	70D	Eastleigh: *Wdn 7/67*
11/62	82G	Templecombe: 83G 10/63	**75076**	70D	Basingstoke
			3/63	70A	Nine Elms
7/64	6C	Croes Newydd	5/65	70D	Eastleigh: *Wdn 7/67*
6/67	5D	Stoke: *Wdn 8/67*	**75077**	70D	Basingstoke
75072	82F	Bath (Green Park)	3/63	70A	Nine Elms
10/62	82G	Templecombe: 83G 10/63	5/65	70D	Eastleigh: *Wdn 7/67*
	83G	Templecombe: *Wdn 12/65*	**75078**	70D	Basingstoke
			3/63	70A	Nine Elms
75073	82F	Bath (Green Park)	5/65	70D	Eastleigh: *Wdn 7/66*
11/62	82G	Templecombe: 83G 10/63	**75079**	70D	Basingstoke
			3/63	71A	Eastleigh: 70D 9/63
	83G	Templecombe: *Wdn 12/65*		70D	Eastleigh: *Wdn 11/66*

Demise of the BR Standard Class 4 4-6-0s

Withdrawals

10/64: 75067
12/64: 75001
3/65: 75007
10/65: 75003
11/65: 75005
12/65: 75000/08/22/25/28/38/72/73
1/66: 75023
2/66: 75031/57/66
3/66: 75044
4/66: 75045
5/66: 75063
6/66: 75036/56
7/66: 75078
8/66: 75054
9/66: 75053/65/69/70
10/66: 75049/51

11/66: 75011/50/79
12/66: 75014
1/67: 75012/17
2/67: 75061
3/67: 75004
4/67: 75060
5/67: 75055/64
6/67: 75018
7/67: 75016/35/59/68/74/75/76/77
8/67: 75002/06/13/29/46/47/52/71
9/67: 75039
10/67: 75010/40
11/67: 75024/42
12/67: 75015/26/30/33/37/43/58
1/68: 75041
2/68: 75021/32/34/62
8/68: 75009/19/20/27/48

BR Standard Class 4 2-6-0
'76XXX'

Introduced: 1952
Purpose: Mixed traffic
Power classification: 4MT
Tractive effort: 24,170lb

Stock Analysis 1959-1968

1/1/59	(115):	76000-99, 76100-14
1/1/60	(115):	76000-99, 76100-14
1/1/61	(115):	76000-99, 76100-14
1/1/62	(115):	76000-99, 76100-14
1/1/63	(115):	76000-99, 76100-14
1/1/64	(115):	76000-99, 76100-14
1/1/65	(108):	76000-27/30/31/33/35-53/55-71/73-96/98/99, 76100-14
1/1/66	(92):	76000-14/16/18-22/24/26/31/33/35-49/51-53/57-59/61/63/64/66/67/69-71/73-96/98/99- 76100-05/08-11/13/14
1/1/67	(39):	76000/05-09/11/26/31/33/36/37/39-41/46/48/51/53/58/61/63/64/66/67/69/75/77/79-81/84/87/88/93-95/98, 76104

Locomotive depot allocations
1959-1967

76000	66B	Motherwell: *Wdn 5/67*		3/60	71A	Eastleigh: 70D 9/63
76001	66B	Motherwell		10/65	70F	Bournemouth: *Wdn 7/67*
	6/60	63B	Fort William			
	8/62	67A	Corkerhill	**76010**	72C	Yeovil Town
	4/64	67D	Ardrossan		1/59	71A	Eastleigh: 70D 9/63
	2/65	67C	Ayr: *Wdn 8/66*		10/65	70F	Bournemouth: *Wdn 9/66*
76002	66B	Motherwell: *Wdn 12/66*				
76003	66B	Motherwell: *Wdn 3/66*	**76011**	72C	Yeovil Town
76004	66B	Motherwell		1/59	71A	Eastleigh: 70D 9/63
	1/63	66D	Greenock (Ladyburn)		10/65	70F	Bournemouth: *Wdn 7/67*
	12/64	66A	Polmadie: *Wdn 10/66*			
76005	72B	Salisbury: 70E 12/62	**76012**	71A	Eastleigh: 70D 9/63
	10/65	70F	Bournemouth: *Wdn 7/67*		6/66	70C	Guildford: *Wdn 9/66*
				76013	71A	Eastleigh: 70D 9/63
76006	72B	Salisbury		9/64	70F	Bournemouth: *Wdn 9/66*
	3/60	71A	Eastleigh: 70D 9/63			
	10/65	70F	Bournemouth: *Wdn 7/67*	**76014**	71A	Eastleigh: 70D 9/63
				9/64	70F	Bournemouth: *Wdn 9/66*
76007	72B	Salisbury: 70E 12/62				
	4/67	70F	Bournemouth: *Wdn 7/67*	**76015**	71A	Eastleigh
				6/61	71B	Bournemouth: 70F 9/63
76008	72B	Salisbury: 70E 12/62		70F	Bournemouth: *Wdn 10/65*
	4/67	70F	Bournemouth: *Wdn 5/67*				
				76016	71A	Eastleigh: 70D 9/63
76009	72C	Yeovil Town		6/66	70C	Guildford: *Wdn 10/66*
	1/59	72B	Salisbury	**76017**	71A	Eastleigh

3/60	72B	Salisbury: 70E 12/62
	70E	Salisbury: *Wdn 7/65*
76018	71A	Eastleigh
3/60	72B	Salisbury: 70E 12/62
8/64	70D	Eastleigh
7/66	70C	Guildford: *Wdn 10/66*
76019	71A	Eastleigh
8/61	71B	Bournemouth: 70F 9/63
8/64	70D	Eastleigh: *Wdn 2/66*
76020	12D	Kirkby Stephen
5/59	2B	Nuneaton
6/59	8G	Sutton Oak
7/62	21D	Aston
12/62	5D	Stoke
10/63	5F	Uttoxeter
12/64	5D	Stoke
7/65	6A	Chester: *Wdn 4/66*
76021	51F	West Auckland
10/63	67B	Hurlford: *Wdn 10/66*
76022	12D	Kirkby Stephen
4/60	24J	Lancaster
2/62	8F	Springs Branch
7/62	21D	Aston
12/62	5D	Stoke
10/63	5F	Uttoxeter
8/64	2C	Stourbridge
11/64	2B	Oxley: *Wdn 8/66*
76023	12D	Kirkby Stephen
4/60	24J	Lancaster
8/60	8G	Sutton Oak
7/62	21D	Aston
12/62	5D	Stoke
10/63	5F	Uttoxeter
6/64	5B	Crewe South
1/65	5D	Stoke: *Wdn 10/65*
76024	51F	West Auckland
6/59	52A	Gateshead
11/59	52B	Heaton
7/60	52G	Sunderland
9/61	50A	York
6/62	51L	Thornaby
10/63	67B	Hurlford: *Wdn 12/66*
76025	71A	Eastleigh
5/61	71B	Bournemouth: 70F 9/63
	70F	Bournemouth: *Wdn 10/65*
76026	71A	Eastleigh
8/61	71B	Bournemouth: 70F 9/63
	70F	Bournemouth: *Wdn 7/67*
76027	71A	Eastleigh
3/62	71B	Bournemouth: 70F 9/63
	70F	Bournemouth: *Wdn 10/65*
76028	71A	Eastleigh: 70D 9/63
	70D	Eastleigh: *Wdn 5/64*
76029	71A	Eastleigh: 70D 9/63
	70D	Eastleigh: *Wdn 10/64*
76030	30A	Stratford
6/60	31A	Cambridge
9/60	31B	March
11/62	75A	Brighton
9/63	70C	Guildford
1/65	70D	Eastleigh: *Wdn 4/65*
76031	30A	Stratford
11/60	31B	March
11/62	75A	Brighton
9/63	70C	Guildford
1/65	70D	Eastleigh
6/66	70C	Guildford: *Wdn 7/67*
76032	30A	Stratford
6/60	31A	Cambridge
9/60	31B	March
11/62	75A	Brighton
9/63	70C	Guildford: *Wdn 8/64*
76033	30A	Stratford
6/60	31A	Cambridge
9/60	31B	March
11/62	75A	Brighton
9/63	70C	Guildford
1/65	70D	Eastleigh
6/66	70C	Guildford: *Wdn 1/67*
76034	30A	Stratford
11/60	32A	Norwich (Thorpe)
9/61	31B	March
11/62	75A	Brighton
9/63	70C	Guildford: *Wdn 9/64*
76035	14D	Neasden
6/62	14A	Cricklewood: 14B 9/63
12/64	1A	Willesden
7/65	6A	Chester: *Wdn 5/66*
76036	14D	Neasden
6/62	14A	Cricklewood: 14B 9/63
7/64	2E	Saltley
3/65	2F	Bescot
11/65	2C	Stourbridge
4/66	6A	Chester: *Wdn 1/67*
76037	14D	Neasden
6/62	14A	Cricklewood: 14B 9/63
12/64	1A	Willesden
9/65	2B	Oxley
2/67	6A	Chester (Midland)
4/67	6C	Croes Newydd: *Wdn 6/67*

76038	14D	Neasden
6/62	14A	Cricklewood: 14B 9/63
7/64	2E	Saltley
6/66	6F	Machynlleth: *Wdn 9/66*
76039	14D	Neasden
6/62	14A	Cricklewood: 14B 9/63
12/64	1A	Willesden
9/65	2B	Oxley
3/67	6A	Chester (Midland)
4/67	6C	Croes Newydd: *Wdn 6/67*
76040	14D	Neasden
6/62	14A	Cricklewood: 14B 9/63
7/64	2E	Saltley
1/65	2J	Aston
10/65	2E	Saltley
9/66	6C	Croes Newydd: *Wdn 4/67*
76041	14D	Neasden
6/62	14A	Cricklewood: 14B 9/63
12/64	1A	Willesden
9/65	2B	Oxley
3/67	6A	Chester: *Wdn 4/67*
76042	14D	Neasden
7/62	14A	Cricklewood: 14B 9/63
7/64	2E	Saltley
3/65	2F	Bescot
11/65	2C	Stourbridge
5/66	2B	Oxley: *Wdn 6/66*
76043	14D	Neasden
7/62	14A	Cricklewood: 14B 9/63
7/64	2E	Saltley
6/66	6F	Machynlleth: *Wdn 9/66*
76044	14D	Neasden
6/62	2F	Woodford Halse: 1G 9/63
6/64	5D	Stoke
3/66	6A	Chester: *Wdn 10/66*
76045	51F	West Auckland
10/63	65F	Grangemouth
10/65	66E	Carstairs: *Wdn 1/66*
76046	51F	West Auckland
10/63	65D	Dawsholm
10/64	65F	Grangemouth
10/65	67A	Corkerhill: *Wdn 5/67*
76047	12D	Kirkby Stephen
6/60	9E	Trafford Park
9/62	14A	Cricklewood: 14B 9/63
9/63	5D	Stoke
10/63	2E	Saltley
3/65	2F	Bescot
3/66	6A	Chester: *Wdn 12/66*
76048	24G	Skipton
5/59	9F	Heaton Mersey
9/62	14A	Cricklewood: 14B 9/63
7/64	2E	Saltley
9/66	6C	Croes Newydd: *Wdn 2/67*
76049	51F	West Auckland
10/63	64G	Hawick
10/65	64A	St. Margarets
1/66	64F	Bathgate: *Wdn 1/66*
76050	51F	West Auckland
10/63	64G	Hawick: *Wdn 9/65*
76051	12D	Kirkby Stephen
4/60	24J	Lancaster
2/62	8F	Springs Branch
7/62	21D	Aston
12/62	5D	Stoke
2/66	16B	Colwick
11/66	8G	Sutton Oak: *Wdn 4/67*
76052	12D	Kirkby Stephen
5/60	14D	Neasden
7/62	2F	Woodford Halse: 1G 9/63
10/63	2E	Saltley
5/65	2B	Oxley
7/65	2E	Saltley
8/65	6A	Chester: *Wdn 12/66*
76053	75B	Redhill
4/60	72B	Salisbury: 70E 12/62
6/64	70C	Guildford
1/65	70B	Feltham
7/65	70D	Eastleigh
6/66	70C	Guildford: *Wdn 1/67*
76054	75B	Redhill
4/60	72B	Salisbury: 70E 12/62
6/64	70C	Guildford: *Wdn 10/64*
76055	75B	Redhill
4/60	72B	Salisbury: 70E 12/62
6/64	70C	Guildford
1/65	70B	Feltham
7/65	70E	Salisbury: *Wdn 10/65*
76056	75B	Redhill
11/59	71A	Eastleigh
12/59	71B	Bournemouth: 70F 9/63
	70F	Bournemouth: *Wdn 10/65*
76057	75B	Redhill
11/59	71A	Eastleigh
12/59	71B	Bournemouth: 70F 9/63
	70F	Bournemouth: *Wdn 10/66*
76058	75B	Redhill

11/59	71A	Eastleigh
12/59	71B	Bournemouth
2/62	71A	Eastleigh: 70D 9/63
6/66	70C	Guildford: *Wdn 3/67*
76059	75B	Redhill
5/59	72B	Salisbury
3/60	71A	Eastleigh: 70D 9/63
6/66	70C	Guildford: *Wdn 9/66*
76060	75B	Redhill
5/59	72B	Salisbury
3/60	71A	Eastleigh: 70D 9/63
	70D	Eastleigh: *Wdn 12/65*
76061	75B	Redhill
5/59	71A	Eastleigh: 70D 9/63
	70D	Eastleigh: *Wdn 1/67*
76062	75B	Redhill
5/59	71A	Eastleigh: 70D 9/63
	70D	Eastleigh: *Wdn 10/65*
76063	71A	Eastleigh: 70D 9/63
	70D	Eastleigh: *Wdn 4/67*
76064	71A	Eastleigh: 70D 9/63
	70D	Eastleigh: *Wdn 7/67*
76065	71A	Eastleigh: 70D 9/63
	70D	Eastleigh: *Wdn 10/65*
76066	71A	Eastleigh
3/60	72B	Salisbury: 70E 12/62
8/64	70C	Guildford
1/65	70B	Feltham
7/65	70D	Eastleigh: *Wdn 7/67*
76067	71A	Eastleigh
3/60	72B	Salisbury: 70E 12/62
4/67	70F	Bournemouth: *Wdn 7/67*
76068	71A	Eastleigh: 70D 9/63
	70D	Eastleigh: *Wdn 10/65*
76069	71A	Eastleigh: 70D 9/63
10/66	70C	Guildford: *Wdn 6/67*
76070	66B	Motherwell
1/63	66D	Greenock (Ladyburn)
4/64	66F	Beattock
12/64	66A	Polmadie: *Wdn 8/66*
76071	66B	Motherwell
1/63	66D	Greenock (Ladyburn)
12/64	66A	Polmadie: *Wdn 1/66*
76072	68B	Dumfries: 67E 7/62
	67E	Dumfries: *Wdn 10/64*
76073	68B	Dumfries: 67E 7/62
4/66	67C	Ayr: *Wdn 6/66*
76074	65A	Eastfield
8/61	65C	Parkhead
10/61	65F	Grangemouth
11/63	65D	Dawsholm
10/64	67E	Dumfries
3/66	67C	Ayr: *Wdn 10/66*
76075	8G	Sutton Oak
10/62	21B	Bescot
1/63	5D	Stoke
2/66	16B	Colwick
11/66	8G	Sutton Oak
6/67	8F	Springs Branch: *Wdn 10/67*
76076	8G	Sutton Oak: *Wdn 11/66*
76077	8G	Sutton Oak
6/67	8F	Springs Branch: *Wdn 12/67*
76078	8G	Sutton Oak: *Wdn 12/66*
76079	8G	Sutton Oak
6/67	8F	Springs Branch: *Wdn 12/67*
76080	24D	Lower Darwen: 10H 9/63
3/65	8G	Sutton Oak
6/67	8F	Springs Branch: *Wdn 12/67*
76081	24D	Lower Darwen: 10H 9/63
3/65	8G	Sutton Oak
6/67	8F	Springs Branch: *Wdn 7/67*
76082	24D	Lower Darwen: 10H 9/63
3/65	8G	Sutton Oak: *Wdn 10/66*
76083	24D	Lower Darwen: 10H 9/63
3/65	8G	Sutton Oak: *Wdn 10/66*
76084	24G	Skipton
2/59	24J	Lancaster
3/59	24D	Lower Darwen: 10H 9/63
3/65	8G	Sutton Oak
6/67	8F	Springs Branch: *Wdn 12/67*
76085	21A	Saltley
1/59	9F	Heaton Mersey
9/62	14A	Cricklewood: 14B 9/63
9/63	5D	Stoke
10/63	2E	Saltley
1/65	5D	Stoke
3/66	16B	Colwick: *Wdn 6/66*
76086	21A	Saltley
1/59	9E	Trafford Park
10/62	14A	Cricklewood: 14B 9/63
9/63	5D	Stoke
10/63	2E	Saltley
3/65	2F	Bescot
3/66	2E	Saltley
6/66	6F	Machynlleth
9/66	6C	Croes Newydd: *Wdn 9/66*
76087	21A	Saltley
1/59	9F	Heaton Mersey
9/62	2F	Woodford Halse: 1G 9/63
10/63	2E	Saltley
3/65	2F	Bescot
3/66	2C	Stourbridge
5/66	2B	Oxley: *Wdn 1/67*
76088	9E	Trafford Park

9/60	14D	Neasden
12/60	9E	Trafford Park
9/62	14A	Cricklewood: 14B 9/63
9/63	5D	Stoke
10/63	2E	Saltley
3/65	2F	Bescot
3/66	2B	Oxley
2/67	6A	Chester (Midland)
	6A	Chester: *Wdn 6/67*
76089	9E	Trafford Park
9/62	14A	Cricklewood: 14B 9/63
12/64	1A	Willesden
1/65	5D	Stoke
2/66	16B	Colwick: *Wdn 9/66*
76090	67A	Corkerhill
1/61	65C	Parkhead
10/61	66B	Motherwell
7/62	66F	Beattock: *Wdn 12/66*
76091	67A	Corkerhill
1/61	65C	Parkhead
10/61	67A	Corkerhill
4/64	67B	Hurlford: *Wdn 12/66*
76092	67A	Corkerhill
4/64	67B	Hurlford: *Wdn 8/66*
76093	67A	Corkerhill
1/61	65C	Parkhead
10/61	67A	Corkerhill: *Wdn 2/67*
76094	67A	Corkerhill
1/61	65C	Parkhead
10/61	67A	Corkerhill
6/64	67B	Hurlford
11/66	66F	Beattock: *Wdn 5/67*
76095	67A	Corkerhill
2/61	65C	Parkhead
12/61	67A	Corkerhill: *Wdn 7/64*
(R)9/64	2E	Saltley
1/65	2J	Aston
8/65	6A	Chester: *Wdn 3/67*
76096	67A	Corkerhill
5/62	67C	Ayr: *Wdn 12/66*
76097	67A	Corkerhill
5/62	67C	Ayr: *Wdn 7/64*
76098	67A	Corkerhill
4/64	67D	Ardrossan
2/65	67C	Ayr
12/65	66F	Beattock: *Wdn 5/67*
76099	67A	Corkerhill
5/62	67C	Ayr
1/63	67A	Corkerhill
4/64	67D	Ardrossan: *Wdn 7/64*
(R)9/64	2E	Saltley
1/65	5D	Stoke
3/66	16B	Colwick: *Wdn 8/66*
76100	65D	Dawsholm
7/60	65C	Parkhead
1/61	65D	Dawsholm
10/64	65F	Grangemouth
10/65	67C	Ayr
12/65	66F	Beattock
6/66	67C	Ayr: *Wdn 8/66*
76101	65D	Dawsholm
10/64	65F	Grangemouth
10/65	67C	Ayr
11/65	67F	Stranraer
3/66	67C	Ayr: *Wdn 12/66*
76102	65C	Parkhead
2/59	65B	St Rollox
7/60	65C	Parkhead
12/60	65D	Dawsholm
10/64	65F	Grangemouth
10/65	67E	Dumfries
6/66	67B	Hurlford: *Wdn 12/66*
76103	65C	Parkhead
3/59	65B	St Rollox
7/60	65C	Parkhead
1/61	65B	St Rollox
10/61	65F	Grangemouth
10/63	65D	Dawsholm
10/64	65F	Grangemouth
10/65	67E	Dumfries
11/65	66A	Polmadie
4/66	66F	Beattock
6/66	67C	Ayr: *Wdn 7/66*
76104	61A	Kittybrewster
6/61	61B	Ferryhill
11/64	64F	Bathgate
1/66	66A	Polmadie: *Wdn 5/67*
76105	61A	Kittybrewster
6/61	61B	Ferryhill
12/61	64C	Dalry Rd
3/64	64F	Bathgate
1/66	66A	Polmadie: *Wdn 1/66*
76106	61A	Kittybrewster
5/60	61C	Keith
6/61	61B	Ferryhill
12/61	64C	Dalry Rd
3/64	64F	Bathgate
8/65	1A	Willesden: *Wdn 9/65*
76107	61A	Kittybrewster
5/60	61C	Keith
6/61	61B	Ferryhill
11/64	64F	Bathgate: *Wdn 10/65*
76108	61A	Kittybrewster
6/61	61B	Ferryhill

1/63	67B	Hurlford: *Wdn 7/66*	**76113**	65B	St. Rollox
76109	62A	Thornton	1/61	65C	Parkhead
1/60	62C	Dunfermline: *Wdn 9/66*	11/61	65B	St. Rollox
76110	62A	Thornton	5/62	65F	Grangemouth
4/60	62C	Dunfermline: *Wdn 12/66*	10/65	66E	Carstairs: *Wdn 12/66*
76111	62A	Thornton	**76114**	65B	St. Rollox
4/60	62C	Dunfermline	7/60	65C	Parkhead
2/62	62A	Thornton	10/61	65B	St. Rollox
11/64	64F	Bathgate: *Wdn 1/66*	5/62	67A	Corkerhill
76112	68C	Stranraer: 67F 7/62	11/66	66F	Beattock: *Wdn 12/66*
	67F	Stranraer: *Wdn 10/65*			

Demise of the BR Standard Class 4 2-6-0s

Withdrawals

5/64: 76028
7/64: 76097
8/64: 76032
9/64: 76034
10/64: 76029/54/72
4/65: 76030
7/65: 76017
9/65: 76050, 76106
10/65: 76015/23/25/27/55/56/62/65/68,
76107/12
12/65: 76060
1/66: 76045/49/71, 76105/11
2/66: 76019
3/66: 76003
4/66: 76020
5/66: 76035
6/66: 76042/73/85
7/66: 76103/08
8/66: 76001/22/70/92/99, 76100
9/66: 76010/12/13/14/38/43/59/86/89,
76109

10/66: 76004/16/18/21/44/57/74/82/83
11/66: 76076
12/66: 76002/24/47/52/78/90/91/96,
76101/02/10/13/14
1/67: 76033/36/53/61/87
2/67: 76048/93
3/67: 76058/95
4/67: 76040/41/51/63
5/67: 76000/08/46/94/98, 76104
6/67: 76037/39/69/88
7/67: 76005/06/07/09/11/26/31/64/66/67/81
10/67: 76075
12/67: 76077/79/80/84

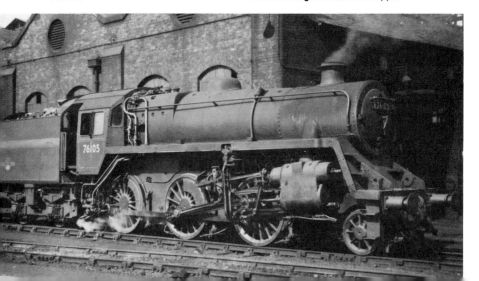

Below:
BR Standard Class 4 2-6-0 No 76105 (64C) at Dalry Road MPD August 1962. *D. J. Dippie*

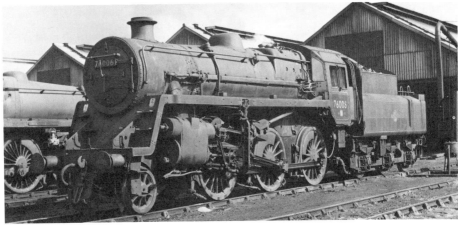

Top:
BR Standard Class 4 2-6-0 No 76042 (14A) at Cricklewood MPD 7 July 1963. *R. A. Panting*

Above:
BR Standard Class 4 2-6-0 No 76006 (71A) at Eastleigh MPD 27 August 1963. No 76006 (70F) was one of the 10 Class 4 2-6-0s that survived to the end of steam on the Southern in July 1967. The others being Nos 76005/07/09/11/26/67 (70F), 76064/66 (70D) and 76031 of Guildford. *J. Scrace*

Below:
BR Standard Class 4 2-6-0 No 76016 (70D) at Weymouth MPD 25 May 1966. *J. Scrace*

BR Standard Class 3 2-6-0
'77XXX'

Introduced: 1954
Purpose: Mixed traffic
Power classification: 3MT
Tractive effort: 21,490lb

Stock Analysis 1959-1967

1/1/59 (20): 77000-19
1/1/60 (20): 77000-19
1/1/61 (20): 77000-19
1/1/62 (20): 77000-19
1/1/63 (20): 77000-19

1/1/64 (20): 77000-19
1/1/65 (20): 77000-19
1/1/66 (19): 77000-09/11-19
1/1/67 (3): 76002/12/14

Locomotive depot allocations
1959-1967

77000	53A	Dairycoates: 50B 1/60
1/63	51A	Darlington
5/64	55B	Stourton: *Wdn 12/66*
77001	53B	Botanic Gardens
6/59	53A	Dairycoates: 50B 1/60
4/62	51L	Thornaby
9/63	55B	Stourton
12/63	55C	Farnley
12/64	55F	Manningham
11/65	50B	Dairycoates
12/65	50D	Goole: *Wdn 1/66*
77002	51F	West Auckland
12/62	51A	Darlington
1/63	50B	Dairycoates
9/63	55B	Stourton
11/64	52D	Tweedmouth
7/66	55B	Stourton
10/66	50A	York: *Wdn 6/67*
77003	51F	West Auckland
2/64	55B	Stourton: *Wdn 12/66*
77004	50G	Whitby
4/59	50B	Neville Hill
5/59	50C	Selby
9/59	50A	York
11/59	50E	Scarborough
4/63	50A	York
11/64	52D	Tweedmouth
7/66	55B	Stourton: *Wdn 12/66*
77005	66C	Hamilton
9/59	66A	Polmadie
5/60	66E	Carstairs
6/63	66B	Motherwell: *Wdn 11/66*
77006	66C	Hamilton
11/62	66E	Carstairs
12/63	65F	Grangemouth
10/65	66B	Motherwell: *Wdn 3/66*
77007	66C	Hamilton
9/59	66A	Polmadie
8/63	67B	Hurlford: *Wdn 11/66*
77008	66A	Polmadie
8/63	66B	Motherwell: *Wdn 6/66*
77009	66A	Polmadie
8/63	66E	Carstairs
10/63	65F	Grangemouth
10/65	66B	Motherwell: *Wdn 5/66*
77010	53A	Dairycoates: 50B 1/60
4/62	51L	Thornaby
4/63	51F	West Auckland
2/64	55B	Stourton: *Wdn 11/65*
77011	52C	Blaydon
9/59	52A	Gateshead
9/60	52H	Tyne Dock
4/61	52F	South Blyth
10/62	51L	Thornaby
9/63	55B	Stourton
11/64	8E	Northwick: *Wdn 2/66*
77012	50A	York
9/63	55B	Stourton
12/63	55C	Farnley
12/64	55F	Manningham
11/65	50B	Dairycoates
12/65	50D	Goole
3/66	52F	South Blyth
4/66	50A	York: *Wdn 6/67*
77013	50G	Whitby
4/59	50B	Neville Hill

5/59	50C	Selby		9/63	55B	Stourton
9/59	50A	York		11/64	8E	Northwich
10/60	50E	Scarborough		3/66	70C	Guildford: *Wdn 7/67*
4/63	50A	York		**77015**	67B	Hurlford: *Wdn 7/66*
9/63	55B	Stourton: *Wdn 3/66*		**77016**	67B	Hurlford: *Wdn 3/66*
77014	52C	Blaydon		**77017**	67B	Hurlford: *Wdn 11/66*
9/59	52A	Gateshead		**77018**	67B	Hurlford: *Wdn 11/66*
9/60	52H	Tyne Dock		**77019**	67B	Hurlford
4/61	52F	South Blyth		2/63	66A	Polmadie
10/62	51L	Thornaby		10/63	67B	Hurlford: *Wdn 11/66*

Demise of the BR Standard Class 3 2-6-0s

Withdrawals

11/65: 77010
1/66: 77001
2/66: 77011
3/66: 77006/13/16
5/66: 77009
6/66: 77008
7/66: 77015
11/66: 77005/07/17/18/19
12/66: 77000/03/04
6/67: 77002/12
7/67: 77014

BR Standard Class 2 2-6-0 '78XXX'

Introduced: 1952
Purpose: Mixed traffic
Power classification: 2MT
Tractive effort: 18,515lb

Stock analysis 1959-1967

1/1/59 (65): 78000-64
1/1/60 (65): 78000-64
1/1/61 (65): 78000-64
1/1/62 (65): 78000-64
1/1/63 (65): 78000-64
1/1/64 (64): 78000-14/16-64
1/1/65 (60): 78000-04/06-08/10-14/16-47/49-52/54-64
1/1/66 (43): 78002/03/07/08/10/12/13/16-23/26/28/31/34/36-41/44-47/49-52/55-64
1/1/67 (12): 78007/12/13/20/21/23/28/37/41/44/55/62

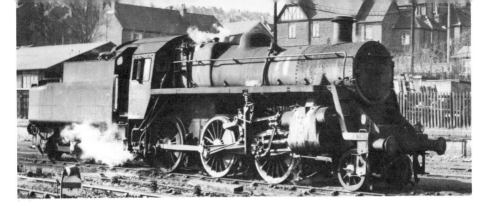

Top:
BR Standard Class 3 2-6-0 No 77014 (70C) at Guildford MPD 18 March 1966 shortly after its transfer from Northwich LMR. The class was rendered extinct with No 77014 when it was withdrawn off Guildford shed in July 1967. *R. E. Ruffell*

Above:
BR Standard Class 3 2-6-0 No 77004 (50A) at Stourton MPD 15 December 1963. *K. Hughes*

Below:
BR Standard Class 3 2-6-0 No 77012 (50A) and Stanier Class 5 4-6-0 No 45256 (8B) raising steam inside Holbeck MPD 13 February 1967. *J. H. Cooper-Smith*

Locomotive depot allocations
1959-1967

78000	89C	Machynlleth		4/64	55F	Manningham
5/63	16A	Nottingham: 16D 9/63		12/64	9G	Gorton
1/64	16C	Derby: *Wdn 6/65*		6/65	9E	Trafford Park: *Wdn 9/65*
78001	85A	Worcester		**78012**	51J	Northallerton
1/64	85C	Gloucester (Barnwood)		3/63	51A	Darlington
4/64	85B	Gloucester (Horton Rd)		11/63	52D	Tweedmouth
	85B	Gloucester: *Wdn 12/65*		12/64	9G	Gorton
78002	89C	Machynlleth		6/65	9E	Trafford Park
8/63	27D	Wigan: 8P 9/63		8/66	9K	Bolton: *Wdn 5/67*
10/63	8K	Bank Hall		**78013**	12D	Kirkby Stephen
6/64	10D	Lostock Hall: *Wdn 6/66*		6/60	16B	Kirby-in-Ashfield
78003	89C	Machynlleth		3/63	16A	Nottingham: 16D 9/63
5/63	6H	Bangor		12/63	15E	Coalville
6/65	1A	Willesden		9/64	15A	Leicester (Midland)
9/65	5E	Nuneaton		7/66	16A	Toton
1/66	6D	Shrewsbury: *Wdn 12/66*		11/66	9K	Bolton: *Wdn 5/67*
78004	85C	Hereford: 86C 1/61		**78014**	51J	Northallerton
1/64	87F	Llanelly		3/63	51A	Darlington
7/64	85B	Gloucester (Horton Rd)		11/63	55C	Farnley
	85B	Gloucester: *Wdn 11/65*		4/64	55F	Manningham
78005	89C	Machynlleth		12/64	9G	Gorton
10/62	85C	Gloucester (Barnwood)		6/65	9E	Trafford Park: *Wdn 9/65*
4/64	85B	Gloucester (Horton Rd)		**78015**	51J	Northallerton
	85B	Gloucester: *Wdn 9/64*		3/63	51A	Darlington: *Wdn 11/63*
78006	89C	Machynlleth		**78016**	51F	West Auckland
9/62	85C	Gloucester (Barnwood)		8/63	66B	Motherwell
4/64	85B	Gloucester (Horton Rd)		10/63	67E	Dumfries
	85B	Gloucester: *Wdn 12/65*		2/64	67F	Stranraer: *Wdn 8/66*
78007	89C	Machynlleth		**78017**	12D	Kirkby Stephen
6/63	5A	Crewe North		4/60	8F	Springs Branch
6/64	5B	Crewe South		6/61	6K	Rhyl
3/65	9G	Gorton		10/61	8D	Widnes
6/65	9E	Trafford Park		3/62	6K	Rhyl
8/66	9K	Bolton: *Wdn 5/67*		4/62	5D	Stoke
78008	85A	Worcester		10/66	6D	Shrewsbury: *Wdn 12/66*
3/62	84A	Wolverhampton		**78018**	12D	Kirkby Stephen
11/62	84B	Oxley: 2B 9/63		4/60	6A	Chester (Midland)
	2B	Oxley: *Wdn 10/66*		6/62	12F	Workington
78009	85A	Worcester		9/62	6A	Chester (Midland)
3/63	85C	Gloucester (Barnwood)		5/63	1A	Willesden
	85C	Gloucester: *Wdn 2/64*		9/65	5E	Nuneaton
78010	51J	Northallerton		4/66	6D	Shrewsbury: *Wdn 11/66*
3/63	66A	Polmadie		**78019**	12D	Kirkby Stephen
5/63	66B	Motherwell		4/60	8F	Springs Branch
6/63	51A	Darlington		6/61	8E	Northwich
11/63	55C	Farnley		5/63	1A	Willesden
4/64	5B	Crewe South: *Wdn 9/66*		9/65	5E	Nuneaton
78011	51J	Northallerton		1/66	5B	Crewe South: *Wdn 11/66*
3/63	51A	Darlington				
11/63	55C	Farnley		**78020**	15B	Kettering

11/59	16A	Nottingham: 16D 9/63		**78028**	15C	Leicester (Midland)
12/63	8P	Wigan Central		1/59	15B	Kettering
4/64	8F	Springs Branch		11/59	16A	Nottingham: 16D 9/63
5/64	16C	Derby		1/64	15E	Coalville
10/66	16A	Toton		9/64	15A	Leicester
11/66	10D	Lostock Hall: *Wdn 5/67*		7/66	16A	Toton
78021	15B	Kettering		11/66	9K	Bolton: *Wdn 2/67*
11/59	16A	Nottingham: 16D 9/63		**78029**	15C	Leicester (Midland)
1/64	16C	Derby		11/59	16A	Nottingham
2/65	15A	Leicester (Midland)		5/63	89D	Oswestry
7/66	16A	Toton		6/63	1C	Watford
11/66	10D	Lostock Hall: *Wdn 5/67*		4/65	1A	Willesden: *Wdn 10/65*
78022	41C	Millhouses		**78030**	5A	Crewe North
1/62	36A	Doncaster		10/64	5B	Crewe South: *Wdn 10/65*
9/62	31B	March				
12/62	12E	Barrow		**78031**	6D	Chester (Northgate)
5/63	27B	Aintree: 8L 9/63		6/59	6K	Rhyl
12/63	10D	Lostock Hall: *Wdn 9/66*		4/62	5B	Crewe South: *Wdn 10/66*
78023	41C	Millhouses				
1/62	36A	Doncaster		**78032**	8D	Widnes
9/62	31B	March		2/60	6A	Chester (Midland)
12/62	12E	Barrow		4/60	12D	Kirkby Stephen
5/63	27B	Aintree: 8L 9/63		5/60	6A	Chester (Midland)
5/64	16D	Nottingham		9/63	6H	Bangor
3/65	9G	Gorton		6/65	1A	Willesden: *Wdn 10/65*
6/65	9E	Trafford Park		**78033**	8D	Widnes
8/66	9K	Bolton: *Wdn 5/67*		2/60	6A	Chester (Midland)
78024	41C	Millhouses		5/63	1A	Willesden: *Wdn 10/65*
1/62	36A	Doncaster		**78034**	8D	Widnes
9/62	31B	March		9/61	6H	Bangor
12/62	51A	Darlington		5/63	1C	Watford
10/63	52D	Tweedmouth		4/65	1A	Willesden
12/64	9G	Gorton: *Wdn 2/65*		9/65	5B	Crewe South: *Wdn 1/66*
78025	41C	Millhouses		**78035**	8D	Widnes
1/62	36A	Doncaster		5/63	1C	Watford
9/62	31B	March		4/65	1A	Willesden
12/62	51A	Darlington		9/65	6D	Shrewsbury: *Wdn 12/65*
1/63	51F	West Auckland		**78036**	24K	Preston
10/63	52D	Tweedmouth		9/61	24C	Lostock Hall
12/64	9G	Gorton: *Wdn 2/65*		9/62	24G	Skipton
78026	41D	Canklow		5/63	5B	Crewe South
1/62	67C	Ayr		11/66	6D	Shrewsbury: *Wdn 12/66*
1/63	67E	Dumfries		**78037**	24K	Preston
2/64	67F	Stranraer		9/61	24C	Lostock Hall
11/64	67A	Corkerhill: *Wdn 8/66*		9/62	24G	Skipton: 10G 9/63
78027	41D	Canklow		3/64	8F	Springs Branch
9/62	31B	March		5/64	16C	Derby
12/62	12E	Barrow		3/65	10D	Lostock Hall: *Wdn 5/67*
6/63	27D	Wigan: 8P 9/63		**78038**	6K	Rhyl
4/64	8F	Springs Branch		11/59	8E	Northwich
5/64	16C	Derby		5/63	1A	Willesden
9/64	15A	Leicester: *Wdn 9/65*		9/65	6D	Shrewsbury: *Wdn 8/66*

78039	8D	Widnes
5/63	1A	Willesden
9/65	5E	Nuneaton
4/66	6D	Shrewsbury: *Wdn 10/66*
78040	27D	Wigan
1/61	27B	Aintree: 8L 9/63
4/64	10D	Lostock Hall: *Wdn 1/66*
78041	27A	Bank Hall: 8K 9/63
6/64	10D	Lostock Hall: *Wdn 5/67*
78042	27A	Bank Hall: 8K 9/63
5/64	16D	Nottingham
4/65	16A	Toton: *Wdn 9/65*
78043	27A	Bank Hall
9/62	27B	Aintree
5/63	1A	Willesden: *Wdn 10/65*
78044	27A	Bank Hall
9/62	27B	Aintree: 8L 9/63
12/63	10D	Lostock Hall
4/64	8L	Aintree
5/64	16D	Nottingham
4/65	16A	Toton
11/66	9K	Bolton: *Wdn 5/67*
78045	61A	Kittybrewster
6/60	61C	Keith
6/61	61B	Ferryhill
6/64	64F	Bathgate: *Wdn 1/66*
78046	64G	Hawick
1/64	64F	Bathgate
9/66	64A	St Margarets: *Wdn 11/66*
78047	64G	Hawick
10/65	64A	St Margarets
1/66	64F	Bathgate
9/66	64A	St Margarets: *Wdn 9/66*
78048	64A	St Margarets
7/60	64G	Hawick: *Wdn 7/64*
78049	64A	St Margarets
6/59	64G	Hawick
1/66	64A	St Margarets: *Wdn 8/66*
78050	66B	Motherwell
10/63	65D	Dawsholm
7/64	64F	Bathgate: *Wdn 1/66*
78051	66B	Motherwell
10/63	65D	Dawsholm
7/64	67E	Dumfries
6/66	67C	Ayr: *Wdn 11/66*
78052	60B	Aviemore
7/62	63A	Perth
11/63	64F	Bathgate: *Wdn 1/66*
78053	61C	Keith
6/61	61B	Ferryhill
1/63	65J	Stirling: *Wdn 7/64*
78054	61C	Keith
6/61	61B	Ferryhill
6/64	64F	Bathgate: *Wdn 12/65*
78055	6D	Chester (Northgate)
6/59	6G	Llandudno Jct
11/59	6K	Rhyl
9/60	8E	Northwich
11/62	5B	Crewe South
5/63	24G	Skipton: 10G 9/63
3/64	8L	Aintree
4/64	8C	Speke Jct
5/64	16D	Nottingham
4/65	16A	Toton
11/66	9K	Bolton: *Wdn 2/67*
78056	6D	Chester (Northgate)
4/59	6K	Rhyl
4/62	5D	Stoke: *Wdn 7/66*
78057	6H	Bangor
11/59	8E	Northwich
5/63	27D	Wigan: 8P 9/63
4/64	8F	Springs Branch
5/64	16C	Derby
3/65	10D	Lostock Hall: *Wdn 5/66*
78058	6D	Chester (Northgate)
6/59	6G	Llandudno Jct
11/59	6H	Bangor
6/65	1A	Willesden
9/65	6D	Shrewsbury: *Wdn 12/66*
78059	6D	Chester (Northgate)
4/59	6G	Llandudno Jct
11/59	6H	Bangor
4/64	6J	Holyhead
10/64	6H	Bangor
6/65	1A	Willesden
9/65	5E	Nuneaton
6/66	5D	Stoke
10/66	5B	Crewe South: *Wdn 11/66*
78060	27D	Wigan
9/62	27B	Aintree
5/63	1A	Willesden
9/65	6D	Shrewsbury: *Wdn 10/66*
78061	27D	Wigan: 8P 9/63
4/64	8F	Springs Branch
5/64	16C	Derby
6/64	15A	Leicester (Midland)
7/66	16A	Toton: *Wdn 11/66*
78062	27D	Wigan: 8P 9/63
4/64	8F	Springs Branch
5/64	16D	Nottingham
4/65	16A	Toton
4/65	9G	Gorton

BR Standard Class 2 2-6-0 No 78015 (51A) in store at Darlington April 1963. No 78015 was the first Standard Class 2 2-6-0 to be taken out of service. It was allocated to Northallerton in January 1959 and to Darlington from March 1963 until its withdrawal in November of that year. *C. S. Freer*

BR Standard Class 2 2-6-0 No 78021 (15A) in open store at Leicester MPD 21 May 1966. *J. S. Hancock*

6/65	9E	Trafford Park		4/66	6D	Shrewsbury: *Wdn 12/66*
11/66	9K	Bolton: *Wdn 5/67*		**78064**	27D	Wigan: 8P 9/63
78063	27D	Wigan		2/64	16C	Derby
5/63	1A	Willesden		10/66	16A	Toton: *Wdn 12/66*
9/65	5E	Nuneaton				

Demise of the BR Standard Class 2 2-6-0s

Withdrawals

11/63:	78015	1/66:	78034/40/45/50/52
2/64:	78009	5/66:	78057
7/64:	78048/53	6/66:	78002
9/64:	78005	7/66:	78056
2/65:	78024/25	8/66:	78016/26/38/49
6/65:	78000	9/66:	78010/22/47
9/65:	78011/14/27/42	10/66:	78008/31/39/60
10/65:	78029/30/32/33/43	11/66:	78018/19/46/51/59/61
11/65:	78004	12/66:	78003/17/36/58/63/64
12/65:	78001/06/35/54	2/67:	78028/55
		5/67:	78007/12/13/20/21/23/37/41/44/62

BR Standard Class 4
2-6-4T '80XXX'

Introduced: 1951
Purpose: Mixed traffic
Power classification: 4MT
Tractive effort: 25,100lb

Stock Analysis 1959-1967

1/1/59 (155): 80000-99, 80100-54
1/1/60 (155): 80000-99, 80100-54
1/1/61 (155): 80000-99, 80100-54
1/1/62 (155): 80000-99, 80100-54
1/1/63 (154): 80000-99, 80100-02/04-54
1/1/64 (154): 80000-99, 80100-02/04-54
1/1/65 (123): 80000-07/11-16/18-20/22-29/32-35/37/39/41-43/45-48/51/54/55/
57-61/63-70/72/78-86/88-99,
80100-02/04/05/08-14/16-24/26/28/30-47/49-54
1/1/66 (79): 80000-02/04-07/11-13/15/16/19/24-28/32-34/37/39/41/43/45-47/51/54/
55/57/58/60/61/63/65/68/69/82/83/85/86/89/91-95,
80111-14/16-18/20-24/26/28/30/32-34/38-46/51/52/54
1/1/67 (25): 80002/04/11/12/15/16/19/32/45/46/85/86,
80116/20/28/33/34/39/40/43/45/46/51/52/54

Above:
BR Standard Class 4 2-6-4T No 80146 (70F
withdrawn July 1967) awaiting disposal at
Salisbury MPD 26 July 1967. With the end of steam
on the Southern, Salisbury became something of a
dumping ground for withdrawn locomotives. Of
the 54 locomotives awaiting disposal in August
1967 32 were of Standard designs. Nos
73029/43/65/85 *Melisande*/93/118 *King
Leodegrance,* were among the last locomotives to
be removed from the depot in March 1968.
J. A. M. Vaughan

Below:
In the aftermath of steam on the Southern. (Left to
right) Nos 80016 (70D wdn July 1967), 76063 (70D
wdn April 1967), 80151 (70D wdn May 1967), 76058
(70C wdn March 1967), 80012 (70A wdn March
1967), 41319 (70A wdn July 1967), 76064 (70D wdn
July 1967) 80145 (70A wdn June 1967), 34040
Crewkerne (70F wdn July 1967) and 80154 (70A
wdn April 1967) all awaiting disposal at Salisbury
MPD 4 August 1967. *J. H. Bird*

Locomotive depot allocations
1959-1967

80000	67A	Corkerhill
9/61	67B	Hurlford
1/62	67A	Corkerhill
9/62	67D	Ardrossan
6/64	67A	Corkerhill: *Wdn 12/66*
80001	66A	Polmadie
5/62	68D	Beattock: 66F 7/62
5/64	66A	Polmadie: *Wdn 7/66*
80002	66A	Polmadie
5/62	68D	Beattock: 66F 7/62
5/64	66A	Polmadie: *Wdn 3/67*
80003	66A	Polmadie
6/62	64A	St Margarets: *Wdn 2/65*
80004	61A	Kittybrewster
6/61	68D	Beattock: 66F 7/62
1/63	65A	Eastfield
8/64	65D	Dawsholm
10/64	67A	Corkerhill: *Wdn 5/67*
80005	61A	Kittybrewster
7/59	67A	Corkerhill
10/64	67C	Ayr
3/65	66F	Beattock
11/65	66A	Polmadie: *Wdn 8/66*
80006	66A	Polmadie
6/61	68D	Beattock
8/61	66A	Polmadie
5/62	64A	St Margarets: *Wdn 9/66*
80007	66A	Polmadie
5/62	64A	St Margarets
11/65	66A	Polmadie: *Wdn 7/66*
80008	67A	Corkerhill: *Wdn 7/64*
80009	67A	Corkerhill: *Wdn 9/64*
80010	75A	Brighton
2/59	75E	Three Bridges
1/63	75F	Tunbridge Wells West
9/63	75A	Brighton: *Wdn 6/64*
80011	75A	Brighton
2/59	75E	Three Bridges
1/63	75F	Tunbridge Wells West
9/63	75A	Brighton
6/64	75B	Redhill
5/65	70D	Eastleigh
10/65	70F	Bournemouth
1/66	70C	Guildford
2/66	70F	Bournemouth: *Wdn 7/67*
80012	75A	Brighton
2/59	75E	Three Bridges
1/63	75D	Stewarts Lane
6/63	70B	Feltham

11/64	70D	Eastleigh
10/65	70A	Nine Elms: *Wdn 3/67*
80013	75F	Tunbridge Wells West
1/59	75A	Brighton
6/64	70F	Bournemouth: *Wdn 6/66*
80014	75F	Tunbridge Wells West
9/63	75A	Brighton
6/64	70D	Eastleigh: *Wdn 5/65*
80015	75F	Tunbridge Wells West
8/63	71A	Eastleigh: 70D 9/63
10/65	70A	Nine Elms: *Wdn 7/67*
80016	75F	Tunbridge Wells West
9/63	75A	Brighton
6/64	70D	Eastleigh: *Wdn 7/67*
80017	75F	Tunbridge Wells West
9/63	75A	Brighton
6/64	70D	Eastleigh: *Wdn 9/64*
80018	75F	Tunbridge Wells West
9/63	75A	Brighton
6/64	70B	Feltham
11/64	70D	Eastleigh: *Wdn 4/65*
80019	75F	Tunbridge Wells West
9/63	75A	Brighton
6/64	75B	Redhill
5/65	70F	Bournemouth: *Wdn 3/67*
80020	61A	Kittybrewster
6/61	67D	Ardrossan
7/61	67A	Corkerhill: *Wdn 6/65*
80021	61A	Kittybrewster
6/61	67D	Ardrossan
7/61	67A	Corkerhill: *Wdn 7/64*
80022	66A	Polmadie
5/62	64A	St Margarets: *Wdn 6/65*
80023	66A	Polmadie
6/62	68C	Stranraer: 67F 7/62
9/62	67B	Hurlford
3/63	67E	Dumfries: *Wdn 10/65*
80024	67A	Corkerhill: *Wdn 8/66*
80025	67A	Corkerhill: *Wdn 8/66*
80026	66A	Polmadie
7/62	64A	St Margarets: *Wdn 9/66*
80027	66A	Polmadie
1/63	65A	Eastfield
12/64	66A	Polmadie: *Wdn 11/66*
80028	61A	Kittybrewster
6/61	67D	Ardrossan
6/62	67B	Hurlford
6/63	67F	Stranraer

11/63	63A	Perth: *Wdn 9/66*
80029	61A	Kittybrewster
6/61	67D	Ardrossan
6/62	67B	Hurlford: *Wdn 12/65*
80030	67A	Corkerhill: *Wdn 6/64*
80031	75A	Brighton
12/63	75B	Redhill: *Wdn 9/64*
80032	75A	Brighton
12/63	75B	Redhill
5/65	70F	Bournemouth: *Wdn 1/67*
80033	75A	Brighton
12/63	75B	Redhill
5/65	70B	Feltham: *Wdn 10/66*
80034	1C	Watford
12/59	73F	Ashford
5/62	73A	Stewarts Lane: 75D 6/62
8/63	75A	Brighton
12/63	75B	Redhill
5/65	70B	Feltham: *Wdn 1/66*
80035	1C	Watford
12/59	73F	Ashford
5/62	72A	Exmouth Jct: 83D 9/63
9/64	83E	Yeovil Town
1/65	83D	Exmouth Jct
2/65	83E	Yeovil Town: *Wdn 3/65*
80036	1C	Watford
12/59	73F	Ashford
5/62	72A	Exmouth Jct: 83D 9/63
	83D	Exmouth Jct: *Wdn 11/64*
80037	1C	Watford
12/59	73F	Ashford
5/61	73J	Tonbridge
6/62	72A	Exmouth Jct: 83D 9/63
1/65	82F	Bath (Green Park)
2/65	83D	Exmouth Jct
6/65	83G	Templecombe: *Wdn 3/66*
80038	1C	Watford
12/59	73F	Ashford
5/61	73J	Tonbridge
6/62	72A	Exmouth Jct
7/63	72C	Yeovil Town: 83E 9/63
10/63	83D	Exmouth Jct: *Wdn 9/64*
80039	1E	Bletchley
12/59	73F	Ashford
5/61	73J	Tonbridge
6/62	72A	Exmouth Jct: 83D 9/63
1/65	82F	Bath (Green Park)
2/65	83D	Exmouth Jct
4/65	83E	Yeovil Town
6/65	83G	Templecombe: *Wdn 2/66*
80040	6A	Chester (Midland)
12/59	73F	Ashford
5/61	73J	Tonbridge
6/62	72A	Exmouth Jct: 83D 9/63
	83D	Exmouth Jct: *Wdn 5/64*
80041	1E	Bletchley
12/59	73F	Ashford
5/61	73J	Tonbridge
6/62	72A	Exmouth Jct: 83D 9/63
6/65	83G	Templecombe: *Wdn 3/66*
80042	1E	Bletchley
12/59	73F	Ashford
5/61	73J	Tonbridge
6/62	72A	Exmouth Jct: 83D 9/63
	83D	Exmouth Jct: *Wdn 1/65*
80043	1E	Bletchley
12/59	73H	Dover
1/60	73F	Ashford
5/61	73J	Tonbridge
6/62	72A	Exmouth Jct: 83D 9/63
9/64	83G	Templecombe: *Wdn 3/66*
80044	26A	Newton Heath
2/60	67A	Corkerhill
7/64	6H	Bangor: *Wdn 11/64*
80045	6A	Chester (Midland)
4/60	67A	Corkerhill
3/65	66F	Beattock
11/65	66A	Polmadie: *Wdn 5/67*
80046	24E	Blackpool
4/60	67A	Corkerhill: *Wdn 5/67*
80047	6A	Chester (Midland)
2/60	67A	Corkerhill: *Wdn 8/66*
80048	6A	Chester (Midland)
5/60	67A	Corkerhill
7/64	6H	Bangor
9/64	6D	Shrewsbury: *Wdn 7/65*
80049	6A	Chester (Midland)
4/60	67A	Corkerhill: *Wdn 6/64*
80050	6A	Chester (Midland)
4/60	67A	Corkerhill
7/64	6H	Bangor: *Wdn 11/64*
80051	6A	Chester (Midland)
4/60	67A	Corkerhill: *Wdn 8/66*
80052	6A	Chester (Midland)
2/60	67A	Corkerhill: *Wdn 7/64*
80053	6A	Chester (Midland)
4/60	67A	Corkerhill: *Wdn 7/64*
80054	66A	Polmadie

7/62	64A	St Margarets
11/65	66D	Greenock (Ladyburn): *Wdn 6/66*
80055	66A	Polmadie
7/62	64A	St Margarets: *Wdn 9/66*
80056	66A	Polmadie
1/63	65A	Eastfield
9/64	10D	Lostock Hall: *Wdn 10/64*
80057	66A	Polmadie
1/63	65A	Eastfield
2/65	66A	Polmadie: *Wdn 12/66*
80058	66A	Polmadie: *Wdn 7/66*
80059	14D	Neasden
12/59	73H	Dover
1/60	73F	Ashford
5/61	73J	Tonbridge
6/62	72A	Exmouth Jct: 83D 9/63
9/64	83G	Templecombe
6/65	82E	Bristol (Barrow Rd)
7/65	82F	Bath (Green Park): *Wdn 11/65*
80060	26A	Newton Heath
2/60	63B	Stirling: 65J 5/60
7/64	66D	Greenock (Ladyburn)
12/65	66A	Polmadie: *Wdn 2/66*
80061	26A	Newton Heath
3/60	63B	Stirling: 65J 5/60
7/64	67E	Dumfries
7/65	66A	Polmadie: *Wdn 12/66*
80062	6C	Birkenhead
2/60	63B	Stirling: 63J 5/60
7/64	66D	Greenock (Ladyburn)
8/64	65J	Stirling: *Wdn 10/64*
80063	6C	Birkenhead
2/60	63B	Stirling: 63J 5/60
7/64	67A	Corkerhill: *Wdn 8/66*
80064	1C	Watford
12/59	73H	Dover
1/60	73F	Ashford
5/61	73J	Tonbridge
6/62	72A	Exmouth Jct: 83D 9/63
5/65	82E	Bristol (Bath Rd): *Wdn 9/65*
80065	1C	Watford
12/59	73H	Dover
1/60	73F	Ashford
5/61	73J	Tonbridge
6/62	71A	Eastleigh: 70D 9/63
	70D	Eastleigh: *Wdn 9/66*
80066	1C	Watford
12/59	73A	Stewarts Lane
1/60	73F	Ashford

5/61	73J	Tonbridge
6/62	71A	Eastleigh: 70D 9/63
	70D	Eastleigh: *Wdn 5/65*
80067	1C	Watford
12/59	73A	Stewarts Lane
5/62	72A	Exmouth Jct: 83D 9/63
9/64	83G	Templecombe
5/65	82E	Bristol (Bath Rd): *Wdn 6/65*
80068	1C	Watford
12/59	73A	Stewarts Lane: 75D 6/62
9/63	75A	Brighton
12/63	75B	Redhill
5/65	70B	Feltham: *Wdn 10/66*
80069	33B	Tilbury
8/62	87D	Swansea East Dock
7/64	70A	Nine Elms: *Wdn 2/66*
80070	33B	Tilbury
8/62	81A	Old Oak Common
12/62	89A	Shrewsbury
2/63	89B	Croes Newydd
3/63	89A	Shrewsbury: 6D 9/63
4/65	70D	Eastleigh: *Wdn 6/65*
80071	33B	Tilbury
9/62	31B	March
12/62	56B	Ardsley
10/63	66E	Carstairs: *Wdn 7/64*
80072	33B	Tilbury
8/62	87D	Swansea East Dock
9/63	2L	Leamington Spa
6/65	6D	Shrewsbury: *Wdn 7/65*
80073	33B	Tilbury
9/62	31B	March
12/62	56B	Ardsley
10/63	66E	Carstairs: *Wdn 7/64*
80074	33B	Tilbury
9/62	31B	March
12/62	56B	Ardsley
10/63	66E	Carstairs: *Wdn 7/64*
80075	33B	Tilbury
9/62	31B	March
12/62	56B	Ardsley
11/63	66E	Carstairs: *Wdn 7/64*
80076	33B	Tilbury
9/62	31B	March
12/62	56B	Ardsley
10/63	67E	Dumfries: *Wdn 7/64*
80077	33B	Tilbury
9/62	31B	March
12/62	56B	Ardsley
10/63	67D	Ardrossan
6/64	67A	Corkerhill: *Wdn 10/64*

80078	33B	Tilbury		5/61	75E	Three Bridges
6/62	30A	Stratford		11/62	71A	Eastleigh
8/62	89A	Shrewsbury		3/63	70C	Guildford
2/63	89B	Croes Newydd: 6C 9/63		9/63	70D	Eastleigh: *Wdn 6/64*
	6C	Croes Newydd: *Wdn 7/65*		**80088**	6H	Bangor
80079	33B	Tilbury		12/59	75E	Three Bridges
6/62	30A	Stratford		1/63	75F	Tunbridge Wells West
8/62	89B	Croes Newydd: 6C 9/63		9/63	75A	Brighton
	6C	Croes Newydd: *Wdn 7/65*		12/63	75B	Redhill: *Wdn 6/65*
80080	33B	Tilbury		**80089**	6H	Bangor
8/62	89B	Croes Newydd: 6C 9/63		12/59	75E	Three Bridges
	6C	Croes Newydd: *Wdn 7/65*		1/63	75D	Stewarts Lane
80081	1E	Bletchley		9/63	75A	Brighton
11/59	1A	Willesden		12/63	75B	Redhill
12/59	73A	Stewarts Lane: 75D 6/62		5/65	70B	Feltham
7/63	71G	Weymouth		11/65	70A	Nine Elms: *Wdn 10/66*
8/63	71B	Bournemouth: 70F 9/63		**80090**	6C	Birkenhead
	70F	Bournemouth: *Wdn 6/65*		2/60	62B	Dundee: *Wdn 3/65*
80082	1E	Bletchley		**80091**	6A	Chester (Midland)
12/59	73B	Bricklayers Arms		4/60	62B	Dundee
6/62	71A	Eastleigh: 70D 9/63		9/60	65B	St Rollox
	70D	Eastleigh: *Wdn 9/66*		5/62	67B	Hurlford
80083	14D	Neasden		4/66	66F	Beattock: *Wdn 11/66*
12/59	73B	Bricklayers Arms		**80092**	6A	Chester (Midland)
6/62	71A	Eastleigh: 70D 9/63		2/60	63A	Perth: *Wdn 9/66*
	70D	Eastleigh: *Wdn 8/66*		**80093**	24E	Blackpool
80084	1E	Bletchley		2/60	63A	Perth: *Wdn 9/66*
11/59	1A	Willesden		**80094**	6H	Bangor
12/59	73B	Bricklayers Arms		12/59	75E	Three Bridges
5/62	73A	Stewarts Lane: 75D 6/62		1/63	75D	Stewarts Lane
9/63	75A	Brighton		9/63	75A	Brighton
12/63	75B	Redhill: *Wdn 6/65*		12/63	75B	Redhill
80085	1E	Bletchley		5/65	70B	Feltham: *Wdn 7/66*
12/59	73B	Bricklayers Arms		**80095**	6H	Bangor
1/61	73F	Ashford		12/59	75F	Tunbridge Wells West
5/61	73J	Tonbridge		11/62	71A	Eastleigh
5/62	73A	Stewarts Lane: 75D 6/62		3/63	70C	Guildford
9/63	75A	Brighton		9/63	70B	Feltham
12/63	75B	Redhill		11/64	70A	Nine Elms: *Wdn 10/66*
5/65	70B	Feltham		**80096**	33A	Plaistow
10/66	70A	Nine Elms: *Wdn 7/67*		11/59	33B	Tilbury
80086	6A	Chester (Midland)		8/62	89A	Shrewsbury
4/60	64C	Dalry Rd		11/62	89B	Croes Newydd
10/60	66E	Carstairs		3/63	89C	Machynlleth: 6F 9/63
11/60	66A	Polmadie: *Wdn 5/67*		10/63	6C	Croes Newydd
80087	6H	Bangor		4/65	70F	Bournemouth: *Wdn 12/65*
12/59	75E	Three Bridges		**80097**	33A	Plaistow
1/60	73F	Ashford		11/59	33B	Tilbury
				6/62	30A	Stratford
				8/62	87D	Swansea East Dock
				7/63	89D	Oswestry: 6E 9/63

6/64	6F	Machynlleth: *Wdn 7/65*
80098	33A	Plaistow
11/59	33B	Tilbury
8/62	81A	Old Oak Common
9/62	89A	Shrewsbury
11/62	89B	Croes Newydd
3/63	89C	Machynlleth: 6F 9/63
	6F	Machynlleth: *Wdn 7/65*
80099	33A	Plaistow
11/59	33B	Tilbury
6/62	30A	Stratford
8/62	87D	Swansea East Dock
7/63	89C	Machynlleth: 6F 9/63
	6F	Machynlleth: *Wdn 5/65*
80100	33A	Plaistow
11/59	33B	Tilbury
6/62	30A	Stratford
8/62	89A	Shrewsbury: 6D 9/63
	6D	Shrewsbury: *Wdn 7/65*
80101	33A	Plaistow
11/59	33B	Tilbury
6/62	30A	Stratford
8/62	89A	Shrewsbury
9/62	89C	Machynlleth
2/63	89B	Croes Newydd
3/63	89C	Machynlleth: 6F 9/63
	6F	Machynlleth: *Wdn 7/65*
80102	33A	Plaistow
11/59	33B	Tilbury
8/62	81A	Old Oak Common
12/62	89A	Shrewsbury: 6D 9/63
6/64	6H	Bangor
9/64	6D	Shrewsbury
4/65	70D	Eastleigh: *Wdn 12/65*
80103	33A	Plaistow
11/59	33B	Tilbury: *Wdn 9/62*
80104	33A	Plaistow
11/59	33B	Tilbury
8/62	81A	Old Oak Common
12/62	89B	Croes Newydd
3/63	89C	Machynlleth: 6F 9/63
	6F	Machynlleth: *Wdn 7/65*
80105	33A	Plaistow
11/59	33B	Tilbury
8/62	89C	Machynlleth
9/62	89A	Shrewsbury
2/63	89B	Croes Newydd
3/63	89C	Machynlleth: 6F 9/63
	6F	Machynlleth: *Wdn 7/65*
80106	66A	Polmadie: *Wdn 10/64*
80107	66A	Polmadie: *Wdn 9/64*
80108	66A	Polmadie: *Wdn 5/65*

80109	66A	Polmadie
3/59	66C	Hamilton
9/59	66A	Polmadie: *Wdn 11/65*
80110	66A	Polmadie
9/63	66E	Carstairs
5/64	66A	Polmadie: *Wdn 5/65*
80111	61A	Kittybrewster
6/61	67A	Corkerhill
7/61	67B	Hurlford
4/66	66F	Beattock: *Wdn 11/66*
80112	61A	Kittybrewster
6/61	67A	Corkerhill
7/61	67B	Hurlford
6/64	67A	Corkerhill: *Wdn 8/66*
80113	61A	Kittybrewster
6/60	61C	Keith
6/61	64G	Hawick
1/66	64A	St Margarets: *Wdn 9/66*
80114	61A	Kittybrewster
10/60	61C	Keith
6/61	64G	Hawick
3/62	64A	St Margarets: *Wdn 12/66*
80115	61A	Kittybrewster
10/60	61C	Keith
6/61	61B	Ferryhill
8/61	66A	Polmadie
1/64	67D	Ardrossan
6/64	67A	Corkerhill
7/64	66A	Polmadie: *Wdn 10/64*
80116	50B	Neville Hill: 55H 1/60
6/63	55A	Holbeck
10/63	67E	Dumfries
11/63	66E	Carstairs
4/64	66A	Polmadie: *Wdn 5/67*
80117	50B	Neville Hill: 55H 1/60
10/63	67E	Dumfries
11/65	66F	Beattock
11/65	66A	Polmadie: *Wdn 3/66*
80118	50B	Neville Hill: 55H 1/60
10/63	66E	Carstairs
4/64	66A	Polmadie: *Wdn 11/66*
80119	50B	Neville Hill: 55H 1/60
10/63	66E	Carstairs
11/63	67E	Dumfries: *Wdn 6/65*
80120	50B	Neville Hill: 55H 1/60
10/63	66E	Carstairs
4/64	66A	Polmadie: *Wdn 5/67*
80121	61C	Keith
6/61	61B	Ferryhill
7/61	66A	Polmadie: *Wdn 6/66*
80122	61C	Keith

6/61	64C	Dalry Rd
5/62	64A	St Margarets
11/65	66D	Greenock: *Wdn 12/66*
80123	62B	Dundee
4/65	66A	Polmadie: *Wdn 8/66*
80124	62B	Dundee
1/66	64A	St Margarets: *Wdn 12/66*
80125	63B	Stirling: 65J 5/60
8/64	10D	Lostock Hall: *Wdn 10/64*
80126	63A	Perth: *Wdn 11/66*
80127	67A	Corkerhill: *Wdn 7/64*
80128	67A	Corkerhill
9/61	67B	Hurlford
1/62	67A	Corkerhill: *Wdn 4/67*
80129	66A	Polmadie
8/64	10D	Lostock Hall: *Wdn 10/64*
80130	66A	Polmadie: *Wdn 8/66*
80131	33A	Plaistow
11/59	33B	Tilbury
8/62	81A	Old Oak Common
9/62	89A	Shrewsbury
1/63	89D	Oswestry: 6E 9/63
1/65	6H	Bangor: *Wdn 5/65*
80132	33A	Plaistow
11/59	33B	Tilbury
8/62	81A	Old Oak Common
12/62	89A	Shrewsbury
1/63	89D	Oswestry: 6E 9/63
1/65	6H	Bangor
4/65	70D	Eastleigh: *Wdn 1/66*
80133	33A	Plaistow
11/59	33C	Shoeburyness
8/62	87D	Swansea East Dock
3/63	87A	Neath
6/64	87F	Llanelly
7/64	70B	Feltham
11/64	70A	Nine Elms: *Wdn 7/67*
80134	33A	Plaistow
11/59	33B	Tilbury
8/62	87D	Swansea East Dock
3/64	87F	Llanelly
7/64	70B	Feltham
8/64	70F	Bournemouth: *Wdn 7/67*
80135	33A	Plaistow
11/59	33B	Tilbury
8/62	89A	Shrewsbury
1/63	89D	Oswestry: 6E 9/63
9/64	6D	Shrewsbury: *Wdn 7/65*
80136	33A	Plaistow
11/59	33B	Tilbury
8/62	89A	Shrewsbury
1/63	89D	Oswestry: 6E 9/63
6/64	6F	Machynlleth
9/64	6D	Shrewsbury: *Wdn 7/65*
80137	14D	Neasden
12/59	75F	Tunbridge Wells West
11/62	71A	Eastleigh
3/63	70C	Guildford
9/63	70B	Feltham
11/64	70A	Nine Elms: *Wdn 10/65*
80138	14D	Neasden
12/59	75F	Tunbridge Wells West
2/61	75A	Brighton
12/63	75B	Redhill
2/65	70F	Bournemouth: *Wdn 10/66*
80139	14D	Neasden
12/59	75F	Tunbridge Wells West
9/63	75A	Brighton
12/63	75B	Redhill
2/65	70D	Eastleigh: *Wdn 7/67*
80140	14D	Neasden
12/59	75F	Tunbridge Wells West
9/63	75A	Brighton
12/63	75B	Redhill
5/65	70B	Feltham
10/66	70A	Nine Elms: *Wdn 7/67*
80141	14D	Neasden
12/59	75F	Tunbridge Wells West
9/63	75A	Brighton
12/63	75B	Redhill
5/65	70B	Feltham
11/65	70A	Nine Elms: *Wdn 2/66*
80142	14D	Neasden
12/59	75F	Tunbridge Wells West
9/63	75A	Brighton
12/63	75B	Redhill
5/65	70E	Salisbury
2/66	70D	Eastleigh: *Wdn 3/66*
80143	14D	Neasden
12/59	75A	Brighton
7/63	70B	Feltham
11/64	70A	Nine Elms: *Wdn 7/67*
80144	14D	Neasden
12/59	75A	Brighton
12/63	75B	Redhill
5/65	70E	Salisbury
11/65	70D	Eastleigh
2/66	70A	Nine Elms: *Wdn 5/66*
80145	75A	Brighton
12/63	75B	Redhill
5/65	70E	Salisbury

2/66	70A	Nine Elms: *Wdn 6/67*
80146	75A	Brighton
8/63	71A	Eastleigh: 70D 9/63
12/63	70F	Bournemouth: *Wdn 7/67*
80147	75A	Brighton
7/63	71G	Weymouth
8/63	71B	Bournemouth: 70F 9/63
	70F	Bournemouth: *Wdn 6/65*
80148	75A	Brighton
6/63	70B	Feltham: *Wdn 6/64*
80149	75A	Brighton
12/63	75B	Redhill: *Wdn 3/65*
80150	75A	Brighton
8/63	71A	Eastleigh: 70D 9/63
	70D	Eastleigh: *Wdn 10/65*
80151	75A	Brighton
12/63	75B	Redhill
5/65	70E	Salisbury
10/66	70D	Eastleigh: *Wdn 5/67*
80152	75A	Brighton
12/63	75B	Redhill
5/65	70E	Salisbury
10/66	70D	Eastleigh: *Wdn 7/67*
80153	75A	Brighton
12/63	75B	Redhill: *Wdn 3/65*
80154	75A	Brighton
7/63	70B	Feltham
11/64	70A	Nine Elms: *Wdn 4/67*

Demise of the BR Standard Class 4 2-6-4Ts

Withdrawals

9/62: 80103
5/64: 80040
6/64: 80010/30/49/87, 80148
7/64: 80008/21/52/53/71/73/74/75/76, 80127
9/64: 80009/17/31/38, 80107
10/64: 80056/62/77, 80106/15/25/29
11/64: 80036/44/50
1/65: 80042
2/65: 80003
3/65: 80035/90, 80149/53
4/65: 80018
5/65: 80014/66/99, 80108/10/31
6/65: 80020/22/67/70/81/84/88, 80119/47
7/65: 80048/72/78/79/80/97/98, 80100/01/04/05/35/36
9/65: 80064
10/65: 80023, 80137/50
11/65: 80059, 80109

12/65: 80029/96, 80102
1/66: 80034, 80132
2/66: 80039/60/69, 80141
3/66: 80037/41/43, 80117/42
5/66: 80144
6/66: 80013/54, 80121
7/66: 80001/07/58/94
8/66: 80005/24/25/47/51/63/83, 80112/23/30
9/66: 80006/26/28/55/65/82/92/93, 80113
10/66: 80033/68/89/95, 80138
11/66: 80027/91, 80111/18/26
12/66: 80000/57/61, 80114/22/24
1/67: 80032
3/67: 80002/12/19
4/67: 80128/54
5/67: 80004/45/46/86, 80116/20/51
6/67: 80145
7/67: 80011/15/16/85, 80133/34/39/40/43/46/52

BR Standard Class 3
2–6–2T '82XXX'

Introduced: 1952
Purpose: Light passenger
Power classification: 3MT
Tractive effort: 21,490lb

Stock Analysis 1959-1967

1/1/59	(45):	82000-44
1/1/60	(45):	82000-44
1/1/61	(45):	82000-44
1/1/62	(45):	82000-44
1/1/63	(45):	82000-44
1/1/64	(45):	82000-44
1/1/65	(35):	82000/01/03-06/09/10/16-24/26-42/44
1/1/66	(15):	82000/03/06/09/18/19/23/24/26-31/34
1/1/67	(2):	82019/29

Locomotive depot allocations 1959-1967

82000	84G	Shrewsbury		**82006**	84H	Wellington
2/59	84K	Wrexham (Rhosddu)		1/60	82A	Bristol (Bath Rd)
2/60	89C	Machynlleth: 6F 9/63		9/60	82E	Bristol (Barrow Rd)
4/65	9H	Patricroft: *Wdn 12/66*		2/61	89C	Machynlleth: 6F 9/63
82001	6E	Chester (West)		4/65	70A	Nine Elms: *Wdn 9/66*
4/60	6A	Chester (Midland)		**82007**	82A	Bristol (Bath Rd)
4/61	82G	Templecombe		9/60	82E	Bristol (Barrow Rd)
9/62	86C	Hereford		2/61	82B	St Phillips Marsh
4/63	72A	Exmouth Jct: 83D 9/63		10/62	82E	Bristol (Bath Rd): *Wdn*
12/63	83B	Taunton				*6/64*
6/64	82E	Bristol (Bath Rd): *Wdn*		**82008**	85A	Worcester
		12/65		7/61	89C	Machynlleth
82002	6E	Chester (West)		9/61	87H	Neyland
4/60	6A	Chester (Midland)		10/61	83B	Taunton: *Wdn 2/64*
4/61	82G	Templecombe		**82009**	84H	Wellington
9/62	86C	Hereford		6/59	84G	Shrewsbury
4/63	72A	Exmouth Jct: 83D 9/63		8/59	84H	Wellington
	83D	Exmouth Jct: *Wdn 2/64*		1/60	82A	Bristol (Bath Rd)
82003	6E	Chester (West)		9/60	82E	Bristol (Barrow Rd)
4/60	6A	Chester (Midland)		10/60	82B	St Phillips Marsh
4/61	82E	Bristol (Barrow Rd)		2/61	89C	Machynlleth: 6F 9/63
2/62	82B	St Phillips Marsh		4/65	9H	Patricroft: *Wdn 11/66*
3/62	87G	Carmarthen		**82010**	72A	Exmouth Jct
6/62	89C	Machynlleth: 6F 9/63		9/62	71A	Eastleigh
4/65	9H	Patricroft: *Wdn 12/66*		10/62	70A	Nine Elms: *Wdn 4/65*
82004	84H	Wellington		**82011**	72A	Exmouth Jct
6/59	84G	Shrewsbury		9/62	71A	Eastleigh
8/59	84H	Wellington		10/62	70A	Nine Elms: *Wdn 8/64*
10/59	82F	Bath (Green Park): *Wdn*		**82012**	71A	Eastleigh
		10/65		11/62	70A	Nine Elms: *Wdn 5/64*
82005	6E	Chester (West)		**82013**	72A	Exmouth Jct
4/60	6A	Chester (Midland)		9/62	71A	Eastleigh
4/61	89A	Shrewsbury		10/62	70A	Nine Elms: *Wdn 6/64*
7/61	89C	Machynlleth		**82014**	71A	Eastleigh
10/61	89A	Shrewsbury		11/62	70A	Nine Elms: *Wdn 5/64*
11/61	89C	Machynlleth: 6F 9/63		**82015**	71A	Eastleigh
4/65	70A	Nine Elms: *Wdn 9/65*		11/62	70C	Guildford

3/63	70A	Nine Elms: *Wdn 12/64*
82016	71A	Eastleigh
11/62	70C	Guildford
3/63	70A	Nine Elms: *Wdn 4/65*
82017	72A	Exmouth Jct
9/62	71A	Eastleigh
10/62	70A	Nine Elms: *Wdn 4/65*
82018	72A	Exmouth Jct
9/62	71A	Eastleigh
10/62	70A	Nine Elms: *Wdn 6/66*
82019	72A	Exmouth Jct
9/62	71A	Eastleigh
10/62	70A	Nine Elms: *Wdn 7/67*
82020	84K	Wrexham (Rhosddu)
1/60	84G	Shrewsbury
3/60	89C	Machynlleth: 6F 9/63
4/65	70A	Nine Elms: *Wdn 9/65*
82021	84K	Wrexham (Rhosddu)
1/60	84G	Shrewsbury
3/60	89C	Machynlleth: 6F 9/63
4/65	70A	Nine Elms: *Wdn 10/65*
82022	72A	Exmouth Jct
9/62	71A	Eastleigh
10/62	70A	Nine Elms: *Wdn 10/65*
82023	72A	Exmouth Jct
9/62	71A	Eastleigh
10/62	70A	Nine Elms: *Wdn 11/66*
82024	72A	Exmouth Jct
9/62	71A	Eastleigh
10/62	70A	Nine Elms: *Wdn 2/66*
82025	72A	Exmouth Jct
9/62	71A	Eastleigh
10/62	70A	Nine Elms: *Wdn 8/64*
82026	50E	Scarborough
12/62	56F	Low Moor
4/63	56C	Copley Hill
9/63	70C	Guildford
12/63	70F	Bournemouth
8/64	70A	Nine Elms: *Wdn 6/66*
82027	50F	Malton
6/60	50E	Scarborough
12/62	50F	Malton
4/63	50A	York
9/63	70C	Guildford
12/63	70F	Bournemouth
8/64	70A	Nine Elms: *Wdn 1/66*
82028	50E	Scarborough
9/61	50F	Malton
4/63	50A	York
9/63	70C	Guildford
12/63	70F	Bournemouth
8/64	70A	Nine Elms: *Wdn 9/66*
82029	50F	Malton
6/60	50E	Scarborough
9/61	50F	Malton
4/63	50A	York
9/63	70C	Guildford
12/63	70F	Bournemouth
8/64	70A	Nine Elms: *Wdn 7/67*
82030	85A	Worcester
4/59	82A	Bristol (Bath Rd)
5/59	85A	Worcester
6/59	85D	Kidderminster
7/59	85A	Worcester
10/59	84H	Wellington
1/60	82A	Bristol (Bath Rd)
9/60	82E	Bristol (Barrow Rd)
10/61	83B	Taunton
6/64	83D	Exmouth Jct
6/65	85B	Gloucester: *Wdn 8/65*
(R)11/65	82F	Bath: *Wdn 1/66*
82031	84G	Shrewsbury
2/59	84K	Wrexham (Rhosddu)
1/60	89C	Machynlleth: 6F 9/63
6/64	6H	Bangor
4/65	9H	Patricroft: *Wdn 12/66*
82032	6E	Chester (West)
4/60	6A	Chester (Midland)
4/61	89A	Shrewsbury
8/61	89C	Machynlleth
11/61	89A	Shrewsbury
7/62	89C	Machynlleth: 6F 9/63
6/64	6H	Bangor: *Wdn 5/65*
82033	82A	Bristol (Bath Rd)
9/60	82E	Bristol (Barrow Rd)
12/60	89C	Machynlleth: 6F 9/63
6/64	6H	Bangor
4/65	70A	Nine Elms: *Wdn 9/65*
82034	6E	Chester (West)
4/60	6A	Chester (Midland)
4/61	89C	Machynlleth: 6F 9/63
4/65	9H	Patricroft: *Wdn 12/66*
82035	82A	Bristol (Bath Rd)
9/60	82E	Bristol (Barrow Rd)
2/62	82B	St Phillips Marsh
10/62	82E	Bristol (Barrow Rd)
3/64	83D	Exmouth Jct
9/64	83E	Yeovil Town: *Wdn 7/65*
82036	6E	Chester (West)
4/60	6A	Chester (Midland)
4/61	89C	Machynlleth
11/61	89A	Shrewsbury
7/62	82B	St Phillips Marsh

Above:
BR Standard Class 3 2-6-2T No 82003 (9H) at Patricroft MPD 23 October 1965. It appears from the photograph to have been unofficially named 'Fanny'. *D. L. Percival*

Below:
BR Standard Class 3 2-6-2T No 82029 (70A) at Nine Elms MPD 5 April 1967. The last two members of the Class Nos 82019/29 were both withdrawn off Nine Elms in July 1967. *J. Scrace*

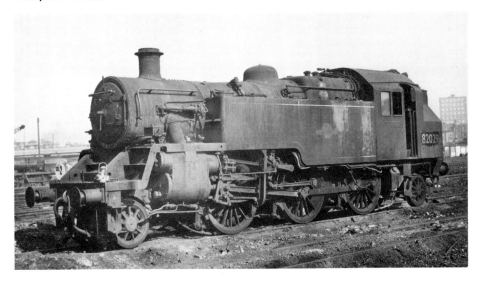

10/62	82E	Bristol (Bath Rd): *Wdn 7/65*
82037	82F	Bath (Green Park)
2/59	84K	Wrexham (Rhosddu)
1/60	82A	Bristol (Bath Rd)
9/60	82E	Bristol (Barrow Rd)
2/62	82B	St Phillips Marsh
10/62	82E	Bristol (Bath Rd): *Wdn 9/65*
82038	85A	Worcester
9/59	84H	Wellington
1/60	82A	Bristol (Bath Rd)
9/60	82B	St Phillips Marsh
10/62	82E	Bristol (Bath Rd): *Wdn 7/65*
82039	82A	Bristol (Bath Rd)
2/59	82G	Templecombe
9/60	82E	Bristol (Barrow Rd)
2/62	82B	St Phillips Marsh
10/62	82E	Bristol (Barrow Rd)
3/64	83D	Exmouth Jct
6/65	85B	Gloucester: *Wdn 7/65*
82040	82A	Bristol (Bath Rd)
9/60	82E	Bristol (Barrow Rd)
2/62	82B	St Phillips Marsh

10/62	82E	Bristol (Barrow Rd)
10/63	83D	Exmouth Jct
6/65	85B	Gloucester: *Wdn 7/65*
82041	82A	Bristol (Bath Rd)
3/59	82F	Bath: *Wdn 12/65*
82042	82A	Bristol (Bath Rd)
9/60	82E	Bristol (Barrow Rd)
9/61	87H	Neyland
10/61	83B	Taunton
6/64	83D	Exmouth Jct
6/65	85B	Gloucester: *Wdn 8/65*
82043	82A	Bristol (Bath Rd)
9/60	82E	Bristol (Barrow Rd)
1/62	83B	Taunton
2/62	82B	St Phillips Marsh
10/62	82E	Bristol (Barrow Rd): *Wdn 2/64*
82044	82A	Bristol (Bath Rd)
9/60	82E	Bristol (Barrow Rd)
9/61	87H	Neyland
10/61	83B	Taunton
6/64	83D	Exmouth Jct
6/65	85B	Gloucester: *Wdn 8/65*
(R)9/65	82F	Bath: *Wdn 11/65*

Demise of the BR Standard Class 3 2–6–2Ts

Withdrawals

2/64: 82002/08/43
5/64: 82012/14
6/64: 82007/13
8/64: 82011/25
12/64: 82015
4/65: 82010/16/17
5/65: 82032
7/65: 82035/36/38/39/40
8/65: 82042
9/65: 82005/20/33/37
10/65: 82004/21/22
11/65: 82044
12/65: 82001/41
1/66: 82027/30
2/66: 82024
6/66: 82018/26
9/66: 82006/28
11/66: 82009/23
12/66: 82000/03/31/34
7/67: 82019/29

BR Standard Class 2
2-6-2T

Introduced: 1953
Purpose: Mixed traffic
Power classification: 2MT
Tractive effort: 18,515lb

Stock Analysis 1959-1965
1/1/59 (30): 84000-29
1/1/60 (30): 84000-29
1/1/61 (30): 84000-29
1/1/62 (30): 84000-29
1/1/63 (30): 84000-29
1/1/64 (29): 84000-11/13-29
1/1/65 (20): 84000/02-06/08-11/13-19/25/26/28

Locomotive depot allocations
1959-1965

84000	6C	Birkenhead		**84006**	17B	Burton
6/61	8B	Warrington (Dallam)		1/59	15A	Wellingborough
4/63	89D	Oswestry: 6E 9/63		12/61	14D	Neasden
1/65	6C	Croes Newydd: *Wdn*		1/62	14E	Bedford
		10/65		3/62	14D	Neasden
84001	6D	Chester (Northgate)		4/62	16D	Annesley: 16B 9/63
1/60	6C	Birkenhead		7/64	15B	Wellingborough
6/61	8B	Warrington (Dallam)		10/64	15A	Leicester: *Wdn 10/65*
12/62	6G	Llandudno Jct: *Wdn*		**84007**	17B	Burton
		10/64		2/59	15A	Wellingborough
84002	1E	Bletchley: *Wdn 4/65*		3/62	16D	Annesley: 16B 9/63
84003	6C	Birkenhead		12/63	15B	Wellingborough: *Wdn*
9/61	6K	Rhyl				*1/64*
2/63	6G	Llandudno Jct		**84008**	17B	Burton
3/64	6C	Croes Newydd		2/59	15A	Wellingborough
6/64	6G	Llandudno Jct: *Wdn 10/65*		6/61	14D	Neasden
84004	1E	Bletchley		7/62	14B	Kentish Town
4/63	89D	Oswestry: 6E 9/63		12/62	15C	Leicester (Midland)
1/65	6C	Croes Newydd: *Wdn*		5/63	15A	Wellingborough: 15B
		10/65				9/63
84005	14E	Bedford		2/64	15A	Leicester (Midland)
6/61	14D	Neasden		5/64	15B	Wellingborough
12/61	14E	Bedford		9/64	15A	Leicester: *Wdn 10/65*
3/62	14D	Neasden		**84009**	55D	Royston
7/62	14B	Kentish Town		6/59	53A	Dairycoates: 50B 1/60
1/63	15A	Wellingborough		12/62	6G	Llandudno Jct
2/63	14E	Bedford		3/64	6C	Croes Newydd
2/63	15A	Wellingborough: 15B		6/64	6G	Llandudno: *Wdn 11/65*
		9/63		**84010**	24B	Rose Grove
2/64	15A	Leicester (Midland)		12/59	24F	Fleetwood: 10C 9/63
5/64	15B	Wellingborough		11/65	70D	Eastleigh
10/64	15A	Leicester: *Wdn 10/65*		12/65	LMR	(for scrap): *Wdn 12/65*

Above:
BR Standard Class 2 2-6-2T No 84014 (26C) at the side of Bolton MPD 17 September 1960. Towards the end of 1965, 10 redundant Standard Class 2s were chosen for possible future use on the Isle of White. The locomotives concerned were Nos 84010/16 (10C), 84013/14/17/26 (9B), 84015/28 (10G) and 84019/25 (9K). The IoW venture did not materialise however, and despite their official transfer to the Southern Region in November 1965

– save for the above loco No 84014, it is doubtful whether any further members of the class reached Eastleigh at all. The class was transferred back to the LMR in December 1965 and subsequently withdrawn. *R. A. Panting*

Below:
BR Standard Class 2 2-6-2T No 84019 (26C) outside Bolton MPD 18 February 1962. *I. G. Holt*

84011	24D	Lower Darwen
3/61	24F	Fleetwood: 10C 9/63
	10C	Fleetwood: *Wdn 4/65*
84012	24D	Lower Darwen
3/61	24F	Fleetwood
2/63	27C	Southport: 8M 9/63
	8M	Southport: *Wdn 10/63*
84013	26E	Lees (Oldham)
4/59	26C	Bolton: 9K 9/63
12/64	9B	Stockport
5/65	15A	Leicester (Midland)
7/65	9B	Stockport
11/65	70D	Eastleigh
12/65	LMR	(for scrap): *Wdn 12/65*
84014	26E	Lees (Oldham)
2/59	26C	Bolton: 9K 9/63
12/64	9B	Stockport
11/65	70D	Eastleigh
12/65	LMR	(for scrap): *Wdn 12/65*
84015	24G	Skipton: 10G 9/63
11/65	70D	Eastleigh
12/65	LMR	(for scrap): *Wdn 12/65*
84016	24F	Fleetwood: 10C 9/63
6/65	9B	Stockport
7/65	10C	Fleetwood
11/65	70D	Eastleigh
12/65	LMR	(for scrap): *Wdn 12/65*
84017	24F	Fleetwood: 10C 9/63
10/63	8M	Southport
6/64	9K	Bolton
6/65	9B	Stockport
11/65	70D	Eastleigh
12/65	LMR	(for scrap): *Wdn 12/65*
84018	24F	Fleetwood: 10C 9/63
	10C	Fleetwood: *Wdn 4/65*
84019	26C	Bolton: 9K 9/63
11/65	70D	Eastleigh
12/65	LMR	(for scrap): *Wdn 12/65*
84020	73F	Ashford
1/61	73A	Stewarts Lane
5/61	72A	Exmouth Jct
9/61	6G	Llandudno Jct: *Wdn 10/64*
84021	73F	Ashford
1/61	73B	Bricklayers Arms
5/61	72A	Exmouth Jct
9/61	6G	Llandudno Jct
7/62	CW	Crewe Works: *Wdn 9/64*
84022	73F	Ashford
1/61	73B	Bricklayers Arms
5/61	72A	Exmouth Jct
9/61	6G	Llandudno Jct
7/62	CW	Crewe Works: *Wdn 9/64*
84023	73F	Ashford
1/61	73B	Bricklayers Arms
5/61	72A	Exmouth Jct
9/61	24J	Lancaster
1/62	8D	Widnes
7/62	CW	Crewe Works: *Wdn 9/64*
84024	73F	Ashford
1/61	73B	Bricklayers Arms
5/61	75A	Brighton
9/61	8B	Warrington (Dallam)
1/62	8D	Widnes
7/62	CW	Crewe Works: *Wdn 9/64*
84025	73G	Ramsgate
5/59	73F	Ashford
5/61	75A	Brighton
9/61	26A	Newton Heath
11/61	26C	Bolton: 9K 9/63
11/65	70D	Eastleigh
12/65	LMR	(for scrap): *Wdn 12/65*
84026	73G	Ramsgate
5/59	73F	Ashford
6/61	75A	Brighton
9/61	26A	Newton Heath
10/61	26C	Bolton
5/63	HW	Horwich Works
12/63	9K	Bolton
12/64	9B	Stockport
11/65	70D	Eastleigh
12/65	LMR	(for scrap): *Wdn 12/65*
84027	73G	Ramsgate
5/59	73F	Ashford
5/61	75A	Brighton
9/61	26A	Newton Heath
10/61	26C	Bolton
1/62	15A	Wellingborough
3/62	16D	Annesley: 16B 9/63
	16B	Annesley: *Wdn 5/64*
84028	73G	Ramsgate
5/59	73F	Ashford
6/61	71A	Eastleigh
9/61	26A	Newton Heath
10/61	24G	Skipton: 10G 9/63
11/65	70D	Eastleigh
12/65	LMR	(for scrap): *Wdn 12/65*
84029	73G	Ramsgate
5/59	73F	Ashford
6/61	71A	Eastleigh
9/61	14E	Bedford
1/62	14D	Neasden
7/62	14B	Kentish Town
1/63	15A	Wellingborough
2/63	15C	Leicester (Midland): 15A 9/63: *Wdn 6/64*

Demise of the BR Standard Class 2 2-6-2Ts

Withdrawals
10/63: 84012
 1/64: 84007
 5/64: 84027
 6/64: 84029
 9/64: 84021/22/23/24
10/64: 84001/20
 4/65: 84002/11/18
10/65: 84000/03/04/05/06/08
11/65: 84009
12/65: 84010/13/14/15/16/17/19/25/26/28

MoS Class WD 2-8-0 'Austerity'

Introduced: 1943
Purpose: Long-distance freight
Power classification: 8F
Tractive effort: 34,215lb

Locomotive name
90732 *Vulcan*

Stock Analysis 1959-1967
1/1/59 (733): 90000-732
1/1/60 (732): 90000-82/84-732
1/1/61 (730): 90000-61/63-82/84-190/192-732
1/1/62 (730): 90000-61/63-82/84-190/192-732
1/1/63 (650): 90000-20/24-27/29-33/35-59/61/63-82/84-86/88-92/94-99,
90100-04/07-27/29-33/35/3638-49/51-62/64-66/68-73/75-90/92-95/97/99,
90200-43/45/46/48-52/54/55/57-69/71-77/79-85/89-97/99,
90300-02/04-06/09-19/21-54/57-75/77-86/88-90/92-99,
90400-13/15-24/26-30/32-35/37-54/56-72/74-93/96-99,
90500-04/06/07/09-11/14-22/24/25/27-31/33-48/51-53/55-58/60/61/63/64/
66-74/76-90/92/93/95-99,
90600-02/04-06/09-15/17-29/31-33/35/36/39-47/49-52/54-56/58-65/67-
89/92/94-99, 90700/02-25/27-31.
1/1/64 (553): 90000-03/05/07-14/16/18/20/24/25/29/30/32/35-45/47/51-57/59/61/63-
65/67-76/78-82/84/85/88/89/91/92/94/96/98/99,
90100/01/03/04/08-17/19-27/29-33/35/36/38-43/45-49/52-58/60-62/64-
66/68/69/71-73/75/78-81/83-85/87-90/94/95/97/99,
90200-05/07-25/27/29/30/32/33/35-37/40-43/45/46/48/52/54/55/57-59/
61-68/71-77/79-85/89-97/99,
90300-02/04-06/09-11/13-19/21-25/27-30/32/33/36/37/39-42/44-54/57/
59-75/77-86/88-90/92-99,
90401-13/15-23/26-30/32-34/37-39/41-45/48-52/54/56-60/62/64-66/68-

96

71/74/76-86/88-93/96/98,
90501/03/06/09-11/14-22/25/28/29/33-35/37/38/40/41/43-48/51-53/55-
58/60/61/63/64/66-70/72-74/77/79-90/92/93/95/96/98/99,
90600-02/05/06/10-13/15/17-22/25-29/31-33/35/36/39-47/49-52/54-56/58/
60/62-65/67-70/72-89/94/95/97-99, 90700/02-12/14/15/17-25/27/30/31

1/1/65 (428): 90000/02/05/07-11/13/14/16/18/20/24/25/29/30/32/35-45/47/51/53-57/59/
61/63/68-76/78/80-82/84/85/88/89/91/92/94/96/99,
90103/04/08/12/13/15-17/19-26/30-33/35/36/39/42/46/48/49/52-56/58/60/
64/66/68/69/71/71/72/75/78/80/81/83/85/87-90/95/99,
90200/02-04/07/10-13/15/17/20-23/25/27/29/30/32/33/35/36/40-43/46/48/
52/54/55/58/59/61/62/65-68/71-77/79-85/90-96,
90300/01/05/06/09/10/14-18/21/25/27/29/30/32/33/36/37/39-42/45-53/57/
60-65/67-70/72/73/77-86/90/93/95-99,
90401/04-07/09/10/13/15/17-23/26-30/32/34/37-39/41-45/48-52/54/56-
60/62/65/66/68/70/71/74/76-82/84/86/89/91-93/96/98,
90501/03/06/09/10/14-18/20/22/28/29/33/34/37/38/40/41/45/47/51/53
/56-58/60/61/63/69/72/73/77/79/80/85-88/93/96,
90600-02/05/06/10/11/13/15/17/19-22/25-29/31-33/36/39-42/44/45/47/
49-52/54-56/58/60/62/64/65/68-70/74/75/77-84/86-89/94/95/97-99,
90702-04/06/07/09-11/18-25/27/30/31

1/1/66 (227): 90001/02/08/09/11/13/14/16/18/20/24/30/32/35/37/39/41/44/47/54/56/57/
61/63/68/69/71/73-76/78/80-82/89/91/94/99,
90104/12/13/16/17/26/32/35/48/49/53-56/60/68/72/78/87/90/99,
90200/10/13/29/30/32/33/36/40/41/43/54/58/62/65/72/74/81/95,
90300/05/09/10/18/21/32/36/37/39/45/47/48/50-52/57/60-63/67/69/70/73/
77-80/82/84-86/95-97,
90404-07/09/10/13/15/17/18/27-30/34/37/41/44/45/49-51/56-59/62/65/68/
70/71/77-79/81/82/84/89/93/98,
90503/06/14/17/18/33/34/37/38/47/51/60/72/86/88/93/96,
90600/05/06/10/11/15/17/20/22/25/27/28/31/33/36/39/40/42/44/45/49-
52/54/55/64/69/70/75/77-80/82-84/87-89/94/95/98/99,
90704/06/07/09/11/18/19/21-23/31

1/1/67 (123): 90008/09/14/16/20/30/47/54/56/57/61/71/74/76/81/89/91/94/99,
90112/16/17/26/32/35/55/60/72,
90200/10/30/33/36/40/43/54/62/65/72/81,
90300/09/18/21/32/37/39/45/47/48/51/52/60-63/70/78/82/85/86/96/97,
90404-07/09/15/17/27/29/30/34/44/50/58/59/62/65/68/78/82/89,
90503/60/88/96,
90606/10/11/15/17/20/25/27/28/31/33/39/42/44/45/49/50/54/55/70/77/78/
80/82/84/88/94/95/98/99, 90704/07/11/21/22

Locomotive depot allocations ▬▬▬▬▬▬▬▬▬▬▬▬▬▬▬▬▬▬▬
1959-1967

90000	40E	Colwick	**90002**	40E	Colwick
2/59	34E	New England	12/65	36A	Doncaster: *Wdn 4/66*
9/62	36C	Frodingham: *Wdn 6/65*	**90003**	40B	Immingham
90001	31B	March	7/61	36E	Retford
9/60	36A	Doncaster	11/61	36A	Doncaster
10/65	40E	Colwick	3/63	41J	Langwith: *Wdn 6/64*
11/65	36A	Doncaster: *Wdn 4/66*	**90004**	62A	Thornton

5/60	66A	Polmadie
2/62	62A	Thornton: *Wdn 12/63*
90005	40E	Colwick
9/63	36E	Retford: *Wdn 4/65*
90006	53A	Dairycoates: 50B 1/60
	50B	Dairycoates: *Wdn 9/63*
90007	41H	Staveley (GC)
2/60	36C	Frodingham: *Wdn 7/65*
90008	53A	Dairycoates: 50B 1/60
	50B	Dairycoates: *Wdn 4/67*
90009	53A	Dairycoates: 50B 1/60
6/67	52G	Sunderland: *Wdn 9/67*
90010	82B	St Phillips Marsh
7/59	18B	Westhouses
6/62	9G	Gorton: *Wdn 2/65*
90011	53A	Dairycoates
6/59	51A	Darlington
3/66	51C	West Hartlepool: *Wdn 6/66*
90012	55E	Normanton: *Wdn 2/64*
90013	36C	Frodingham
3/66	36A	Doncaster: *Wdn 4/66*
90014	51L	Thornaby
6/60	51A	Darlington
3/66	51C	West Hartlepool: *Wdn 4/67*
90015	40E	Colwick
2/59	34E	New England: *Wdn 5/63*
90016	51L	Thornaby
4/59	56A	Wakefield
6/60	51A	Darlington
12/62	52H	Tyne Dock
12/63	56A	Wakefield
2/65	51C	West Hartlepool
3/66	50B	Dairycoates
12/66	50D	Goole: *Wdn 6/67*
90017	62C	Dunfermline: *Wdn 9/63*
90018	31B	March
2/61	30A	Stratford
6/61	31B	March
9/61	36A	Doncaster: *Wdn 4/66*
90019	62A	Thornton: *Wdn 12/63*
90020	62A	Thornton: *Wdn 4/67*
90021	55E	Normanton: *Wdn 11/62*
90022	53A	Dairycoates: 50B 1/60
2/60	51L	Thornaby: *Wdn 10/62*
90023	31B	March
12/59	31F	Spital Bridge
2/60	33B	Tilbury: *Wdn 9/62*
90024	40E	Colwick
2/60	34E	New England
9/62	36C	Frodingham: *Wdn 2/66*
90025	40E	Colwick
10/60	36C	Frodingham: *Wdn 7/65*
90026	50B	Neville Hill
12/59	50A	York: *Wdn 12/63*
90027	51L	Thornaby: *Wdn 5/63*
90028	31B	March
4/59	30A	Stratford
5/60	41F	Mexborough
11/62	41D	Canklow: *Wdn 12/62*
90029	40B	Immingham: *Wdn 7/65*
90030	53A	Dairycoates: 50B 1/60
9/61	50A	York
3/65	50B	Dairycoates
10/65	50D	Goole: *Wdn 4/67*
90031	36C	Frodingham
11/61	34E	New England: *Wdn 5/63*
90032	36C	Frodingham: *Wdn 2/66*
90033	2F	Woodford Halse: *Wdn 5/63*
90034	33B	Tilbury: *Wdn 9/62*
90035	40B	Immingham
9/65	36C	Frodingham: *Wdn 2/66*
90036	40B	Immingham
10/60	40E	Colwick: *Wdn 12/65*
90037	40E	Colwick
12/65	40B	Immingham
2/66	36A	Doncaster: *Wdn 4/66*
90038	40E	Colwick: *Wdn 7/65*
90039	66A	Polmadie
8/63	62C	Dunfermline: *Wdn 9/66*
90040	2F	Woodford Halse: 1G 9/63
12/63	16D	Nottingham
4/64	10F	Rose Grove: *Wdn 7/65*
90041	61B	Ferryhill
4/66	62C	Dunfermline: *Wdn 12/66*
90042	31B	March
1/60	33B	Tilbury
6/61	36A	Doncaster: *Wdn 1/65*
90043	41J	Langwith: *Wdn 12/65*
90044	50D	Starbeck
9/59	53E	Goole: 50D 1/60
11/63	50B	Dairycoates: *Wdn 12/66*
90045	50B	Neville Hill
12/59	50A	York: *Wdn 10/65*
90046	2F	Woodford Halse
10/60	18B	Westhouses
6/62	9G	Gorton: *Wdn 3/63*
90047	56A	Wakefield: *Wdn 6/67*
90048	51C	West Hartlepool
7/59	51L	Thornaby: *Wdn 5/63*

90049	65A	Eastfield
12/61	65D	Dawsholm
3/62	62C	Dunfermline: *Wdn 9/63*
90050	40E	Colwick
2/60	34E	New England: *Wdn 5/63*
90051	41J	Langwith
6/59	41D	Canklow
9/59	40E	Colwick: *Wdn 10/65*
90052	40E	Colwick
4/59	41G	Barnsley
6/59	41F	Mexborough
11/62	36A	Doncaster
1/63	41D	Canklow: *Wdn 3/64*
90053	40E	Colwick
4/60	40B	Immingham
10/60	36C	Frodingham: *Wdn 7/65*
90054	50D	Starbeck
9/59	56A	Wakefield
12/62	56F	Low Moor
1/64	56A	Wakefield
7/66	55D	Royston
9/66	55E	Normanton: *Wdn 1/67*
90055	41H	Staveley (GC)
2/60	41J	Langwith
5/60	34E	New England
9/62	40B	Immingham: *Wdn 3/65*
90056	56A	Wakefield
10/62	56B	Ardsley
9/65	56A	Wakefield
12/66	52G	Sunderland: *Wdn 5/67*
90057	53A	Dairycoates
6/59	51A	Darlington
12/62	52H	Tyne Dock
12/63	50B	Dairycoates
12/66	50D	Goole: *Wdn 6/67*
90058	62A	Thornton: *Wdn 12/63*
90059	36C	Frodingham: *Wdn 4/65*
90060	66A	Polmadie: *Wdn 6/62*
90061	56A	Wakefield
11/66	51C	West Hartlepool: *Wdn 6/67*
90062	30A	Stratford: *Wdn 1/60*
90063	31F	Spital Bridge
2/60	31B	March
9/60	36A	Doncaster: *Wdn 4/66*
90064	40E	Colwick
4/59	41G	Barnsley
6/59	41F	Mexborough
12/62	41D	Canklow: *Wdn 1/64*
90065	2F	Woodford Halse: 1G 9/63
	1G	Woodford Halse: *Wdn 3/64*
90066	2F	Woodford Halse: *Wdn 5/63*
90067	51C	West Hartlepool: *Wdn 10/64*
90068	50A	York
11/59	56F	Low Moor
9/61	56D	Mirfield
1/64	56A	Wakefield: *Wdn 7/66*
90069	86A	Newport (Ebbw Jct)
10/59	86C	Cardiff (Canton): 88A 10/60
9/62	81C	Southall
12/62	36A	Doncaster
1/63	41D	Canklow
4/65	41H	Staveley (GC)
6/65	41J	Langwith: *Wdn 1/66*
90070	36C	Frodingham: *Wdn 2/65*
90071	66B	Motherwell
7/63	62C	Dunfermline: *Wdn 4/67*
90072	53A	Dairycoates: 50B 1/60
2/60	51L	Thornaby
8/63	50D	Goole: *Wdn 12/65*
90073	40E	Colwick
12/59	34E	New England
4/63	36A	Doncaster: *Wdn 2/66*
90074	51L	Thornaby
12/62	52H	Tyne Dock
12/63	56A	Wakefield
10/66	52G	Sunderland
3/67	51C	West Hartlepool: *Wdn 9/67*
90075	40E	Colwick
2/60	34E	New England
9/62	40B	Immingham
9/65	36C	Frodingham
3/66	36A	Doncaster: *Wdn 4/66*
90076	51L	Thornaby
4/59	56A	Wakefield
7/67	55E	Normanton
8/67	51C	West Hartlepool: *Wdn 9/67*
90077	66A	Polmadie
3/61	66E	Carstairs
6/61	61B	Ferryhill: *Wdn 5/63*
90078	53A	Dairycoates: 50B 1/60
9/61	50A	York
10/66	52G	Sunderland: *Wdn 11/66*
90079	31B	March
9/60	36A	Doncaster
11/61	36C	Frodingham: *Wdn 1/64*

No.	Shed	Location
90080	2F	Woodford Halse
9/62	9G	Gorton
12/64	8L	Aintree
12/64	9G	Gorton
1/65	10F	Rose Grove
6/65	40E	Colwick
12/65	36C	Frodingham: *Wdn 2/66*
90081	51L	Thornaby
8/63	50D	Goole: *Wdn 6/67*
90082	51E	Stockton
6/59	51A	Darlington
3/63	66A	Polmadie
6/63	51A	Darlington
1/64	51L	Thornaby
5/64	51C	West Hartlepool: *Wdn 6/66*
90083	31B	March: *Wdn 12/59*
90084	40E	Colwick
1/65	41E	Barrow Hill: *Wdn 6/65*
90085	41H	Staveley (GC)
2/60	41J	Langwith
3/60	41D	Canklow
1/64	41E	Barrow Hill: *Wdn 5/65*
90086	51G	Haverton Hill
6/59	51L	Thornaby
3/63	52H	Tyne Dock: *Wdn 8/63*
90087	41H	Staveley (GC)
2/60	36C	Frodingham: *Wdn 10/62*
90088	41J	Langwith: *Wdn 7/65*
90089	56A	Wakefield: *Wdn 1/67*
90090	51L	Thornaby
3/63	52H	Tyne Dock: *Wdn 5/63*
90091	51L	Thornaby
8/63	50B	Dairycoates
11/63	50D	Goole: *Wdn 6/67*
90092	51C	West Hartlepool
3/63	66A	Polmadie
6/63	51C	West Hartlepool
8/63	50B	Dairycoates: *Wdn 10/65*
90093	33B	Tilbury
6/59	31B	March
10/59	33A	Plaistow
11/59	33B	Tilbury: *Wdn 8/62*
90094	53E	Goole: 50D 1/60
	50D	Goole: *Wdn 6/67*
90095	2F	Woodford Halse: *Wdn 6/63*
90096	34E	New England
4/63	36A	Doncaster: *Wdn 9/65*
90097	61B	Ferryhill: *Wdn 8/63*
90098	51L	Thornaby
5/63	51A	Darlington: *Wdn 11/64*
90099	53A	Dairycoates: 50B 1/60
11/63	50D	Goole: *Wdn 6/67*
90100	56A	Wakefield
6/62	56B	Ardsley: *Wdn 1/64*
90101	27B	Aintree: 8L 9/63
	8L	Aintree: *Wdn 5/64*
90102	26C	Bolton: 9K 9/63: *Wdn 10/63*
90103	40E	Colwick: *Wdn 11/65*
90104	40E	Colwick: 16B 1/66
	16B	Colwick: *Wdn 2/66*
90105	26A	Newton Heath: *Wdn 12/62*
90106	33B	Tilbury
6/59	31B	March
10/59	33A	Plaistow
11/59	33B	Tilbury
11/61	34E	New England: *Wdn 9/62*
90107	27B	Aintree: 8L 9/63
	8L	Aintree: *Wdn 11/63*
90108	36A	Doncaster
2/60	36E	Retford
11/60	36C	Frodingham: *Wdn 7/65*
90109	24B	Rose Grove: 10F 9/63
	10F	Rose Grove: *Wdn 5/64*
90110	26C	Bolton
2/62	26B	Agecroft: 9J 9/63
10/63	9K	Bolton
11/63	9J	Agecroft: *Wdn 3/64*
90111	36C	Frodingham: *Wdn 4/64*
90112	56A	Wakefield
11/66	52G	Sunderland: *Wdn 1/67*
90113	56E	Sowerby Bridge
1/64	56A	Wakefield: *Wdn 9/66*
90114	65D	Dawsholm
1/63	65A	Eastfield
11/63	65F	Grangemouth: *Wdn: 6/64*
90115	40E	Colwick
10/60	36C	Frodingham: *Wdn 5/65*
90116	56A	Wakefield
11/66	51C	West Hartlepool: *Wdn 6/67*
90117	62A	Thornton: *Wdn 1/67*
90118	40E	Colwick: *Wdn 11/63*
90119	41F	Mexborough
8/62	36C	Frodingham: *Wdn 1/65*
90120	40E	Colwick
10/60	36C	Frodingham: *Wdn 4/65*
90121	27D	Wigan
2/60	26C	Bolton: 9K 9/63
9/64	41J	Langwith

1/65	41H	Staveley (GC)
6/65	41E	Barrow Hill: *Wdn 6/65*
90122	56E	Sowerby Bridge
1/64	56A	Wakefield: *Wdn 9/65*
90123	26E	Lees: 9P 9/63
4/64	9D	Newton Heath
6/64	8L	Aintree
7/64	10H	Lower Darwen
11/64	10F	Rose Grove: *Wdn 3/65*
90124	56A	Wakefield: *Wdn 6/65*
90125	86C	Canton: 88A 10/60
9/62	8B	Warrington
1/63	27B	Aintree
7/63	8F	Springs Branch
9/63	10D	Lostock Hall
12/63	16E	Kirkby-in-Ashfield
4/64	10D	Lostock Hall: *Wdn 7/65*
90126	56D	Mirfield
11/60	56A	Wakefield
6/61	56D	Mirfield
6/62	56B	Ardsley
10/65	56A	Wakefield: *Wdn 1/67*
90127	55C	Farnley
10/61	55D	Royston: *Wdn 10/64*
90128	62A	Thornton
6/59	65A	Eastfield
12/61	65F	Grangemouth: *Wdn 11/62*
90129	31B	March
4/59	30A	Stratford
4/60	34B	Hornsey
6/61	34E	New England
9/62	40B	Immingham: *Wdn 7/64*
90130	40E	Colwick
5/60	34E	New England
4/63	36E	Retford
6/65	40E	Colwick: *Wdn 10/65*
90131	40B	Immingham
9/63	36E	Retford: *Wdn 3/65*
90132	51L	Thornaby
8/63	50D	Goole: *Wdn 4/67*
90133	36C	Frodingham: *Wdn 10/65*
90134	66A	Polmadie
10/61	65D	Dawsholm
12/61	65B	St Rollox: *Wdn 7/62*
90135	51A	Darlington
11/59	56D	Mirfield
12/60	56A	Wakefield
6/61	56D	Mirfield
3/64	56B	Ardsley
7/65	56A	Wakefield
12/66	52G	Sunderland: *Wdn 9/67*
90136	41F	Mexborough
12/62	41D	Canklow: *Wdn 4/65*
90137	2F	Woodford Halse: *Wdn 12/62*
90138	24B	Rose Grove: 10F 9/63
	10F	Rose Grove: *Wdn 3/64*
90139	41F	Mexborough
12/62	41D	Canklow: *Wdn 5/65*
90140	26E	Lees
9/62	26F	Patricroft
1/63	8D	Widnes
3/63	8F	Springs Branch
6/63	26B	Agecroft: 9J 9/63
	9J	Agecroft: *Wdn 9/64*
90141	26E	Lees
9/62	26F	Patricroft
1/63	8D	Widnes
2/63	27B	Aintree: 8L 9/63
	8L	Aintree: *Wdn 2/64*
90142	26A	Newton Heath
4/61	26B	Agecroft: 9J 9/63
9/64	40B	Immingham: *Wdn 12/65*
90143	24B	Rose Grove: 10F 9/63
	10F	Rose Grove: *Wdn 5/64*
90144	36A	Doncaster: *Wdn 12/63*
90145	40B	Immingham
9/59	41D	Canklow
4/61	41J	Langwith: *Wdn 6/64*
90146	40E	Colwick
5/60	34E	New England
4/63	36E	Retford: *Wdn 6/65*
90147	6B	Mold Jct
2/60	5C	Stafford
5/60	6B	Mold Jct
4/62	8D	Widnes
3/63	9G	Gorton
6/63	8G	Sutton Oak
7/63	8F	Springs Branch: *Wdn 5/64*
90148	84C	Banbury
12/61	85C	Gloucester (Barnwood)
2/62	84F	Stourbridge Jct
7/62	8F	Springs Branch
3/65	8G	Sutton Oak
4/65	10H	Lower Darwen
6/65	41E	Barrow Hill
10/65	40E	Colwick
12/65	36C	Frodingham
3/66	36A	Doncaster: *Wdn 3/66*
90149	86A	Newport (Ebbw Jct)
10/59	86C	Canton: 88A 10/60
9/62	81C	Southall

12/62	41F	Mexborough
2/64	41D	Canklow
6/65	41J	Langwith: *Wdn 1/66*
90150	31B	March
9/62	36A	Doncaster: *Wdn 9/62*
90151	34E	New England: *Wdn 5/63*
90152	81C	Southall
7/59	18B	Westhouses
6/62	9G	Gorton
11/64	10H	Lower Darwen: *Wdn 5/65*
90153	41F	Mexborough
12/62	41D	Canklow
6/65	41J	Langwith: *Wdn 2/66*
90154	40E	Colwick
12/59	34E	New England
9/63	36A	Doncaster: *Wdn 4/66*
90155	51E	Stockton
6/59	51A	Darlington
1/63	56A	Wakefield: *Wdn 1/67*
90156	31B	March
4/59	30A	Stratford
4/60	34B	Hornsey
6/61	36A	Doncaster: *Wdn 4/66*
90157	6B	Mold Jct
8/59	8D	Widnes
3/61	12H	Tebay
6/62	6C	Birkenhead
9/62	8D	Widnes
3/63	8F	Springs Branch: *Wdn 7/64*
90158	34E	New England
11/63	36E	Retford
6/65	36A	Doncaster: *Wdn 12/65*
90159	24B	Rose Grove: 10F 9/63
	10F	Rose Grove: *Wdn 11/63*
90160	53A	Dairycoates: 50B 1/60
2/60	50D	Goole
7/64	56A	Wakefield: *Wdn 6/67*
90161	40E	Colwick
4/60	40B	Immingham
10/60	36C	Frodingham: *Wdn 2/64*
90162	41J	Langwith
6/59	41D	Canklow
9/59	40B	Immingham
1/60	41D	Canklow: *Wdn 2/64*
90163	26A	Newton Heath: *Wdn 12/62*
90164	27B	Aintree
9/62	24B	Rose Grove: 10F 9/63
4/64	9G	Gorton
9/64	41J	Langwith: *Wdn 4/65*
90165	34E	New England
9/62	36C	Frodingham
1/63	41F	Mexborough
9/63	36A	Doncaster: *Wdn 4/64*
90166	40E	Colwick
4/60	40B	Immingham
10/60	36C	Frodingham: *Wdn 5/65*
90167	87G	Carmarthen
6/60	87F	Llanelly
9/60	86C	Canton: 88A 10/60: *Wdn 3/62*
90168	62A	Thornton: *Wdn 8/66*
90169	34E	New England
6/62	40E	Colwick
9/63	36E	Retford
6/65	36A	Doncaster: *Wdn 8/65*
90170	12A	Kingmoor
9/60	21B	Bescot
10/60	8G	Sutton Oak
6/63	26B	Agecroft: *Wdn 8/63*
90171	24B	Rose Grove: 10F 9/63
	10F	Rose Grove: *Wdn 7/65*
90172	51E	Stockton
6/59	51A	Darlington
3/63	66A	Polmadie
6/63	51A	Darlington
8/63	50B	Dairycoates
11/63	50D	Goole: *Wdn 6/67*
90173	6C	Birkenhead
4/60	8F	Springs Branch
11/62	24J	Lancaster
7/63	8F	Springs Branch: *Wdn 7/64*
90174	81C	Southall: *Wdn 11/62*
90175	40B	Immingham: *Wdn 4/65*
90176	82B	St Phillips Marsh
7/59	18B	Westhouses
6/62	9G	Gorton: *Wdn 2/63*
90177	62C	Dunfermline: *Wdn 5/63*
90178	6B	Mold Jct
8/59	8D	Widnes
2/60	24L	Carnforth
9/60	8G	Sutton Oak
5/65	36C	Frodingham: *Wdn 2/66*
90179	87G	Carmarthen
6/60	87F	Llanelly
5/62	9G	Gorton: *Wdn 4/64*
90180	34E	New England
9/62	40B	Immingham: *Wdn 3/65*
90181	24B	Rose Grove: 10F 9/63
	10F	Rose Grove: *Wdn 5/65*
90182	62A	Thornton: *Wdn 12/63*

90183	24B	Rose Grove		9D	Newton Heath: *Wdn*
1/60	26F	Patricroft			*5/64*
1/63	26A	Newton Heath: 9D 9/63	**90198**	66A	Polmadie
12/63	8F	Springs Branch	2/62	61B	Ferryhill
5/65	36C	Frodingham: *Wdn 8/65*	3/62	67D	Ardrossan
90184	51E	Stockton	4/62	67C	Ayre: *Wdn 12/62*
6/59	51A	Darlington	**90199**	66A	Polmadie
11/59	56D	Mirfield: *Wdn 10/64*	1/63	65A	Eastfield
90185	40E	Colwick	11/63	65F	Grangemouth
5/60	34E	New England	11/65	62C	Dunfermline: *Wdn*
9/62	40B	Immingham: *Wdn 3/65*			*11/66*
90186	53E	Goole: 50D 1/60: *Wdn*	**90200**	51A	Darlington
		8/63	2/59	50A	York
90187	6B	Mold Jct	11/59	56F	Low Moor
3/61	24L	Carnforth: 10A 9/63	6/61	56E	Sowerby Bridge
12/63	16E	Kirkby-in-Ashfield	1/64	56A	Wakefield
4/64	8G	Sutton Oak	8/66	52G	Sunderland: *Wdn 7/67*
7/64	10H	Lower Darwen	**90201**	86C	Canton: 88A 10/60
6/65	40E	Colwick	3/61	81E	Didcot
12/65	36A	Doncaster: *Wdn 2/66*	7/71	86A	Newport (Ebbw Jct)
90188	86C	Canton: 88A 10/60	5/62	9G	Gorton: *Wdn 7/64*
10/60	84C	Banbury	**90202**	40E	Colwick
12/60	86A	Newport (Ebbw Jct)	2/60	41D	Canklow: *Wdn 4/65*
12/62	41F	Mexborough	**90203**	41F	Mexborough
1/64	41E	Barrow Hill: *Wdn 4/65*	5/63	41D	Canklow
90189	40E	Colwick	6/65	36A	Doncaster: *Wdn 10/65*
2/60	36C	Frodingham	**90204**	27B	Aintree: 8L 9/63
1/64	41E	Barrow Hill	4/65	10H	Lower Darwen: *Wdn*
10/65	41J	Langwith: *Wdn 11/65*			*6/65*
90190	41F	Mexborough	**90205**	26D	Bury: 9M 9/63
11/62	36A	Doncaster	12/63	16E	Kirkby-in-Ashfield
1/63	41F	Mexborough	1/64	9M	Bury: *Wdn 3/64*
3/64	41D	Canklow	**90206**	26C	Bolton: *Wdn 4/63*
7/64	41J	Langwith	**90207**	87G	Carmarthen
1/65	41E	Barrow Hill	6/60	87F	Llanelly
10/65	40E	Colwick	5/62	9G	Gorton
12/65	40B	Immingham: *Wdn 2/66*	2/65	10F	Rose Grove: *Wdn 5/65*
90191	31B	March: *Wdn 2/60*	**90208**	31B	March
90192	86G	Pontypool Rd	9/61	36A	Doncaster: *Wdn 1/64*
2/60	6C	Birkenhead	**90209**	41F	Mexborough
9/62	8D	Widnes	1/63	41J	Langwith: *Wdn 7/64*
3/63	8F	Springs Branch: *Wdn*	**90210**	56E	Sowerby Bridge
		5/63	1/64	56A	Wakefield
90193	65D	Dawsholm	8/66	52G	Sunderland
7/62	62A	Thornton: *Wdn 8/63*	3/67	51C	West Hartlepool: *Wdn*
90194	26D	Bury			*7/67*
12/60	26E	Lees: 9P 9/63: *Wdn 3/64*	**90211**	41F	Mexborough
90195	41F	Mexborough	5/63	41D	Canklow
8/62	36A	Doncaster: *Wdn 10/65*	6/65	36A	Doncaster: *Wdn 7/65*
90196	33A	Plaistow	**90212**	6C	Birkenhead
11/59	33B	Tilbury: *Wdn 9/62*	1/60	24L	Carnforth
90197	26A	Newton Heath: 9D 9/63	8/60	24K	Preston

9/60	8G	Sutton Oak	**90227**	6B	Mold Jct
5/65	36C	Frodingham: *Wdn 8/65*	4/62	6C	Birkenhead
90213	53E	Goole: 50D 1/60	9/62	8B	Warrington
5/64	50B	Dairycoates: *Wdn 2/66*	3/63	26D	Bury
90214	6E	Chester (West)	5/63	26C	Bolton: 9K 9/63
4/60	8F	Springs Branch	9/64	41J	Langwith
6/60	18B	Westhouses	1/65	41H	Staveley (GC)
6/62	9G	Gorton: *Wdn 3/64*	6/65	41E	Barrow Hill: *Wdn 9/65*
90215	40E	Colwick	**90228**	53E	Goole: 50D 1/60: *Wdn*
5/60	34E	New England			*9/63*
9/62	40B	Immingham: *Wdn 4/65*	**90229**	66A	Polmadie
90216	27B	Aintree: 8L 9/63	6/63	62C	Dunfermline: *Wdn 9/66*
	8L	Aintree: *Wdn 8/64*	**90230**	50A	York
90217	53A	Dairycoates: 50B 1/60	11/59	56A	Wakefield
9/61	50A	York: *Wdn 6/65*	8/61	56B	Ardsley
90218	2F	Woodford Halse: 1G	10/65	51C	West Hartlepool: *Wdn*
		9/63			*5/67*
12/63	16A	Toton	**90231**	24B	Rose Grove: *Wdn 8/63*
3/64	1G	Woodford Halse: *Wdn*	**90232**	36C	Frodingham: *Wdn 1/66*
		4/64	**90233**	53A	Dairycoates
90219	26D	Bury	6/59	51A	Darlington
11/60	27B	Aintree	9/59	51L	Thornaby
9/62	24B	Rose Grove: 10F 9/63	11/59	56D	Mirfield
	10F	Rose Grove: *Wdn 5/64*	6/60	56E	Sowerby Bridge
90220	41F	Mexborough	1/64	56A	Wakefield
5/63	41D	Canklow	2/66	56D	Mirfield
6/65	41E	Barrow Hill	1/67	56A	Wakefield: *Wdn 5/67*
10/65	41J	Langwith: *Wdn 11/65*	**90234**	66A	Polmadie
90221	40B	Immingham: *Wdn 1/65*	7/62	65F	Grangemouth: *Wdn*
90222	26A	Newton Heath			*11/63*
2/60	26F	Patricroft	**90235**	40E	Colwick
1/63	26B	Agecroft: 9J 9/63	10/60	36A	Doncaster: *Wdn 10/65*
9/64	10F	Rose Grove	**90236**	50A	York
10/64	8L	Aintree: *Wdn 8/65*	11/59	56F	Low Moor
90223	40B	Immingham	9/61	56D	Mirfield
2/59	34E	New England	6/62	56B	Ardsley
9/62	40A	Lincoln	10/65	56A	Wakefield
9/63	36E	Retford	7/67	55E	Normanton: *Wdn 9/67*
6/65	36C	Frodingham: *Wdn 8/65*	**90237**	2F	Woodford Halse: 1G
90224	40B	Immingham			9/63
7/61	36E	Retford	12/63	16A	Toton
11/61	36A	Doncaster	1/64	1G	Woodford Halse: *Wdn*
3/63	41J	Langwith: *Wdn 3/64*			*2/64*
90225	86A	Newport (Ebbw Jct)	**90238**	86C	Canton
6/60	87F	Llanelly	7/59	18B	Westhouses
9/60	86A	Newport (Ebbw Jct)	6/62	9G	Gorton: *Wdn 3/63*
12/62	41F	Mexborough	**90239**	34E	New England
9/63	36A	Doncaster	9/62	36C	Frodingham: *Wdn 11/63*
1/65	41E	Barrow Hill: *Wdn 4/65*	**90240**	51L	Thornaby
90226	26D	Bury	6/62	56B	Ardsley
10/59	26E	Lees	10/65	50B	Dairycoates: *Wdn 1/67*
11/59	26D	Bury: 9M 9.63:*Wdn 12/63*	**90241**	24B	Rose Grove: 10F 9/63

6/65	40E	Colwick
12/65	36C	Frodingham: *Wdn 1/66*
90242	6B	Mold Jct
8/59	8D	Widnes
3/63	9G	Gorton
6/63	8F	Springs Branch
11/63	10C	Fleetwood
12/63	8L	Aintree
9/64	40B	Immingham: *Wdn 9/65*
90243	55G	Huddersfield
4/59	55C	Farnley
6/59	55D	Royston
8/64	55E	Normanton: *Wdn 6/67*
90244	33B	Tilbury
6/59	31B	March
10/59	33A	Plaistow
11/59	33B	Tilbury: *Wdn 8/62*
90245	26A	Newton Heath
12/59	27B	Aintree: 8L 9/63
	8L	Aintree: *Wdn 5/64*
90246	34E	New England
11/63	36E	Retford: *Wdn 4/65*
90247	55E	Normanton: *Wdn 11/62*
90248	26A	Newton Heath
9/62	26F	Patricroft
1/63	26A	Newton Heath: 9D 9/63
3/64	9K	Bolton
9/64	8L	Aintree
4/65	36C	Frodingham: *Wdn 11/65*
90249	55G	Huddersfield
11/59	55E	Normanton: *Wdn 12/63*
90250	41F	Mexborough: *Wdn 3/63*
90251	81F	Oxford
7/59	18B	Westhouses
9/59	2F	Woodford Halse
12/59	18B	Westhouses
6/62	9G	Gorton: *Wdn 5/63*
90252	41F	Mexborough
9/63	36A	Doncaster: *Wdn 9/65*
90253	34E	New England: *Wdn 12/62*
90254	55C	Farnley
11/59	55E	Normanton
8/62	55D	Royston
6/63	55C	Farnley
12/63	55D	Royston
5/64	55E	Normanton
9/65	56A	Wakefield
11/65	50A	York
9/66	51C	West Hartlepool: *Wdn 1/67*
90255	36A	Doncaster: *Wdn 12/65*

90256	33A	Plaistow
11/59	33B	Tilbury: *Wdn 8/62*
90257	6B	Mold Jct
8/59	8D	Widnes
11/59	6C	Birkenhead
4/60	8F	Springs Branch: *Wdn 8/64*
90258	24C	Lostock Hall: 10D 9/63
9/64	41J	Langwith
1/65	41H	Staveley (GC)
6/65	41E	Barrow Hill
10/65	41J	Langwith: *Wdn 1/66*
90259	41J	Langwith
5/60	40E	Colwick: *Wdn 10/65*
90260	53E	Goole: 50D 1/60: *Wdn 9/63*
90261	84G	Shrewsbury
8/59	84C	Banbury
2/62	84F	Stourbridge Jct
7/62	8F	Springs Branch
6/63	26B	Agecroft: 9J 9/63
10/64	10F	Rose Grove
11/64	10H	Lower Darwen: *Wdn 7/65*
90262	53E	Goole: 50D 1/60
11/63	50B	Dairycoates: *Wdn 6/67*
90263	40B	Immingham
8/59	40E	Colwick: *Wdn 1/64*
90264	24B	Rose Grove: 10F 9/63
1/64	10D	Lostock Hall: *Wdn 8/64*
90265	53E	Goole: 50D 1/60
11/63	50B	Dairycoates
11/65	50D	Goole: *Wdn 6/67*
90266	24C	Lostock Hall
8/62	24B	Rose Grove: 10F 9/63
5/64	9G	Gorton
9/64	41J	Langwith
1/65	41H	Staveley (GC)
6/65	41E	Barrow Hill: *Wdn 7/65*
90267	26C	Bolton: 9K 9/63
9/64	8L	Aintree: *Wdn 3/65*
90268	81C	Southall
6/59	84C	Banbury
12/61	85C	Gloucester (Barnwood)
2/62	84F	Stourbridge Jct
7/62	8F	Springs Branch
6/63	26B	Agecroft: 9J 9/63
10/64	9G	Gorton
11/64	10H	Lower Darwen: *Wdn 4/65:*
90269	40E	Colwick
2/59	34E	New England: *Wdn 5/63*

90270	41F	Mexborough
11/61	34E	New England: *Wdn* 12/62
90271	26A	Newton Heath: 9D 9/63
6/64	8L	Aintree
7/64	10F	Rose Grove
9/64	41J	Langwith: *Wdn 7/65*
90272	53A	Dairycoates: 50B 1/60
5/67	50D	Goole: *Wdn 6/67*
90273	51L	Thornaby
8/63	50D	Goole: *Wdn 10/65*
90274	24B	Rose Grove: 10F 9/63
5/64	9G	Gorton
12/64	8L	Aintree
4/65	36C	Frodingham: *Wdn 1/66*
90275	41J	Langwith: *Wdn 7/65*
90276	41H	Staveley (GC)
2/60	41J	Langwith
3/60	41H	Staveley (GC)
4/60	41D	Canklow: *Wdn 2/65*
90277	24C	Lostock Hall: 10D 9/63
9/64	36A	Doncaster: *Wdn 10/65*
90278	27B	Aintree: *Wdn 12/62*
90279	31B	March
9/61	36A	Doncaster: *Wdn 6/65*
90280	40B	Immingham
9/63	36E	Retford
6/65	36C	Frodingham: *Wdn 9/65*
90281	53E	Goole
6/59	56D	Mirfield
6/60	56E	Sowerby Bridge
1/64	56A	Wakefield: *Wdn 6/67*
90282	27B	Aintree: 8L 9/63
9/64	40E	Colwick: *Wdn 1/65*
90283	27B	Aintree: 8L 9/63
7/64	8F	Springs Branch
9/64	36C	Frodingham: *Wdn 10/65*
90284	81F	Oxford
7/59	18B	Westhouses
6/62	9G	Gorton
12/64	8L	Aintree: *Wdn 3/65*
90285	40B	Immingham
9/63	36E	Retford: *Wdn 6/65*
90286	41F	Mexborough
12/60	36A	Doncaster: *Wdn 8/62*
90287	41J	Langwith
5/60	40E	Colwick: *Wdn 12/62*
90288	40E	Colwick
4/60	40B	Immingham
8/60	40E	Colwick
10/60	36C	Frodingham: *Wdn 9/62*
90289	26A	Newton Heath: 9D 9/63
6/64	8L	Aintree
7/64	10F	Rose Grove: *Wdn 11/64*
90290	41F	Mexborough
5/60	41J	Langwith
8/60	41D	Canklow: *Wdn 5/65*
90291	26A	Newton Heath: 9D 9/63
6/64	10F	Rose Grove: *Wdn 2/65*
90292	26B	Agecroft
6/63	9G	Gorton
9/64	41J	Langwith: *Wdn 10/65*
90293	31B	March
9/61	36A	Doncaster: *Wdn 9/65*
90294	40B	Immingham: *Wdn 7/65*
90295	24C	Lostock Hall
2/62	24B	Rose Grove: 10F 9/63
6/65	41E	Barrow Hill
10/65	40E	Colwick: 16B & *Wdn 1/66*
90296	40E	Colwick
10/60	36A	Doncaster: *Wdn 8/65*
90297	26C	Bolton
4/60	27B	Aintree
6/61	24D	Lower Darwen
4/63	24B	Rose Grove: 10F 9/63
1/64	10D	Lostock Hall: *Wdn 9/64*
90298	30A	Stratford
1/60	33B	Tilbury: *Wdn 8/62*
90299	2F	Woodford Halse: 1G 9/63
3/64	16A	Toton
4/64	1G	Woodford Halse: *Wdn 4/64*
90300	53E	Goole
6/59	56D	Mirfield
1/64	56A	Wakefield: *Wdn 6/67*
90301	41F	Mexborough
5/60	41J	Langwith
1/65	41H	Staveley (GC)
6/65	41J	Langwith: *Wdn 9/65*
90302	41J	Langwith: *Wdn 8/64*
90303	40E	Colwick: *Wdn 12/62*
90304	41F	Mexborough
11/61	34E	New England
6/62	40E	Colwick: *Wdn 9/64*
90305	31B	March
10/61	36A	Doncaster: *Wdn 3/66*
90306	26E	Lees
10/61	26B	Agecroft: 9J 9/63
10/64	8L	Aintree
5/65	10F	Rose Grove
6/65	41E	Barrow Hill: *Wdn 6/65*
90307	26B	Agecroft: *Wdn 12/62*

90308	55C	Farnley		2/61	67D	Ardrossan
1/61	55G	Huddersfield: *Wdn*		7/62	67C	Ayr
		11/62		11/63	62A	Thornton: *Wdn 6/64*
90309	55E	Normanton		**90320**	66A	Polmadie: *Wdn 7/62*
6/61	51A	Darlington		**90321**	56A	Wakefield
3/63	66A	Polmadie		12/66	52G	Sunderland: *Wdn 7/67*
6/63	51A	Darlington		**90322**	55C	Farnley
3/66	51C	West Hartlepool: *Wdn*		6/59	56D	Mirfield
		7/67		1/60	56F	Low Moor
90310	56E	Sowerby Bridge		9/61	56D	Mirfield
12/62	56F	Low Moor		1/64	56A	Wakefield: *Wdn 8/64*
8/64	56D	Mirfield: *Wdn 12/66*		**90323**	86C	Canton: 88A 10/60
90311	41F	Mexborough		10/60	84C	Banbury
1/63	41D	Canklow: *Wdn 8/64*		11/60	86A	Newport (Ebbw Jct)
90312	86C	Canton		5/62	9G	Gorton: *Wdn 5/64*
3/60	81C	Southall		**90324**	26B	Agecroft: 9J 9/63
3/61	81E	Didcot			9J	Agecroft: *Wdn 5/64*
5/61	86A	Newport (Ebbw Jct)		**90325**	55G	Huddersfield: *Wdn 9/65*
9/61	87F	Llanelly		**90326**	56A	Wakefield: *Wdn 11/63*
5/62	9G	Gorton: *Wdn 12/63*		**90327**	24J	Lancaster
90313	84C	Banbury		1/59	27B	Aintree
12/62	41F⸓	Mexborough		9/62	24B	Rose Grove: 10F 9/63
9/63	41D	Canklow: *Wdn 4/64*		1/64	9K	Bolton
90314	24B	Rose Grove: 10F 9/63		8/64	8L	Aintree: *Wdn 1/65*
	10F	Rose Grove: *Wdn 4/65*		**90328**	24C	Lostock Hall
90315	86G	Pontypool Rd		1/59	26A	Newton Heath
4/60	85E	Gloucester (Barnwood)		9/62	26F	Patricroft
6/60	84C	Banbury		1/63	26A	Newton Heath: 9D 9/63
8/62	8B	Warrington			9D	Newton Heath: *Wdn*
1/63	24J	Lancaster				*5/64*
8/63	26B	Agecroft: 9J 9/63		**90329**	56E	Sowerby Bridge
10/63	9K	Bolton		9/63	56A	Wakefield: *Wdn 9/65*
7/64	9J	Agecroft		**90330**	41F	Mexborough
9/64	36C	Frodingham: *Wdn 11/65*		9/63	41D	Canklow
90316	24J	Lancaster		6/65	36A	Doncaster: *Wdn 12/65*
1/59	27B	Aintree		**90331**	24C	Lostock Hall
6/61	24D	Lower Darwen		9/61	26E	Lees
1/63	24J	Lancaster: 10J 9/63		9/62	26F	Patricroft
1/64	8L	Aintree		2/63	26A	Newton Heath: 9D 9/63
2/64	9K	Bolton			9D	Newton Heath: *Wdn*
3/64	8F	Springs Branch				*11/63*
9/64	40E	Colwick: *Wdn 12/65*		**90332**	55G	Huddersfield
90317	6B	Mold Jct		1/67	55E	Normanton: *Wdn 1/67*
8/59	8D	Widnes		**90333**	56F	Low Moor
11/59	6C	Birkenhead		9/61	56D	Mirfield
4/60	8F	Springs Branch: *Wdn*		3/64	56A	Wakefield: *Wdn 10/65*
		3/65		**90334**	55E	Normanton
90318	55C	Farnley		1/59	55C	Farnley: *Wdn 11/63*
11/59	55E	Normanton		**90335**	24C	Lostock Hall
9/65	55D	Royston		2/62	24F	Fleetwood: 10C 9/63
1/67	55E	Normanton: *Wdn 9/67*			10C	Fleetwood: *Wdn 11/63*
90319	67C	Ayr		**90336**	55C	Farnley

6/59	55D	Royston
10/63	56A	Wakefield: *Wdn 1/66*
90337	55E	Normanton
9/65	55D	Royston
9/66	55E	Normanton: *Wdn 1/67*
90338	26A	Newton Heath: 9D 9/63
	9D	Newton Heath: *Wdn 11/63*
90339	56A	Wakefield
9/66	51C	West Hartlepool: *Wdn 7/67*
90340	31B	March
10/61	36A	Doncaster
1/64	41E	Barrow Hill: *Wdn 7/65*
90341	56A	Wakefield: *Wdn 7/65*
90342	56A	Wakefield: *Wdn 11/65*
90343	27B	Aintree: 8L 9/63
	8L	Aintree: *Wdn 12/63*
90344	51C	West Hartlepool: *Wdn 11/64*
90345	55G	Huddersfield
9/63	55D	Royston
5/64	55E	Normanton
9/65	56A	Wakefield: *Wdn 6/67*
90346	2F	Woodford Halse: 1G 9/63
12/63	16A	Toton
4/64	9D	Newton Heath
6/64	8L	Aintree
5/65	10F	Rose Grove
6/65	41E	Barrow Hill
10/65	40E	Colwick: *Wdn 10/65*
90347	55G	Huddersfield
9/65	56A	Wakefield
11/65	50A	York
9/66	51C	West Hartlepool: *Wdn 5/67*
90348	56A	Wakefield
10/66	52G	Sunderland: *Wdn 9/67*
90349	34E	New England
11/63	36E	Retford: *Wdn 6/65*
90350	62A	Thornton: *Wdn 8/66*
90351	55C	Farnley
6/59	56D	Mirfield
1/60	56F	Low Moor
8/64	56D	Mirfield
1/67	56A	Wakefield
7/67	55E	Normanton: *Wdn 9/67*
90352	53A	Dairycoates: 50B 1/60
4/67	50D	Goole: *Wdn 6/67*
90353	56A	Wakefield: *Wdn 2/65*
90354	26B	Agecroft: 9J 9/63
	9J	Agecroft: *Wdn 10/64*
90355	81C	Southall: *Wdn 11/62*
90356	81C	Southall: *Wdn 11/62*
90357	55E	Normanton
9/65	56A	Wakefield
8/66	52G	Sunderland: *Wdn 9/66*
90358	41F	Mexborough
1/63	41D	Canklow: *Wdn 11/63*
90359	26B	Agecroft: 9J 9/63
	9J	Agecroft: *Wdn 9/64*
90360	56E	Sowerby Bridge
9/63	56A	Wakefield
7/67	55E	Normanton
8/67	51C	West Hartlepool: *Wdn 9/67*
90361	56A	Wakefield
6/60	56B	Ardsley
9/65	56A	Wakefield
12/66	52G	Sunderland: *Wdn 4/67*
90362	55E	Normanton
3/65	55G	Huddersfield
1/67	55E	Normanton: *Wdn 6/67*
90363	56A	Wakefield: *Wdn 6/67*
90364	26D	Bury: 9M 9/63
12/63	9K	Bolton
9/64	9G	Gorton
1/65	10F	Rose Grove
6/65	36A	Doncaster
11/65	40B	Immingham: *Wdn 12/65*
90365	2F	Woodford Halse: 1G 9/63
12/63	16A	Toton
4/64	9G	Gorton
9/64	36A	Doncaster: *Wdn 6/65*
90366	26A	Newton Heath: 9D 9/63
	9D	Newton Heath: *Wdn 1/64*
90367	24C	Lostock Hall
2/62	24F	Fleetwood
4/63	26C	Bolton: 9K 9/63
9/64	9G	Gorton
1/65	10F	Rose Grove
6/65	41E	Barrow Hill
10/65	40E	Colwick
12/65	36C	Frodingham: *Wdn 2/66*
90368	40E	Colwick
9/59	41D	Canklow
1/64	41E	Barrow Hill: *Wdn 6/65*
90369	6C	Birkenhead
9/62	8B	Warrington
3/63	24L	Carnforth: 10A 9/63
12/63	16D	Nottingham

4/64	8F	Springs Branch
9/64	36A	Doncaster: *Wdn 4/66*
90370	56A	Wakefield
11/66	52G	Sunderland: *Wdn 5/67*
90371	24B	Rose Grove
1/61	26F	Patricroft
1/63	26A	Newton Heath: 9D 9/63
	9D	Newton Heath: *Wdn 4/64*
90372	26B	Agecroft: 9J 9/63
9/64	56A	Wakefield: *Wdn 12/65*
90373	51L	Thornaby
6/60	51A	Darlington
1/63	56A	Wakefield: *Wdn 9/66*
90374	24A	Accrington
1/60	24B	Rose Grove
2/60	24A	Accrington
2/61	24B	Rose Grove: 10F 9/63
	10F	Rose Grove: *Wdn 3/64*
90375	27B	Aintree
6/61	24D	Lower Darwen: 10H 9/63
	10H	Lower Darwen: *Wdn 7/64*
90376	26A	Newton Heath: *Wdn 12/62*
90377	51E	Stockton
6/59	51A	Darlington
9/59	51L	Thornaby
12/62	55D	Royston
12/63	55E	Normanton
3/65	55D	Royston: *Wdn 2/66*
90378	53A	Dairycoates: 50B 1/60
7/67	52G	Sunderland: *Wdn 9/67*
90379	56A	Wakefield: *Wdn 3/66*
90380	56A	Wakefield
2/66	56D	Mirfield: *Wdn 3/66*
90381	27B	Aintree: 8L 9/63
4/65	36C	Frodingham: *Wdn 10/65*
90382	56A	Wakefield
12/66	52G	Sunderland: *Wdn 9/67*
90383	40B	Immingham
10/60	40E	Colwick
1/65	41E	Barrow Hill: *Wdn 4/65*
90384	41F	Mexborough
2/64	41D	Canklow
6/65	41E	Barrow Hill
10/65	40E	Colwick
12/65	36C	Frodingham: *Wdn 2/66*
90385	56A	Wakefield: *Wdn 3/67*
90386	66B	Motherwell
5/63	61B	Ferryhill

6/63	62C	Dunfermline
12/66	52G	Sunderland
2/67	62C	Dunfermline: *Wdn 4/67*
90387	66A	Polmadie: *Wdn 8/62*
90388	26A	Newton Heath: 9D 9/63
6/64	10F	Rose Grove: *Wdn 7/64*
90389	26A	Newton Heath: 9D 9/63
6/64	10F	Rose Grove: *Wdn 10/64*
90390	26A	Newton Heath
9/62	26F	Patricroft
1/63	26A	Newton Heath: 9D 9/63
1/64	9G	Gorton
3/64	8G	Sutton Oak
5/65	36C	Frodingham: *Wdn 9/65*
90391	41H	Staveley (GC)
12/59	41D	Canklow: *Wdn 8/62*
90392	6C	Birkenhead
9/62	8B	Warrington
3/63	24L	Carnforth
7/63	9G	Gorton
11/63	10C	Fleetwood
12/63	9G	Gorton: *Wdn 12/64*
90393	40B	Immingham
10/60	40E	Colwick: *Wdn 8/65*
90394	40E	Colwick
4/60	40B	Immingham: *Wdn 4/64*
90395	55C	Farnley
1/60	55D	Royston
12/63	55E	Normanton
9/65	56A	Wakefield
11/65	50A	York
10/66	52G	Sunderland: *Wdn 10/66*
90396	56A	Wakefield: *Wdn 6/67*
90397	51G	Haverton Hill
6/59	51L	Thornaby
11/59	56D	Mirfield
1/60	56F	Low Moor
8/64	56D	Mirfield
1/67	56A	Wakefield: *Wdn 5/67*
90398	24C	Lostock Hall
9/61	26D	Bury
8/62	24B	Rose Grove: 10F 9/63
4/64	9P	Lees
5/64	9D	Newton Heath
6/64	10H	Lower Darwen
9/64	41J	Langwith: *Wdn 7/65*
90399	24A	Accrington
1/60	26F	Patricroft
1/63	26A	Newton Heath: 9D 9/63
6/64	8L	Aintree
7/64	8F	Springs Branch: *Wdn 3/65*

90400	41F	Mexborough: *Wdn 12/63*
90401	41F	Mexborough
2/64	41D	Canklow
4/65	41H	Staveley (GC)
6/65	41J	Langwith: *Wdn 11/65*
90402	26E	Lees: 9P 9/63
2/64	9G	Gorton: *Wdn 3/64*
90403	2F	Woodford Halse
9/62	9G	Gorton
12/63	16D	Nottingham
4/64	9G	Gorton: *Wdn 5/64*
90404	56A	Wakefield: *Wdn 6/67*
90405	50A	York
11/59	56A	Wakefield
6/60	51A	Darlington
11/61	56B	Ardsley
9/65	56A	Wakefield
7/67	55E	Normanton: *Wdn 9/67*
90406	51A	Darlington
9/59	51L	Thornaby
8/63	50D	Goole: *Wdn 6/67*
90407	55C	Farnley
10/61	55D	Royston
10/63	56A	Wakefield: *Wdn 5/67*
90408	26D	Bury: 9M 9/63
12/63	16E	Kirkby-in-Ashfield
4/64	9M	Bury: *Wdn 5/64*
90409	51L	Thornaby
6/62	56B	Ardsley
7/65	56A	Wakefield: *Wdn 6/67*
90410	41F	Mexborough
3/64	41D	Canklow
6/65	41E	Barrow Hill
10/65	40E	Colwick
11/65	36C	Frodingham
2/66	36A	Doncaster: *Wdn 4/66*
90411	41J	Langwith
6/59	41D	Canklow
9/59	40B	Immingham
1/60	41D	Canklow
8/60	41J	Langwith: *Wdn 8/64*
90412	56E	Sowerby Bridge
9/63	56A	Wakefield: *Wdn 10/64*
90413	24C	Lostock Hall
9/61	26D	Bury
9/62	24F	Fleetwood: 10C 9/63
12/63	8L	Aintree
9/64	40E	Colwick: 16B 1/66
	16B	Colwick: *Wdn 2/66*
90414	56A	Wakefield
8/59	41D	Canklow: *Wdn 12/62*
90415	56A	Wakefield: *Wdn 1/67*
90416	27B	Aintree: 8L 9/63
	8L	Aintree: *Wdn 5/64*
90417	56A	Wakefield
10/66	52G	Sunderland: *Wdn 9/67*
90418	41H	Staveley (GC)
2/60	41J	Langwith
4/60	41B	Grimesthorpe
4/61	41J	Langwith: *Wdn 1/66*
90419	26D	Bury: 9M 9/63
12/63	9K	Bolton
8/64	8L	Aintree
9/64	41E	Barrow Hill: *Wdn 4/65*
90420	24B	Rose Grove: 10F 9/63
	10F	Rose Grove: *Wdn 8/65*
90421	41F	Mexborough
9/63	36A	Doncaster
1/64	41E	Barrow Hill
6/64	36A	Doncaster: *Wdn 7/65*
90422	36C	Frodingham: *Wdn 6/65*
90423	6B	Mold Jct
8/59	8D	Widnes
3/63	8F	Springs Branch
9/64	40E	Colwick: *Wdn 12/65*
90424	50A	York: *Wdn 12/63*
90425	36C	Frodingham: *Wdn 12/62*
90426	51L	Thornaby
2/62	51C	West Hartlepool
4/62	56A	Wakefield
1/64	56B	Ardsley: *Wdn 3/65*
90427	53A	Dairycoates: 50B 1/60
11/63	50D	Goole: *Wdn 6/67*
90428	34E	New England
4/63	36A	Doncaster: *Wdn 1/66*
90429	56A	Wakefield: *Wdn 4/67*
90430	51E	Stockton
6/59	51A	Darlington
1/63	56A	Wakefield
7/67	55E	Normanton: *Wdn 9/67*
90431	41J	Langwith: *Wdn 12/62*
90432	40E	Colwick: *Wdn 10/65*
90433	2F	Woodford Halse: 1G 9/63
12/63	16A	Toton
4/64	1G	Woodford Halse: *Wdn 5/64*
90434	51L	Thornaby
6/63	52H	Tyne Dock
6/65	51C	West Hartlepool: *Wdn 6/67*
90435	51L	Thornaby
2/62	50D	Goole

4/62	50B	Dairycoates: *Wdn 9/63*
90436	65D	Dawsholm: *Wdn 6/62*
90437	40E	Colwick
12/65	36A	Doncaster: *Wdn 4/66*
90438	41J	Langwith
5/60	40E	Colwick: *Wdn 10/65*
90439	34E	New England
4/63	36C	Frodingham: *Wdn 11/65*
90440	65D	Dawsholm
7/62	8F	Springs Branch: *Wdn 8/63*
90441	62A	Thornton: *Wdn 10/66*
90442	33B	Tilbury
11/61	36A	Doncaster
3/63	41J	Langwith: *Wdn 4/65*
90443	40B	Immingham: *Wdn 6/65*
90444	62B	Dundee (Tay Bridge)
6/63	62A	Thornton: *Wdn 1/67*
90445	50A	York
11/59	56A	Wakefield
6/60	51A	Darlington
1/64	51L	Thornaby
5/64	51C	West Hartlepool: *Wdn 7/66*
90446	51L	Thornaby: *Wdn 11/63*
90447	31F	Spital Bridge
2/60	31B	March
10/61	36A	Doncaster: *Wdn 11/63*
90448	2F	Woodford Halse: 1G 9/63
3/64	16A	Toton
4/64	9J	Agecroft
10/64	10F	Rose Grove
6/65	36A	Doncaster
11/65	40B	Immingham: *Wdn 12/65*
90449	41J	Langwith: *Wdn 1/66*
90450	53A	Dairycoates: 50B 1/60
	50B	Dairycoates: *Wdn 6/67*
90451	51L	Thornaby
8/63	50D	Goole: *Wdn 12/66*
90452	51L	Thornaby
6/63	52H	Tyne Dock
12/63	50B	Dairycoates: *Wdn 6/65*
90453	36A	Doncaster
11/61	36C	Frodingham: *Wdn 10/63*
90454	34E	New England
11/63	36E	Retford: *Wdn 6/65*
90455	61B	Ferryhill: *Wdn 9/62*
90456	36C	Frodingham: *Wdn 2/66*
90457	50D	Starbeck
9/59	56D	Mirfield
1/64	56A	Wakefield: *Wdn 1/66*

90458	53A	Dairycoates: 50B 1/60
5/67	50D	Goole: *Wdn 6/67*
90459	51L	Thornaby
6/63	52H	Tyne Dock
6/65	51C	West Hartlepool: *Wdn 6/67*
90460	40B	Immingham
11/60	40A	Lincoln
9/63	36E	Retford: *Wdn 6/65*
90461	51L	Thornaby
2/62	50D	Goole: *Wdn 9/63*
90462	51L	Thornaby
8/63	50B	Dairycoates: *Wdn 1/67*
90463	67C	Ayr
1/61	67D	Ardrossan: *Wdn 11/63*
90464	12A	Kingmoor
9/60	8G	Sutton Oak: *Wdn 3/64*
90465	51L	Thornaby
6/62	56B	Ardsley
10/65	55E	Normanton: *Wdn 1/67*
90466	84C	Banbury
2/59	81C	Southall
8/62	8B	Warrington
1/63	26C	Bolton: 9K 9/63
9/64	40E	Colwick: *Wdn 12/65*
90467	50B	Neville Hill
6/59	50A	York: *Wdn 11/63*
90468	66B	Motherwell
8/63	62A	Thornton: *Wdn 4/67*
90469	36C	Frodingham: *Wdn 11/64*
90470	56E	Sowerby Bridge
1/64	56A	Wakefield: *Wdn 12/66*
90471	40B	Immingham
9/59	41D	Canklow
6/65	41E	Barrow Hill
10/65	40E	Colwick
11/65	36C	Frodingham
3/66	36A	Doncaster: *Wdn 4/66*
90472	62A	Thornton: *Wdn 12/63*
90473	40E	Colwick: *Wdn 9/62*
90474	2F	Woodford Halse: 1G 9/63
5/64	8L	Aintree
9/64	41E	Barrow Hill: *Wdn 7/65*
90475	50A	York
6/60	50D	Goole: *Wdn 8/63*
90476	40E	Colwick
10/60	36A	Doncaster: *Wdn 7/65*
90477	31B	March
10/61	36A	Doncaster
11/65	40B	Immingham
2/66	36A	Doncaster: *Wdn 3/66*

90478	53E	Goole: 50D 1/60		3/64	41D	Canklow
11/63	50B	Dairycoates		4/64	41E	Barrow Hill: *Wdn 9/65*
7/67	51C	West Hartlepool: *Wdn 9/67*		**90492**	41J	Langwith
				5/60	40E	Colwick: *Wdn 10/65*
90479	51G	Haverton Hill		**90493**	65D	Dawsholm
6/59	51L	Thornaby		8/62	8F	Springs Branch
6/63	51C	West Hartlepool		4/65	36C	Frodingham: *Wdn 2/66*
3/66	50B	Dairycoates: *Wdn 9/66*		**90494**	33B	Tilbury
90480	31B	March		11/61	36A	Doncaster: *Wdn 9/62*
4/59	30A	Stratford		**90495**	41F	Mexborough: *Wdn 12/62*
4/60	34B	Hornsey				
6/61	36A	Doncaster: *Wdn 7/65*		**90496**	40E	Colwick
90481	51L	Thornaby		10/60	36A	Doncaster
2/62	56D	Mirfield		1/65	41E	Barrow Hill: *Wdn 4/65*
6/62	56B	Ardsley		**90497**	56A	Wakefield: *Wdn 3/63*
10/65	55E	Normanton		**90498**	30A	Stratford
6/66	55D	Royston: *Wdn 10/66*		10/60	36A	Doncaster
90482	53A	Dairycoates: 50B 1/60		9/65	36C	Frodingham: *Wdn 2/66*
7/64	56A	Wakefield		**90499**	41F	Mexborough: *Wdn 12/63*
9/66	51C	West Hartlepool: *Wdn 7/67*				
				90500	51L	Thornaby
90483	84D	Leamington Spa		3/63	52H	Tyne Dock: *Wdn 8/63*
8/59	84C	Banbury		**90501**	31F	Spital Bridge
12/62	41J	Langwith: *Wdn 3/64*		2/60	31B	March
90484	31B	March		11/60	30A	Stratford
11/60	30A	Stratford		3/61	31A	Cambridge
6/61	36A	Doncaster: *Wdn 3/66*		4/61	33B	Tilbury
90485	87G	Carmarthen		6/61	31B	March
11/59	81D	Reading		10/61	36A	Doncaster
1/60	81C	Southall		3/63	36E	Retford
2/60	86C	Canton		6/65	36C	Frodingham
4/60	85E	Gloucester (Barnwood)		11/65	36A	Doncaster: *Wdn 11/65*
6/60	86C	Canton: 88A 10/60		**90502**	41H	Staveley (GC)
10/61	84C	Banbury		1/60	34B	Hornsey
12/62	41F	Mexborough		2/60	34E	New England: *Wdn 5/63*
3/64	41D	Canklow: *Wdn 8/64*		**90503**	53A	Dairycoates: 50B 1/60
90486	2F	Woodford Halse: 1G 9/63		2/60	51L	Thornaby
				12/62	55C	Farnley
1/64	16D	Nottingham		12/63	55D	Royston
4/64	9K	Bolton		9/66	55E	Normanton: *Wdn 1/67*
9/64	8L	Aintree: *Wdn 4/65*		**90504**	2F	Woodford Halse: *Wdn 5/63*
90487	55E	Normanton: *Wdn 8/63*				
90488	51L	Thornaby		**90505**	67C	Ayr
4/59	55D	Royston: *Wdn 12/64*		1/61	67D	Ardrossan: *Wdn 6/62*
90489	65A	Eastfield		**90506**	41F	Mexborough
12/61	65D	Dawsholm		12/60	36A	Doncaster
11/63	65F	Grangemouth		11/65	40B	Immingham: *Wdn 1/66*
11/65	62C	Dunfermline: *Wdn 4/67*		**90507**	2F	Woodford Halse
90490	36C	Frodingham		3/59	8F	Springs Branch: *Wdn 6/63*
11/61	34E	New England				
9/62	40B	Immingham: *Wdn 2/64*		**90508**	30A	Stratford
90491	41F	Mexborough				

5/60	41F	Mexborough: *Wdn 12/62*
90509	2F	Woodford Halse
3/59	8F	Springs Branch
9/64	41E	Barrow Hill: *Wdn 8/65*
90510	40B	Immingham
10/60	40E	Colwick: *Wdn 7/65*
90511	53A	Dairycoates: 50B 1/60
2/60	55D	Royston
10/63	56A	Wakefield: *Wdn 6/64*
90512	36C	Frodingham: *Wdn 9/62*
90513	62A	Thornton: *Wdn 7/62*
90514	33B	Tilbury
6/59	31B	March
10/59	33A	Plaistow
11/59	33B	Tilbury
11/61	34E	New England
11/63	36E	Retford
6/65	40E	Colwick
12/65	36C	Frodingham: *Wdn 1/66*
90515	62B	Dundee
1/63	62C	Dunfermline: *Wdn 11/65*
90516	2F	Woodford Halse: 1G 9/63
12/63	16A	Toton
4/64	9D	Newton Heath
9/64	8L	Aintree
4/65	36C	Frodingham
11/65	36A	Doncaster: *Wdn 11/65*
90517	51L	Thornaby
12/62	50A	York: *Wdn 5/66*
90518	50D	Starbeck
9/59	50A	York: *Wdn 2/66*
90519	40E	Colwick
4/59	41G	Barnsley
6/59	41F	Mexborough
3/64	41D	Canklow
4/64	41E	Barrow Hill: *Wdn 9/64*
90520	2F	Woodford Halse: 1G 9/63
12/63	16A	Toton
4/64	9D	Newton Heath
6/64	8L	Aintree
8/64	9D	Newton Heath
9/64	8L	Aintree: *Wdn 2/65*
90521	41F	Mexborough
3/64	41D	Canklow
4/64	41E	Barrow Hill: *Wdn 10/64*
90522	31B	March
11/60	30A	Stratford
3/61	31A	Cambridge

4/61	33B	Tilbury
6/61	31B	March
10/61	36A	Doncaster
3/63	36E	Retford: *Wdn 5/65*
90523	26A	Newton Heath: *Wdn 12/62*
90524	86C	Canton
7/59	18B	Westhouses
10/59	2F	Woodford Halse: *Wdn 5/63*
90525	26E	Lees: 9P 9/63
4/64	9D	Newton Heath: *Wdn 5/64*
90526	41F	Mexborough: *Wdn 12/62*
90527	27B	Aintree: *Wdn 5/63*
90528	31F	Spital Bridge
2/60	31B	March
11/60	30A	Stratford
9/61	36A	Doncaster
3/63	36E	Retford
6/65	40E	Colwick: *Wdn 9/65*
90529	87G	Carmarthen
6/60	87F	Llanelly
6/62	86A	Newport (Ebbw Jct)
12/62	41F	Mexborough
3/64	41D	Canklow
4/64	41E	Barrow Hill
10/65	41J	Langwith: *Wdn 11/65*
90530	26A	Newton Heath
2/60	26F	Patricroft
1/63	26A	Newton Heath: *Wdn 5/63*
90531	53E	Goole: 50D 1/60: *Wdn 9/63*
90532	6B	Mold Jct
7/59	6F	Bidston
8/59	6B	Mold Jct
4/62	8D	Widnes: *Wdn 12/62*
90533	26A	Newton Heath: 9D 9/63
2/64	9J	Agecroft
10/64	9G	Gorton
2/65	8L	Aintree
4/65	36E	Retford
6/65	40E	Colwick: 16B 1/66
	16B	Colwick: *Wdn 2/66*
90534	62A	Thornton
1/63	62C	Dunfermline: *Wdn 10/66*
90535	27B	Aintree
7/63	8F	Springs Branch
9/63	10D	Lostock Hall: *Wdn 10/64*

90536	66A	Polmadie
3/62	61B	Ferryhill: *Wdn 9/63*
90537	36A	Doncaster
11/60	36C	Frodingham
11/65	36A	Doncaster: *Wdn 2/66*
90538	36A	Doncaster
11/65	40B	Immingham
2/66	36A	Doncaster: *Wdn 4/66*
90539	62A	Thornton
12/59	65F	Grangemouth: *Wdn 11/63*
90540	36C	Frodingham: *Wdn 7/65*
90541	24C	Lostock Hall: 10D 9/63
11/64	10F	Rose Grove: *Wdn 5/65*
90542	62C	Dunfermline: *Wdn 7/63*
90543	50A	York
11/59	56A	Wakefield: *Wdn 2/65*
90544	86A	Newport (Ebbw Jct)
10/62	81C	Southall
12/62	36C	Frodingham
1/63	41F	Mexborough
3/64	41D	Canklow
4/64	41E	Barrow Hill: *Wdn 6/64*
90545	41J	Langwith
5/60	40E	Colwick: *Wdn 10/65*
90546	26B	Agecroft: 9J 9/63
	9J	Agecroft: *Wdn 2/64*
90547	62C	Dunfermline: *Wdn 10/66*
90548	26A	Newton Heath
4/62	26F	Patricroft
1/63	26A	Newton Heath: 9D 9/63
	9D	Newton Heath: *Wdn 5/64*
90549	66A	Polmadie
10/60	67C	Ayr
2/61	67D	Ardrossan
4/62	67C	Ayr: *Wdn 12/62*
90550	36A	Doncaster
2/60	36C	Frodingham: *Wdn 9/62*
90551	30A	Stratford
10/60	36A	Doncaster
5/63	36E	Retford
6/65	36C	Frodingham
11/65	36A	Doncaster: *Wdn 4/66*
90552	27B	Aintree: 8L 9/63
	8L	Aintree: *Wdn 5/64*
90553	62C	Dunfermline
1/63	65F	Grangemouth: *Wdn 10/65*
90554	41J	Langwith
5/60	40E	Colwick: *Wdn 9/62*

90555	26D	Bury
6/63	26B	Agecroft: 9J 9/63
	9J	Agecroft: *Wdn 6/64*
90556	24C	Lostock Hall
9/61	24D	Lower Darwen: 10H 9/63
	10H	Lower Darwen: *Wdn 3/65*
90557	24B	Rose Grove: 10F 9/63
9/64	41D	Canklow
6/65	36A	Doncaster: *Wdn 9/65*
90558	26B	Agecroft
6/63	9G	Gorton
9/64	41D	Canklow
6/65	41J	Langwith: *Wdn 11/65*
90559	31B	March
4/59	32A	Ipswich
2/60	31B	March
11/60	30A	Stratford
6/61	31B	March
10/61	36A	Doncaster: *Wdn 12/62*
90560	62C	Dunfermline
1/63	65F	Grangemouth
11/65	62C	Dunfermline
12/66	52G	Sunderland
2/67	62C	Dunfermline: *Wdn 4/67*
90561	26A	Newton Heath
1/59	27D	Wigan
2/60	26A	Newton Heath: 9D 9/63
6/64	8L	Aintree
7/64	8F	Springs Branch: *Wdn 3/65*
90562	55C	Farnley: *Wdn 11/62*
90563	82B	St Phillips Marsh
7/59	18B	Westhouses
12/59	2F	Woodford Halse: 1G 9/63
2/64	16D	Nottingham
4/64	8L	Aintree: *Wdn 8/65*
90564	26B	Agecroft
6/60	24C	Lostock Hall
10/61	26B	Agecroft
6/63	9G	Gorton
9/63	9P	Lees
2/64	9D	Newton Heath: *Wdn 4/64*
90565	86C	Canton
11/59	85E	Gloucester (Barnwood)
7/60	86A	Newport (Ebbw Jct)
11/60	81C	Southall
3/61	81E	Didcot
4/61	84C	Banbury

114

9/61	81C	Southall: *Wdn 11/62*
90566	6B	Mold Jct
11/61	6C	Birkenhead
9/62	8B	Warrington
1/63	8G	Sutton Oak: *Wdn 7/64*
90567	41F	Mexborough
3/64	41D	Canklow
4/64	41E	Barrow Hill: *Wdn 11/64*
90568	26D	Bury
1/61	26F	Patricroft
1/63	26A	Newton Heath: 9D 9/63
	9D	Newton Heath: *Wdn 1/64*
90569	36A	Doncaster
7/65	40B	Immingham: *Wdn 10/65*
90570	27D	Wigan
2/60	26A	Newton Heath
3/60	26F	Patricroft
2/63	2F	Woodford Halse: 1G 9/63
1/64	16E	Kirkby-in-Ashfield
3/64	1G	Woodford Halse: *Wdn 4/64*
90571	53A	Dairycoates: 50B 1/60
9/61	50A	York: *Wdn 11/63*
90572	86C	Canton
6/59	81C	Southall
7/59	86C	Canton: 88A 10/60
9/62	81C	Southall
12/62	41F	Mexborough
1/64	41E	Barrow Hill
10/65	41J	Langwith: *Wdn 2/66*
90573	86C	Canton: 88A 10/60
9/62	81C	Southall
12/62	36C	Frodingham
1/63	41F	Mexborough
3/64	41D	Canklow
4/64	41E	Barrow Hill: *Wdn 8/65*
90574	2F	Woodford Halse
3/59	8F	Springs Branch: *Wdn 2/64*
90575	62C	Dunfermline: *Wdn 7/62*
90576	26A	Newton Heath
4/60	27B	Aintree
7/62	24B	Rose Grove: *Wdn 3/63*
90577	41J	Langwith
5/60	40E	Colwick
11/60	40A	Lincoln
9/63	36E	Retford: *Wdn 5/65*
90578	50A	York: *Wdn 12/63*
90579	86C	Canton: 88A 10/60
9/62	81C	Southall

12/62	41F	Mexborough
3/64	41D	Canklow
4/64	41E	Barrow Hill: *Wdn 2/65*
90580	41F	Mexborough
3/64	41D	Canklow
4/64	41E	Barrow Hill
6/64	36A	Doncaster: *Wdn 8/65*
90581	56A	Wakefield: *Wdn 11/64*
90582	41F	Mexborough: *Wdn 3/64*
90583	40B	Immingham
9/63	36E	Retford: *Wdn 4/64*
90584	24H	Hellifield
6/60	24C	Lostock Hall
8/62	24B	Rose Grove: 10F 9/63
	10F	Rose Grove: *Wdn 9/64*
90585	84C	Banbury
8/62	8F	Springs Branch
4/63	9G	Gorton
6/63	8F	Springs Branch: *Wdn 4/65*
90586	53A	Dairycoates: 50B 1/60
	50B	Dairycoates: *Wdn 2/66*
90587	41F	Mexborough
3/64	41D	Canklow
4/64	41E	Barrow Hill
10/65	41J	Langwith: *Wdn 11/65*
90588	55C	Farnley
4/63	55G	Huddersfield
12/63	51L	Thornaby
10/64	51C	West Hartlepool: *Wdn 2/67*
90589	26A	Newton Heath
4/62	26F	Patricroft
1/63	2F	Woodford Halse: 1G 9/63
2/64	16E	Kirkby-in-Ashfield
3/64	1G	Woodford Halse: *Wdn 4/64*
90590	41F	Mexborough: *Wdn 3/64*
90591	55C	Farnley
2/61	55G	Huddersfield
3/62	55D	Royston: *Wdn 11/62*
90592	24B	Rose Grove
6/61	24D	Lower Darwen: 10H 9/63
	10H	Lower Darwen: *Wdn 6/64*
90593	51A	Darlington
9/59	51L	Thornaby
5/64	51C	West Hartlepool: *Wdn 6/66*
90594	41J	Langwith

5/60	40E	Colwick: *Wdn 9/62*	**90617**	55E	Normanton: *Wdn 6/67*
90595	24H	Hellifield	**90618**	40E	Colwick
1/59	24J	Lancaster: 10J 9/63	5/60	34E	New England
	10J	Lancaster: *Wdn 2/64*	9/62	40B	Immingham: *Wdn 5/64*
90596	66A	Polmadie	**90619**	55G	Huddersfield
9/63	61B	Ferryhill	9/65	56A	Wakefield: *Wdn 10/65*
4/66	62A	Thornton: *Wdn 4/67*	**90620**	56A	Wakefield: *Wdn 6/67*
90597	36C	Frodingham: *Wdn 7/63*	**90621**	55G	Huddersfield
90598	36C	Frodingham: *Wdn 2/64*	11/64	51C	West Hartlepool: *Wdn 11/65*
90599	27D	Wigan	**90622**	56D	Mirfield
2/60	26B	Agecroft	1/64	56A	Wakefield: *Wdn 9/66*
3/60	27B	Aintree: 8L 9/63	**90623**	53A	Dairycoates: 50B 1/60
	8L	Aintree: *Wdn 7/64*	9/61	50A	York: *Wdn 12/63*
90600	62C	Dunfermline	**90624**	55G	Huddersfield: *Wdn 12/63*
1/63	65F	Grangemouth	**90625**	56A	Wakefield
11/65	62C	Dunfermline	6/62	56B	Ardsley
12/65	62A	Thornton: *Wdn 8/66*	10/65	56A	Wakefield: *Wdn 6/67*
90601	36C	Frodingham: *Wdn 6/65*	**90626**	26D	Bury
90602	36A	Doncaster	11/60	26B	Agecroft
11/60	36C	Frodingham: *Wdn 1/65*	6/63	9G	Gorton
90603	51L	Thornaby: *Wdn 2/62*	11/64	10H	Lower Darwen: *Wdn 3/65*
90604	56A	Wakefield: *Wdn 12/63*	**90627**	53A	Dairycoates: 50B 1/60
90605	51L	Thornaby	6/67	51C	West Hartlepool: *Wdn 9/67*
6/59	55D	Royston	**90628**	66B	Motherwell
1/67	55E	Normanton: *Wdn 9/67*	8/63	62C	Dunfermline
90606	6B	Mold Jct	6/64	62A	Thornton: *Wdn 1/67*
6/60	6C	Birkenhead	**90629**	40E	Colwick: *Wdn 9/65*
9/62	8G	Sutton Oak	**90630**	81C	Southall: *Wdn 11/62*
9/64	40E	Colwick: 16B 1/66	**90631**	56A	Wakefield: *Wdn 1/67*
	16B	Colwick: *Wdn 2/66*	**90632**	26B	Agecroft: 9J 9/63
90607	56A	Wakefield: *Wdn 11/62*	10/64	8F	Springs Branch
90608	41F	Mexborough: *Wdn 12/62*	1/65	8L	Aintree: *Wdn 5/65*
90609	53A	Dairycoates: 50B 1/60	**90633**	56A	Wakefield
	50B	Dairycoates: *Wdn 8/63*	1/67	56F	Low Moor: *Wdn 7/67*
90610	55E	Normanton	**90634**	40E	Colwick: *Wdn 12/62*
1/61	55D	Royston	**90635**	56A	Wakefield: *Wdn 1/64*
10/63	56A	Wakefield: *Wdn 5/67*	**90636**	36A	Doncaster: *Wdn 4/66*
90611	50A	York	**90637**	55E	Normanton: *Wdn 11/62*
4/59	55D	Royston	**90638**	2F	Woodford Halse: *Wdn 12/62*
10/63	56A	Wakefield	**90639**	56A	Wakefield: *Wdn 1/67*
7/67	55E	Normanton: *Wdn 8/67*	**90640**	66A	Polmadie
90612	41F	Mexborough: *Wdn 3/64*	7/62	65F	Grangemouth
90613	34E	New England	9/62	61B	Ferryhill
4/63	36C	Frodingham: *Wdn 5/65*	4/66	62A	Thornton: *Wdn 8/66*
90614	62A	Thornton	**90641**	26C	Bolton: 9K 9/63
1/63	65F	Grangemouth: *Wdn 11/63*	9/64	8L	Aintree: *Wdn 8/65*
90615	56A	Wakefield	**90642**	56D	Mirfield
7/66	55D	Royston			
1/67	55E	Normanton: *Wdn 9/67*			
90616	66A	Polmadie: *Wdn 6/62*			

12/60	56A	Wakefield		9/62	40B	Immingham: *Wdn 8/65*
8/61	56B	Ardsley		**90663**	50B	Neville Hill
9/65	56A	Wakefield		6/59	50A	York: *Wdn 4/64*
7/66	55D	Royston		**90664**	55C	Farnley
1/67	55E	Normanton: *Wdn 9/67*		6/59	55D	Royston
90643	27B	Aintree: 8L 9/63		9/59	55E	Normanton
	8L	Aintree: *Wdn 2/64*		9/65	56A	Wakefield: *Wdn 10/66*
90644	56A	Wakefield		**90665**	34E	New England
6/60	56B	Ardsley		9/62	36C	Frodingham
10/65	55E	Normanton: *Wdn 6/67*		7/65	40E	Colwick: *Wdn 12/65*
90645	55C	Farnley		**90666**	55C	Farnley
12/63	55D	Royston: *Wdn 1/67*		6/59	55G	Huddersfield: *Wdn*
90646	36C	Frodingham: *Wdn 5/64*				*11/62*
90647	36C	Frodingham: *Wdn 3/65*		**90667**	2F	Woodford Halse
90648	40B	Immingham		3/59	8F	Springs Branch: *Wdn*
8/59	40E	Colwick				*5/64*
8/60	40B	Immingham		**90668**	41F	Mexborough
10/60	36C	Frodingham: *Wdn 8/62*		3/64	41D	Canklow
90649	55C	Farnley		4/64	41E	Barrow Hill: *Wdn 4/65*
6/59	55G	Huddersfield		**90669**	26A	Newton Heath
1/67	55D	Royston: *Wdn 1/67*		1/60	26F	Patricroft
90650	55C	Farnley		1/63	2F	Woodford Halse: 1G
11/60	55D	Royston				9/63
2/64	55E	Normanton		1/64	16E	Kirkby-in-Ashfield
3/65	55D	Royston		4/64	8F	Springs Branch
1/67	55E	Normanton: *Wdn 6/67*		4/65	36E	Retford
90651	56A	Wakefield: *Wdn 10/66*		6/65	36C	Frodingham
90652	55E	Normanton: *Wdn 9/66*		7/65	40E	Colwick: 16B 1/66
90653	33A	Plaistow			16B	Colwick: *Wdn 2/66*
11/59	33B	Tilbury: *Wdn 9/62*		**90670**	53A	Dairycoates: 50B 1/60
90654	56A	Wakefield: *Wdn 6/67*		5/67	50D	Goole: *Wdn 6/67*
90655	56D	Mirfield		**90671**	26E	Lees: *Wdn 9/63*
12/60	56A	Wakefield		**90672**	2F	Woodford Halse: 1G
6/61	56D	Mirfield				9/63
1/67	56A	Wakefield: *Wdn 4/67*		12/63	16D	Nottingham
90656	56A	Wakefield: *Wdn 2/65*		3/64	1G	Woodford Halse: *Wdn*
90657	41J	Langwith: *Wdn 9/62*				*4/64*
90658	24C	Lostock Hall		**90673**	55E	Normanton: *Wdn 3/64*
9/62	24F	Fleetwood: 10C 9/63		**90674**	40B	Immingham
12/63	10F	Rose Grove		10/60	40E	Colwick: *Wdn 7/65*
9/64	41D	Canklow		**90675**	26A	Newton Heath
6/65	41J	Langwith: *Wdn 11/65*		2/59	24C	Lostock Hall: 10D 9/63
90659	34E	New England: *Wdn 5/63*		9/64	36A	Doncaster: *Wdn 4/66*
90660	30A	Stratford		**90676**	86A	Newport (Ebbw Jct)
4/60	34B	Hornsey		9/61	87F	Llanelly
6/61	34E	New England		5/62	9G	Gorton: *Wdn 1/64*
9/62	40B	Immingham: *Wdn 7/65*		**90677**	53A	Dairycoates: 50B 1/60
90661	51G	Haverton Hill		7/67	51C	West Hartlepool: *Wdn*
4/59	55D	Royston				*9/67*
9/59	55E	Normanton: *Wdn 12/63*		**90678**	56D	Mirfield
90662	40E	Colwick		11/60	56A	Wakefield
5/60	34E	New England		6/61	56D	Mirfield

1/64	56A	Wakefield: *Wdn 6/67*		1/67	55D	Royston: *Wdn 1/67*
90679	56A	Wakefield		**90695**	53A	Dairycoates: 50B 1/60
2/66	56D	Mirfield: *Wdn 9/66*		7/67	51C	West Hartlepool: *Wdn 9/67*
90680	55G	Huddersfield				
1/67	55D	Royston: *Wdn 1/67*		**90696**	36A	Doncaster
90681	24C	Lostock Hall		2/60	36C	Frodingham: *Wdn 7/63*
2/62	24F	Fleetwood: 10C 9/63		**90697**	2F	Woodford Halse: 1G 9/63
12/63	10F	Rose Grove: *Wdn 7/65*		12/63	16A	Toton
90682	55E	Normanton: *Wdn 9/67*		4/64	9D	Newton Heath
90683	31B	March		7/64	8F	Springs Branch
12/60	36A	Doncaster: *Wdn 2/66*		9/64	41D	Canklow
90684	55C	Farnley		6/65	41E	Barrow Hill
10/61	55D	Royston		10/65	41J	Langwith: *Wdn 11/65*
10/63	56A	Wakefield: *Wdn 1/67*		**90698**	51A	Darlington
90685	86C	Canton		7/59	51L	Thornaby
11/59	85E	Gloucester (Barnwood)		11/59	56D	Mirfield
6/60	86A	Newport (Ebbw Jct)		12/62	56F	Low Moor
10/60	81C	Southall		1/64	56A	Wakefield
12/62	36A	Doncaster		12/66	52G	Sunderland: *Wdn 7/67*
1/63	41D	Canklow: *Wdn 11/64*		**90699**	55C	Farnley
90686	6E	Chester (West)		12/63	55D	Royston
4/60	8F	Springs Branch		4/64	55E	Normanton: *Wdn 9/67*
3/63	9G	Gorton		**90700**	41F	Mexborough
6/63	8F	Springs Branch: *Wdn 4/65*		1/63	41D	Canklow: *Wdn 2/64*
90687	27B	Aintree: 8L 9/63		**90701**	86G	Pontypool Rd
7/64	8F	Springs Branch		7/59	18B	Westhouses
8/64	8L	Aintree		9/59	2F	Woodford Halse: *Wdn 12/62*
9/64	36A	Doncaster: *Wdn 1/66*		**90702**	6B	Mold Jct
90688	53A	Dairycoates: 50B 1/60		4/60	8F	Springs Branch
5/67	50D	Goole: *Wdn 6/67*		8/60	24K	Preston
90689	24C	Lostock Hall		9/60	8G	Sutton Oak
2/62	24F	Fleetwood: 10C 9/63		10/63	8L	Aintree
12/63	9K	Bolton		7/64	8G	Sutton Oak
9/64	8L	Aintree		5/65	36C	Frodingham: *Wdn 7/65*
4/65	36E	Retford		**90703**	40E	Colwick
6/65	36C	Frodingham		5/60	34E	New England
7/65	40E	Colwick: 16B 1/66		6/62	40E	Colwick: *Wdn 7/65*
	16B	Colwick: *Wdn 2/66*		**90704**	53A	Dairycoates
90690	62A	Thornton		11/59	53E	Goole: 50D 1/60
1/60	66A	Polmadie		11/63	50B	Dairycoates
5/62	66B	Motherwell: *Wdn 9/62*		12/66	50D	Goole: *Wdn 6/67*
90691	86C	Canton		**90705**	62A	Thornton
10/60	84C	Banbury: *Wdn 5/62*		1/60	66A	Polmadie
90692	56A	Wakefield		5/62	66B	Motherwell
11/60	56B	Ardsley		9/63	61B	Ferryhill
6/61	56E	Sowerby Bridge: *Wdn 12/63*		12/63	62A	Thornton: *Wdn 7/64*
90693	86C	Canton: 88A 10/60		**90706**	24H	Hellifield
2/61	84C	Banbury		1/59	24J	Lancaster
9/61	81C	Southall: *Wdn 11/62*		9/60	21B	Bescot
90694	55G	Huddersfield		10/60	24J	Lancaster: 10J 9/63

5/64	8L	Aintree
6/65	41E	Barrow Hill
10/65	40E	Colwick: 16B 1/66
	16B	Colwick: *Wdn 2/66*
90707	56D	Mirfield
12/60	56A	Wakefield
6/61	56D	Mirfield
1/64	56A	Wakefield: *Wdn 1/67*
90708	26E	Lees: 9P 9/63
4/64	9D	Newton Heath: *Wdn 5/64*
90709	31B	March
12/60	36A	Doncaster: *Wdn 4/66*
90710	56A	Wakefield: *Wdn 2/65*
90711	56F	Low Moor
8/66	56A	Wakefield
10/66	56F	Low Moor: *Wdn 1/67*
90712	27B	Aintree: 8L 9/63
	8L	Aintree: *Wdn 8/64*
90713	26B	Agecroft
6/60	24C	Lostock Hall: 10D 9/63
	10D	Lostock Hall: *Wdn 10/63*
90714	36C	Frodingham: *Wdn 12/64*
90715	26A	Newton Heath: 9D 9/63
	9D	Newton Heath: *Wdn 5/64*
90716	84G	Shrewsbury
7/59	18B	Westhouses
6/62	9G	Gorton: *Wdn 10/63*
90717	40E	Colwick
5/60	34E	New England
6/62	40E	Colwick
9/63	36E	Retford: *Wdn 3/64*
90718	26D	Bury
11/59	26E	Lees: 9P 9/63
4/64	9D	Newton Heath
9/64	8L	Aintree
4/65	36E	Retford
6/65	36A	Doncaster: *Wdn 2/66*
90719	56A	Wakefield
8/59	41D	Canklow
4/65	41H	Staveley (GC)
6/65	41J	Langwith: *Wdn 2/66*
90720	24C	Lostock Hall: 10D 9/63
	10D	Lostock Hall: *Wdn 7/65*
90721	56D	Mirfield
2/62	56F	Low Moor
1/64	56A	Wakefield
7/66	55D	Royston
9/66	55E	Normanton: *Wdn 9/67*
90722	55E	Normanton: *Wdn 6/67*
90723	56D	Mirfield
2/62	56F	Low Moor
10/64	52H	Tyne Dock
1/65	56F	Low Moor
8/66	56A	Wakefield: *Wdn 11/66*
90724	27B	Aintree
9/62	24B	Rose Grove: 10F 9/63
1/64	9K	Bolton
7/64	8F	Springs Branch
1/65	8L	Aintree: *Wdn 6/65*
90725	26C	Bolton
9/62	24F	Fleetwood: 10C 9/63
3/64	9J	Agecroft
10/64	8F	Springs Branch
11/64	10F	Rose Grove: *Wdn 8/65*
90726	55C	Farnley: *Wdn 11/62*
90727	62C	Dunfermline
1/63	67C	Ayr
11/63	62A	Thornton: *Wdn 9/65*
90728	55C	Farnley: *Wdn 12/63*
90729	26C	Bolton: *Wdn 4/63*
90730	34E	New England
9/62	36C	Frodingham
1/64	41E	Barrow Hill: *Wdn 10/65*
90731	56D	Mirfield
3/64	56B	Ardsley
6/65	56F	Low Moor
10/66	56A	Wakefield: *Wdn 11/66*
90732	36A	Doncaster
2/60	36C	Frodingham: *Wdn 9/62*

Demise of the MoS Class WD 2-8-0s ∎

Withdrawals

12/59: 90083
1/60: 90062
2/60: 90191
2/62: 90603
3/62: 90167
5/62: 90691

6/62: 90060, 90436, 90505, 90616
7/62: 90134, 90320, 90513/75
8/62: 90093, 90244/56/86/98, 90387/91, 90648
9/62: 90023/34, 90106/50/96, 90288, 90455/73/94, 90512/50/54/94, 90653/57/90, 90732

Above:
WD 2-8-0 No 90732 *Vulcan,* the only named
member of this large class, at Stratford MPD
August 1950. No 90732 was allocated to Doncaster
in January 1959, it was re-allocated to Frodingham
in February 1960 and withdrawn off that depot in
September 1962. *H. C. Casserley*

Below:
WD 2-8-0 No 90084 (40E) at New England MPD
October 1960. *P. N. Townend*

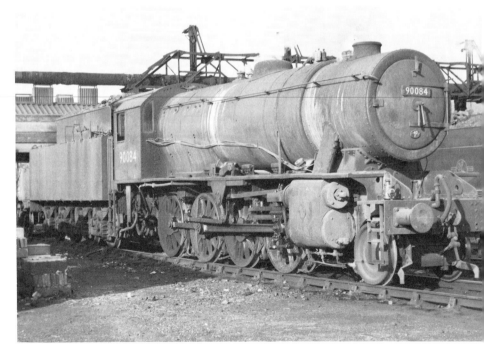

Above:
WD 2-8-0 No 90449 (41J) at Doncaster MPD 26 August 1963. *N. E. Preedy*

Below:
WD 2-8-0 No 90682 (55E) in shabby external condition, at Normanton MPD 5 September 1964. The first member of this once 733 strong class to be taken out of service was No 90083 withdrawn off March MPD in December 1959. Withdrawals progressed steadily from 1962 onwards until September 1967 when the last 24 all allocated to the NER went to the scrap yard. No 90682 (55E) was amongst the last survivors the others being Nos 90074/76/360/478/627/77/95 (51C), 90009/135/348/78/82/417 (52G) and 90236/318/51/405/30/605/15/42/99/721 (55E). *N. E. Preedy*

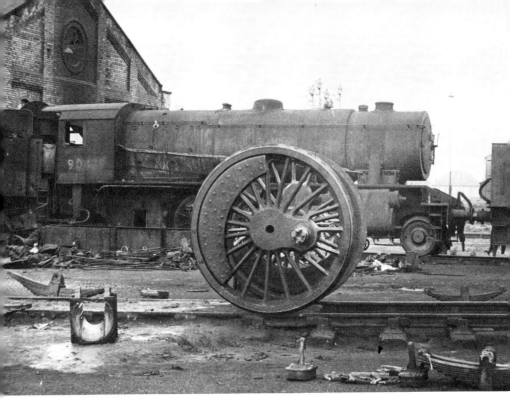

Above:
WD 2-8-0 No 90439 (36C) under repair at Burton MPD 26 September 1965 two months before withdrawal. A total of 18 WD 2-8-0s survived to the end of steam on the Eastern. The locos concerned were Nos 90001/02/13/18/37/63/75/154/56/369/410/37/71/538/51/636/75/709 all 36A. They went for scrap with the closure of Doncaster MPD in April 1966. *A. Walker*

Below:
WD 2-8-0 No 90678 (56D) at Stockport Edgeley MPD, 24 February 1963. *A. W. Martin*

Below:
WD 2-10-0 No 90774 (65F) at Grangemouth MPD 23 April 1962. With the exception of No 90763 on the LMR. The entire class was allocated to the Scottish Region. First withdrawals occurred in 1961 with Nos 90752-54, followed in 1962 by the remaining 22; 17 of which went in December .

Bottom:
WD 2-10-0 No 90768 (66E) withdrawn in July 1962, awaiting disposal at Carstairs MPD 30 September 1962. *D. G. Smith*

10/62: 90022/87
11/62: 90021, 90128/74, 90247,
90308/55/56, 90562/65/91,
90607/30/37/66/93, 90726
12/62: 90028, 90105/37/63/98,
90253/70/78/87, 90303/07/76,
90414/25/31/95,
90508/23/26/32/49/59,
90608/34/38, 90701
2/63: 90176
3/63: 90046, 90238/50, 90497, 90576
4/63: 90206, 90729
5/63: 90015/27/31/33/48/50/66/77/90,
90151/77/92, 90251/69,
90502/04/24/27/30, 90659
6/63: 90095, 90507
7/63: 90542/97, 90696
8/63: 90086/97, 90170/86/93, 90231,
90440/75/87, 90500, 90609
9/63: 90006/17/49, 90228/60, 90435/61,
90531/36, 90671
10/63: 90102, 90453, 90713/16
11/63: 90107/18/59, 90234/39,
90326/31/34/35/38/58,
90446/47/63/67, 90539/71, 90614
12/63: 90004/19/26/58, 90144/82,
90226/49, 90312/43,
90400/24/72/99, 90578,
90604/23/24/61/92, 90728
1/64: 90064/79, 90100, 90208/63,
90366, 90568, 90635/76
2/64: 90012, 90141/61/62, 90237,
90490, 90546/74/95/98, 90643,
90700
3/64: 90052/65, 90110/38/94,
90205/14/24, 90374, 90402/64/83,
90582/90, 90612/73, 90717
4/64: 90111/65/79, 90218/99,
90313/71/94, 90564/70/83/89,
90663/72
5/64: 90101/09/43/47/97, 90219/45,
90323/24/28, 90403/08/16/33,
90525/48/52, 90618/46/67,
90708/15
6/64: 90003, 90114/45, 90319,
90511/44/55/92
7/64: 90129/57/73, 90201/09, 90375/88,
90566/99, 90705
8/64: 90216/57/64, 90302/11/22,
90411/85, 90712
9/64: 90140, 90297, 90304/59,
90519/84

10/64: 90067, 90127/84, 90354/89,
90412, 90521/35
11/64: 90098, 90289, 90344, 90469,
90567/81, 90685
12/64: 90392, 90488, 90714
1/65: 90042, 90119, 90221/82, 90327,
90602
2/65: 90010/70, 90276/91, 90353,
90520/43/79, 90656, 90710
3/65: 90055, 90123/31/80/85, 90267/84,
90317/99, 90426, 90556/61,
90626/47
4/65: 90005/59, 90120/36/64/75/88,
90202/15/25/46/68, 90314/83,
90419/42/86/96, 90585, 90668/86
5/65: 90085, 90115/39/52/66/81,
90207/90, 90522/41/77, 90613/32
6/65: 90000/84, 90121/24/46,
90204/17/79/85, 90306/49/65/68,
90422/43/52/54/60, 90601, 90724
7/65: 90007/25/29/38/40/53/88,
90108/25/71,
90211/61/66/71/75/94,
90340/41/98, 90421/74/76/80,
90510/40, 90660/74/81,
90702/03/20
8/65: 90169/83, 90212/22/23/96, 90393,
90420, 90509/63/73/80, 90641/62,
90725
9/65: 90096, 90122, 90227/42/52/80/93,
90301/25/29/90, 90491, 90528/57,
90629, 90727
10/65: 90045/51/92, 90130/33/95,
90203/35/59/73/77/83/92,
90333/46/81, 90432/38/92,
90545/53/69, 90619, 90730
11/65: 90103/89, 90220/48, 90315/42,
90401/39, 90501/15/16/29/58/87,
90621/58/97
12/65: 90036/43/72, 90142/58, 90255,
90316/30/64/72, 90423/48/66,
90665
1/66: 90069, 90149, 90232/41/58/74/95,
90336, 90418/28/49/57, 90506/14,
90687
2/66: 90024/32/35/73/80,
90104/53/78/87/90, 90213,
90367/77/84, 90413/56/93/98,
90518/33/37/72/86,
90606/69/83/89, 90706/18/19
3/66: 90148, 90305/79/80, 90477/84

4/66: 90001/02/13/18/37/63/75,
90154/56, 90369, 90410/37/71,
90538/51, 90636/75, 90709
5/66: 90517
6/66: 90011/82, 90593
7/66: 90068, 90445
8/66: 90168, 90350, 90600/40
9/66: 90039, 90113, 90229, 90357/73,
90479, 90622/52/79
10/66: 90395, 90441/81, 90534/47,
90651/64
11/66: 90078, 90199, 90723/31
12/66: 90041/44, 90310, 90451/70
1/67: 90054/89, 90112/17/26/55,
90240/54, 90332/37,
90415/44/62/65, 90503,
90628/31/39/45/49/80/84/94,
90707/11
2/67: 90588
3/67: 90385

4/67: 90008/14/20/30/71, 90132,
90361/86, 90429/68/89, 90560/96,
90655
5/67: 90056, 90230/33, 90347/70/97,
90407, 90610
6/67: 90016/47/57/61/81/91/94/99,
90116/60/72, 90243/62/65/72/81,
90300/45/52/62/63/96,
90404/06/09/27/34/50/58/59,
90617/20/25/44/50/54/70/78/88,
90704/22
7/67: 90200/10, 90309/21/39, 90482,
90633/98
8/67: 90611
9/67: 90009/74/76, 90135, 90236,
90318/48/51/60/78/82,
90405/17/30/78,
90605/15/27/42/77/82/95/99,
90721

MoS Class WD 2-10-0 'Austerity'

Introduced: 1943
Purpose: Long-distance freight
Power classification: 8F
Tractive effort: 34,215lb

Stock Analysis 1959-1962
1/1/59 (25): 90750-74
1/1/60 (25): 90750-74
1/1/61 (25): 90750-74
1/1/62 (22): 90750/51/55-74

Locomotive depot allocations
1959-1962

90750	66B	Motherwell: *Wdn 5/62*	**90758**	66B	Motherwell: *Wdn 12/62*
90751	66A	Polmadie	**90759**	65F	Grangemouth: *Wdn*
	10/61	66B	Motherwell: *Wdn 12/62*		*12/62*
90752	66A	Polmadie: *Wdn 12/61*	**90760**	66B	Motherwell: *Wdn 5/62*
90753	64D	Carstairs: 66E 5/60	**90761**	66B	Motherwell: *Wdn 11/62*
	66E	Carstairs: *Wdn 7/61*	**90762**	66B	Motherwell: *Wdn 12/62*
90754	66B	Motherwell: *Wdn 7/61*	**90763**	12A	Kingmoor
90755	65F	Grangemouth: *Wdn*	8/59	6F	Bidston
		12/62	6/60	12A	Kingmoor: *Wdn 12/62*
90756	66B	Motherwell: *Wdn 12/62*	**90764**	66C	Hamilton
90757	65F	Grangemouth: *Wdn*	9/59	66B	Motherwell: *Wdn 5/62*
		12/62			

90765	65F	Grangemouth: *Wdn* 12/62	90770	66B	Motherwell: *Wdn* 12/62
90766	65F	Grangemouth: *Wdn* 12/62	90771	66C	Hamilton
			9/59	66B	Motherwell: *Wdn* 12/62
90767	66A	Polmadie	90772	66C	Carstairs
10/61	66B	Motherwell: *Wdn* 12/62	11/62	66B	Motherwell: *Wdn* 12/62
90768	64D	Carstairs: 66E 5/60	90773	65F	Grangemouth: *Wdn* 12/62
	66E	Carstairs: *Wdn* 7/62			
90769	65F	Grangemouth: *Wdn* 12/62	90774	65F	Grangemouth: *Wdn* 12/62

Demise of the MoS Class WD 2-10-0s

Withdrawals

7/61: 90753/54
12/61: 90752
5/62: 90750/60/64
7/62: 90768
11/62: 90761
12/62: 90751/55/56/57/58/59/62/63/65/66/67/69/70/71/72/73/74

BR Standard Class 9
2-10-0 '92XXX'

Introduced: 1954
Purpose: Heavy mineral freight
Power classification: 9F
Tractive effort: 39,670 lb

Locomotive names

92220 *Evening Star*

Stock analysis 1959-1968

1/1/59 (233): 92000-92202/21-50
1/1/60 (248): 92000-92217/21-50
1/1/61 (251): 92000-92250
1/1/62 (251): 92000-92250
1/1/63 (251): 92000-92250
1/1/64 (251): 92000-92250
1/1/65 (235): 92000-33/35/37-99, 92100-68/72-74/78-95/97, 92200-06/08/09/11-28/30/31/33-44/46-50
1/1/66 (170): 92001/02/04/06/08-32/35/43/45-56/58-65/67-99, 92100-39/45/46/50-67/72/73/82/83, 92201/03-06/08/11-13/15/17/18/23/24/27/28/31/33/34/39/47/49
1/1/67 (125): 92001/02/04/06/08/09/11/12/14-27/29-32/45-52/ 54-56/58/65/69-71/73/74/76-80/82-84/86-91/93/94/96, 92100-14/17-23/25-29/31-33/35/37-39/50-54/56/57/59/60/62/63/65-67, 92203-06/08/11/12/15/18/23/24/27/28/33/34/49
1/1/68 (18): 92004/09/54/69/77/88/91/94, 92118/53/60/65/67, 92212/18/23/33/49

Class 9F 2-10-0 variants ■■■

Introduced: 1955. Fitted with Crosti boiler – 92020-29
Introduced: 1957. Fitted with double chimney – 92000/79, 92178/83-99, 92200-50
Introduced: 1958. Fitted with mechanical stoker – 92165-67

Locomotive depot allocations ■■■■
1959-1968

92000	86A	Newport (Ebbw Jct)	10/66	56A	Wakefield: *Wdn 4/67*
6/61	82F	Bath (Green Park)	**92007**	86A	Newport (Ebbw Jct)
9/61	84C	Banbury	12/60	82E	Bristol (Barrow Rd)
3/62	81A	Old Oak Common	2/65	85B	Gloucester (Horton Rd)
7/62	84E	Tyseley	6/65	88A	Cardiff East Dock
12/62	82E	Bristol (Barrow Rd)	7/65	86E	Seven Tunnel Jct
2/65	85B	Gloucester: *Wdn 7/65*	10/65	85B	Gloucester: *Wdn 12/65*
92001	86A	Newport (Ebbw Jct)	**92008**	21A	Saltley
6/61	82F	Bath (Green Park)	11/59	17C	Rowsley
10/61	88A	Canton	1/62	18A	Toton
7/62	82F	Bath (Green Park)	2/62	17C	Rowsley
9/62	81F	Oxford	6/62	21A	Saltley
11/62	84E	Tyseley: 2A 9/63	7/63	17C	Rowsley: 16J 9/63
10/66	56A	Wakefield: *Wdn 1/67*	4/64	16E	Kirkby-in-Ashfield
92002	86A	Newport (Ebbw Jct)	12/64	8C	Speke Jct
4/63	84E	Tyseley: 2A 9/63	8/67	8B	Warrington: *Wdn 10/67*
7/64	2D	Banbury	**92009**	21A	Saltley
11/64	2A	Tyseley	11/59	17C	Rowsley
11/66	2E	Saltley	6/62	21A	Saltley
12/66	8H	Birkenhead: *Wdn 11/67*	7/62	18B	Westhouses: 16G 9/63
92003	86C	Canton: 88A 10/60	10/63	16J	Rowsley
9/62	88L	Cardiff East Dock: 88A 9/63	4/64	15C	Kettering
			6/64	12A	Kingmoor
	88A	Cardiff East Dock: *Wdn 3/65*	1/68	10A	Carnforth: *Wdn 3/68*
			92010	16D	Annesley
92004	86A	Newport (Ebbw Jct)	3/63	15A	Wellingborough
9/59	86C	Canton	6/63	15C	Leicester (M): 15A 9/63
2/60	81C	Southall	4/64	9D	Newton Heath
10/60	86A	Newport (Ebbw Jct)	6/64	12A	Kingmoor: *Wdn 4/66*
1/61	82E	Bristol (Barrow Rd)	**92011**	16D	Annesley: 16B 9/63
3/63	84C	Banbury: 2D 9/63	8/65	8H	Birkenhead: *Wdn 11/67*
10/66	12A	Kingmoor	**92012**	16D	Annesley
1/68	10A	Carnforth: *Wdn 3/68*	8/63	17C	Rowsley: 16J 9/63
92005	86C	Canton: 88A 10/60	4/64	15C	Kettering
5/61	86A	Newport (Ebbw Jct)	6/64	12A	Kingmoor: *Wdn 10/67*
9/63	50A	York: *Wdn 8/65*	**92013**	16D	Annesley: 16B 9/63
92006	86A	Newport (Ebbw Jct)	6/65	2D	Banbury
7/61	82F	Bath (Green Park)	9/66	2E	Saltley: *Wdn 10/66*
9/61	86A	Newport (Ebbw Jct)	**92014**	16D	Annesley
9/63	50A	York	4/60	21A	Saltley

127

Above:
BR Standard Class 9 2-10-0 No 92241 (88A)
alongside withdrawn Class 94XX 0-6-0PT No 8451
(81C wdn November 1961) at Swindon, 7 January
1962. *R. A. Panting*

Below:
BR Standard Class 9 2-10-0 No 92022 (15A) fitted
with Franco-Crosti boiler, at Wellingborough MPD
18 February 1962. The locomotive had been placed
in store pending conversion at Crewe Works.
P. H. Wells

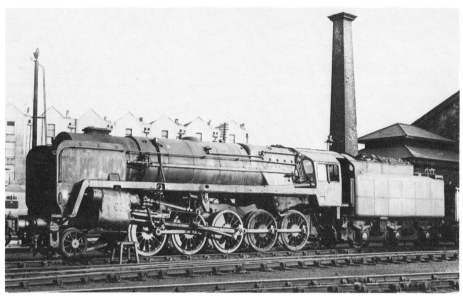

129

9/60	18A	Toton		7/65	8H	Birkenhead: *Wdn 11/67*
7/61	14A	Cricklewood		**92025**	15A	Wellingborough: 15B
10/61	16D	Annesley: 16B 9/63				9/63
5/65	8H	Birkenhead: *Wdn 10/67*		1/64	15C	Kettering
92015	26A	Newton Heath		4/64	16B	Annesley
9/62	26C	Bolton		11/64	8C	Speke Jct
12/62	26A	Newton Heath: 9D 9/63		2/67	8H	Birkenhead: *Wdn 11/67*
6/64	12A	Kingmoor: *Wdn 4/67*		**92026**	15A	Wellingborough
92016	26A	Newton Heath		3/61	21A	Saltley
9/62	26C	Bolton		4/61	15A	Wellingborough
12/62	26A	Newton Heath: 9D 9/63		8/63	15C	Kettering: 15C 9/63
6/67	10A	Carnforth: *Wdn 10/67*		11/63	16E	Kirkby-in-Ashfield
92017	26A	Newton Heath		9/64	9D	Newton Heath
9/62	26C	Bolton		5/65	8H	Birkenhead: *Wdn 11/67*
12/62	26A	Newton Heath: 9D 9/63		**92027**	15A	Wellingborough: 15B
6/64	12A	Kingmoor: *Wdn 12/67*				9/63
92018	15A	Wellingborough		1/64	15C	Kettering
3/62	17C	Rowsley: 16J 9/63		4/64	16B	Annesley
4/64	16E	Kirkby-in-Ashfield		11/64	8C	Speke Jct: *Wdn 8/67*
9/64	9D	Newton Heath		**92028**	15A	Wellingborough
8/66	12A	Kingmoor: *Wdn 4/67*		12/60	15B	Kettering
92019	15A	Wellingborough		10/62	21A	Saltley: 2E 9/63
1/62	18A	Toton		11/63	8H	Birkenhead
3/62	17C	Rowsley		4/64	2E	Saltley
4/62	15A	Wellingborough: 15B		3/65	2D	Banbury
		9/63		7/65	2E	Saltley: *Wdn 10/66*
1/64	15C	Kettering		**92029**	15A	Wellingborough
6/64	12A	Kingmoor: *Wdn 6/67*		12/60	15B	Kettering
92020	15A	Wellingborough: 15B		10/62	21A	Saltley: 2E 9/63
		9/63		11/63	8H	Birkenhead
11/63	16E	Kirkby-in-Ashfield		4/64	2E	Saltley
9/64	8C	Speke Jct		5/66	6C	Croes Newydd
1/65	8H	Birkenhead: *Wdn 10/67*		8/66	2E	Saltley
92021	15A	Wellingborough: 15B		12/66	8H	Birkenhead: *Wdn 11/67*
		9/63		**92030**	16D	Annesley: 16B 9/63
1/64	15C	Kettering		6/65	2D	Banbury
6/64	12A	Kingmoor		10/66	2E	Saltley
7/65	8H	Birkenhead: *Wdn 11/67*		10/66	56A	Wakefield: *Wdn 2/67*
92022	15A	Wellingborough		**92031**	16D	Annesley: 16B 9/63
7/63	17C	Rowsley: 16J 9/63		7/65	16G	Westhouses
4/64	15C	Kettering		7/65	9D	Newton Heath: *Wdn*
6/64	9D	Newton Heath				*1/67*
2/66	8C	Speke Jct		**92032**	16D	Annesley: 16B 9/63
2/67	8H	Birkenhead: *Wdn 11/67*		7/65	16E	Kirkby-in-Ashfield
92023	15A	Wellingborough		7/65	8H	Birkenhead: *Wdn 4/67*
8/63	15B	Kettering: 15C 9/63		**92033**	16D	Annesley: 16B 9/63
5/64	12A	Kingmoor		6/65	2D	Banbury
7/65	8H	Birkenhead: *Wdn 11/67*		7/65	1H	Northampton: *Wdn*
92024	15A	Wellingborough: 15B				*9/65*
		9/63		**92034**	34E	New England
1/64	15C	Kettering		1/59	36C	Frodingham
5/64	12A	Kingmoor		4/59	34E	New England

6/63	40B	Immingham: *Wdn 5/64*	**92047**	6F	Bidston
92035	34E	New England	1/63	6C	Birkenhead: 8H 9/63:
1/59	36C	Frodingham			*Wdn 11/67*
4/59	34E	New England	**92048**	21A	Saltley
6/63	40B	Immingham: *Wdn 2/66*	11/59	17C	Rowsley: 16J 9/63
92036	34E	New England	4/64	16A	Toton
9/62	36A	Doncaster	3/65	8B	Warrington
6/63	40E	Colwick	5/65	8H	Birkenhead: *Wdn 9/67*
11/63	34E	New England	**92049**	21A	Saltley
1/64	40E	Colwick	11/59	17C	Rowsley: 16J 9/63
6/64	34E	New England: *Wdn*	4/64	16A	Toton
		12/64	3/65	8B	Warrington
92037	34E	New England	2/66	8H	Birkenhead: *Wdn 11/67*
6/63	40B	Immingham: *Wdn 2/65*	**92050**	18A	Toton
92038	34E	New England	11/59	17C	Rowsley: 16J 9/63
6/63	40B	Immingham	4/64	16E	Kirkby-in-Ashfield
6/64	34E	New England	10/64	9D	Newton Heath
1/65	41J	Langwith: *Wdn 4/65*	2/66	8C	Speke Jct
92039	34E	New England	8/67	8B	Warrington: *Wdn 9/67*
2/59	40B	Immingham	**92051**	21A	Saltley
9/61	34E	New England	11/59	17C	Rowsley: 16J 9/63
9/62	36A	Doncaster	4/64	16E	Kirkby-in-Ashfield
6/63	40E	Colwick	10/64	9D	Newton Heath
11/63	40B	Immingham	11/65	12A	Kingmoor: *Wdn 10/67*
6/64	36A	Doncaster	**92052**	15A	Wellingborough
6/65	41J	Langwith: *Wdn 10/65*	5/61	21A	Saltley
92040	34E	New England	6/61	18A	Toton
6/63	40E	Colwick	10/61	16D	Annesley
9/64	41E	Barrow Hill	3/62	17C	Rowsley
1/65	41J	Langwith: *Wdn 8/65*	4/62	18A	Toton
92041	34E	New England	7/63	17C	Rowsley
6/63	40E	Colwick	7/63	18A	Toton
9/64	41E	Barrow Hill	8/63	15A	Wellingborough: 15B
1/65	41J	Langwith: *Wdn 8/65*			9/63
92042	34E	New England	10/63	16E	Kirkby-in-Ashfield
6/63	40E	Colwick	10/64	9D	Newton Heath
1/65	41J	Langwith	6/67	12A	Kingmoor: *Wdn 8/67*
11/65	40E	Colwick: *Wdn 12/65*	**92053**	21A	Saltley
92043	16D	Annesley: 16B 9/63	11/59	15A	Wellingborough
12/65	16F	Burton	9/62	18A	Toton: 16A 9/63
1/66	12A	Kingmoor: *Wdn 7/66*	3/65	8B	Warrington: *Wdn 2/66*
92044	34E	New England	**92054**	15A	Wellingborough
9/62	36A	Doncaster	9/62	15C	Leicester (Midland)
6/63	40E	Colwick	12/62	18B	Westhouses: 16G 9/63
9/64	41E	Barrow Hill	6/64	8C	Speke Jct: *Wdn 5/68*
1/65	41J	Langwith: *Wdn 4/65*	**92055**	15A	Wellingborough
92045	6F	Bidston	9/60	18A	Toton
1/63	6C	Birkenhead: 8H 9/63:	3/61	6F	Bidston
		Wdn 9/67	4/61	18A	Toton
92046	6F	Bidston	3/62	17C	Rowsley
1/63	6C	Birkenhead: 8H 9/63:	4/62	18A	Toton
		Wdn 10/67	7/62	15A	Wellingborough

9/62	18A	Toton: 16A 9/63
3/65	8B	Warrington
10/67	8C	Speke Jct: *Wdn 12/67*
92056	15A	Wellingborough
9/60	18A	Toton
3/62	21A	Saltley
5/62	15A	Wellingborough
9/62	17C	Rowsley: 16J 9/63
4/64	16E	Kirkby-in-Ashfield
10/64	9D	Newton Heath
8/66	12A	Kingmoor: *Wdn 11/67*
92057	18A	Toton
1/60	18B	Westhouses
5/60	14A	Cricklewood
10/61	16D	Annesley
4/63	18A	Toton: 16A 9/63
10/63	2E	Saltley
4/64	8H	Birkenhead: *Wdn 10/65*
92058	15A	Wellingborough
9/60	18A	Toton
7/62	18B	Westhouses: 16G 9/63
4/64	15A	Leicester (Midland)
3/65	8B	Warrington
6/67	8C	Speke Jct
8/67	12A	Kingmoor: *Wdn 11/67*
92059	15A	Wellingborough
9/60	18A	Toton: 16A 9/63
3/65	8B	Warrington
5/65	8H	Birkenhead: *Wdn 9/66*
92060	52H	Tyne Dock: *Wdn 10/66*
92061	52H	Tyne Dock: *Wdn 9/66*
92062	52H	Tyne Dock: *Wdn 6/66*
92063	52H	Tyne Dock: *Wdn 11/66*
92064	52H	Tyne Dock: *Wdn 11/66*
92065	52H	Tyne Dock
11/66	56A	Wakefield: *Wdn 4/67*
92066	52H	Tyne Dock: *Wdn 5/65*
92067	16D	Annesley: 16B 9/63
6/65	2D	Banbury
10/66	12A	Kingmoor: *Wdn 11/66*
92068	16D	Annesley: 16B 9/63
12/65	16C	Derby: *Wdn 1/66*
92069	16D	Annesley: 16B 9/63
5/65	8H	Birkenhead
11/67	8C	Speke Jct: *Wdn 5/68*
92070	16D	Annesley
4/60	21A	Saltley
9/60	18A	Toton
6/62	18B	Westhouses
3/63	15A	Wellingborough
5/63	15C	Leicester (Midland): 15A 9/63
3/65	8B	Warrington
5/65	8H	Birkenhead: *Wdn 11/67*
92071	16D	Annesley: 16B 9/63
7/65	9D	Newton Heath
11/65	12A	Kingmoor: *Wdn 11/67*
92072	16D	Annesley: 16B 9/63
7/65	16E	Kirkby-in-Ashfield: *Wdn 1/66*
92073	16D	Annesley: 16B 9/63
6/65	2D	Banbury
9/66	8H	Birkenhead: *Wdn 11/67*
92074	16D	Annesley: 16B 9/63
6/65	2D	Banbury
1/66	2E	Saltley
5/66	6C	Croes Newydd
12/66	12A	Kingmoor: *Wdn 4/67*
92075	16D	Annesley
4/63	18A	Toton: 16A 9/63
10/63	16B	Annesley
7/65	16E	Kirkby-in-Ashfield
4/66	12A	Kingmoor: *Wdn 9/66*
92076	16D	Annesley: 16B 9/63
10/63	16J	Rowsley
4/64	16E	Kirkby-in-Ashfield
10/64	9D	Newton Heath
1/65	12A	Kingmoor: *Wdn 2/67*
92077	18A	Toton
8/63	15A	Wellingborough: 15B 9/63
10/63	16E	Kirkby-in-Ashfield
6/64	9D	Newton Heath
4/67	10A	Carnforth: *Wdn 6/68*
92078	18A	Toton: 16A 9/63
3/65	8B	Warrington: *Wdn 5/67*
92079	85F	Bromsgrove: 85D 1/61
10/63	8H	Birkenhead: *Wdn 11/67*
92080	15A	Wellingborough
8/63	15B	Kettering: 15C 9/63
6/64	9D	Newton Heath
8/66	12A	Kingmoor: *Wdn 5/67*
92081	16D	Annesley
4/59	18A	Toton
11/59	15A	Wellingborough
8/63	15B	Kettering: 15C 9/63
6/64	9D	Newton Heath: *Wdn 2/66*
92082	15A	Wellingborough
1/62	18A	Toton
3/62	15A	Wellingborough
2/63	16D	Annesley
3/63	21A	Saltley: 2E 9/63
11/63	8H	Birkenhead: *Wdn 11/67*

92083	15A	Wellingborough	7/65	16E	Kirkby-in-Ashfield
11/60	16D	Annesley	1/66	12A	Kingmoor: *Wdn 9/67*
2/61	15A	Wellingborough	**92094**	18A	Toton
2/63	16D	Annesley	4/59	16D	Annesley: 16B 9/63
3/63	15A	Wellingborough: 15B	5/65	8H	Birkenhead
		9/63	11/67	8C	Speke Jct: *Wdn 5/68*
1/64	15C	Kettering	**92095**	16D	Annesley: 16B 9/63
10/64	15A	Leicester (Midland)	7/65	16E	Kirkby-in-Ashfield
1/65	16B	Annesley	5/66	8B	Warrington: *Wdn 10/66*
5/65	8H	Birkenhead: *Wdn 2/67*	**92096**	16D	Annesley: 16B 9/63
92084	15A	Wellingborough: 15B	12/65	16C	Derby
		9/63	1/66	12A	Kingmoor: *Wdn 2/67*
1/64	15C	Kettering	**92097**	52H	Tyne Dock: *Wdn 10/66*
9/64	8C	Speke Jct	**92098**	52H	Tyne Dock: *Wdn 7/66*
1/65	8H	Birkenhead: *Wdn 11/67*	**92099**	52H	Tyne Dock: *Wdn 9/66*
92085	15A	Wellingborough	**92100**	15C	Leicester (Midland)
12/60	15B	Kettering	12/59	18A	Toton
10/62	21A	Saltley: 2E 9/63	1/60	18B	Westhouses
11/63	2A	Tyseley	3/63	15A	Wellingborough
9/64	1A	Willesden	5/63	15C	Leicester (Midland):
12/64	8H	Birkenhead: *Wdn 12/66*			15A 9/63
92086	18A	Toton	4/65	8H	Birkenhead: *Wdn 5/67*
3/62	15A	Wellingborough: 15B	**92101**	15C	Leicester (Midland)
		9/63	1/60	15A	Wellingborough
1/64	15C	Kettering	4/60	15C	Leicester (Midland):
10/64	15A	Leicester (Midland)			15A 9/63
3/65	8B	Warrington	4/65	8H	Birkenhead: *Wdn 10/67*
6/65	8H	Birkenhead: *Wdn 11/67*	**92102**	15C	Leicester (Midland):
92087	16D	Annesley: 16B 9/63			15A 9/63
6/65	2D	Banbury	4/65	8H	Birkenhead: *Wdn 11/67*
7/65	1H	Northampton	**92103**	15C	Leicester (Midland):
9/65	2A	Tyseley			15A 9/63
11/66	10A	Carnforth *Wdn 2/67*	4/65	8H	Birkenhead: *Wdn 5/67*
92088	16D	Annesley	**92104**	15C	Leicester (Midland)
5/63	18A	Toton	4/62	18B	Westhouses: 16G 9/63
8/63	16D	Annesley: 16B 9/63	12/64	8C	Speke Jct
6/65	16A	Toton	5/64	8H	Birkenhead: *Wdn 2/67*
7/65	8H	Birkenhead	**92105**	15B	Kettering
11/67	10A	Carnforth: *Wdn : 4/68*	3/63	15A	Wellingborough: 15B
92089	16D	Annesley			9/63
2/63	15C	Leicester (Midland):	1/64	15C	Kettering
		15A 9/63	10/64	15A	Leicester (Midland)
9/64	8C	Speke Jct	5/65	8H	Birkenhead: *Wdn 1/67*
1/65	8H	Birkenhead: *Wdn 2/67*	**92106**	15B	Kettering: 15C 9/63
92090	16D	Annesley: 16B 9/63	10/64	15C	Leicester (Midland)
5/65	8H	Birkenhead: *Wdn 5/67*	4/65	8H	Birkenhead: *Wdn 7/67*
92091	16D	Annesley: 16B 9/63	**92107**	15A	Wellingborough
7/65	8C	Speke Jct	12/61	21A	Saltley: 2E 9/63
5/68	10A	Carnforth: *Wdn 5/68*	11/63	2D	Banbury
92092	16D	Annesley: 16B 9/63	9/64	1A	Willesden
5/65	8H	Birkenhead: *Wdn 10/66*	12/64	8H	Birkenhead: *Wdn 2/67*
92093	16D	Annesley: 16B 9/63	**92108**	14A	Cricklewood

4/59	15A	Wellingborough
3/60	15C	Leicester (Midland)
2/62	15A	Wellingborough
9/62	15C	Leicester (Midland): 15A 9/63
4/65	8H	Birkenhead: *Wdn 11/67*
92109	15C	Leicester (Midland): 15A 9/63
11/63	16B	Annesley
4/64	15A	Leicester (Midland)
4/65	8H	Birkenhead: *Wdn 11/67*
92110	14A	Cricklewood
4/59	15A	Wellingborough
3/60	15C	Leicester (Midland)
7/62	15A	Wellingborough
9/62	15C	Leicester (Midland): 15A 9/63
11/63	16E	Kirkby-in-Ashfield
9/64	9D	Newton Heath
5/65	12A	Kingmoor: *Wdn 12/67*
92111	14A	Cricklewood
4/59	15A	Wellingborough
3/60	15C	Leicester (Midland): 15A 9/63
11/63	16E	Kirkby-in-Ashfield
9/64	8C	Speke Jct
1/65	8H	Birkenhead: *Wdn 10/67*
92112	14A	Cricklewood
4/59	15A	Wellingborough
3/60	15C	Leicester (Midland): 15A 9/63
4/65	8H	Birkenhead: *Wdn 11/67*
92113	18B	Westhouses
6/60	18A	Toton
3/61	6F	Bidston
4/61	18A	Toton
4/62	17C	Rowsley: 16J 9/63
2/64	15B	Wellingborough
3/64	16A	Toton
10/64	16B	Annesley
7/65	16G	Westhouses
8/65	8H	Birkenhead: *Wdn 10/67*
92114	18B	Westhouses
6/60	18A	Toton
4/62	17C	Rowsley: 16J 9/63
4/64	16E	Kirkby-in-Ashfield
9/64	9D	Newton Heath
5/65	12A	Kingmoor: *Wdn 7/67*
92115	18B	Westhouses: 16G 9/63
6/64	8C	Speke Jct: *Wdn 2/66*
92116	18B	Westhouses
3/63	15A	Wellingborough: 15B 9/63
2/64	15C	Kettering
3/65	8B	Warrington: *Wdn 11/66*
92117	18B	Westhouses
10/61	16D	Annesley
3/62	17C	Rowsley
4/62	15A	Wellingborough: 15B 9/63
2/64	15C	Kettering
10/64	8C	Speke Jct: *Wdn 12/67*
92118	18B	Westhouses
11/59	15A	Wellingborough
1/62	21A	Saltley: 2E 9/63
7/64	2D	Banbury
11/64	2A	Tyseley
11/66	10A	Carnforth: *Wdn 5/68*
92119	15C	Leicester (Midland)
1/59	16A	Nottingham
4/59	15C	Leicester (Midland): 15A 9/63
3/65	8B	Warrington
6/67	8C	Speke Jct
8/67	12A	Kingmoor: *Wdn 9/67*
92120	21A	Saltley
11/59	15A	Wellingborough
3/60	15C	Leicester (Midland)
11/60	16D	Annesley
10/61	15C	Leicester (Midland): 15A 9/63
4/65	8H	Birkenhead: *Wdn 7/67*
92121	15C	Leicester (Midland): 15A 9/63
4/65	8H	Birkenhead: *Wdn 7/67*
92122	15A	Wellingborough
3/60	15C	Leicester (Midland)
7/62	15A	Wellingborough
9/62	15C	Leicester (Midland): 15A 9/63
4/65	8H	Birkenhead: *Wdn 11/67*
92123	15A	Wellingborough
3/60	15C	Leicester (Midland):15A 9/63
4/65	8H	Birkenhead: *Wdn 10/67*
92124	15A	Wellingborough: 15B 9/63
2/64	15C	Kettering
3/65	8B	Warrington: *Wdn 12/66*
92125	15A	Wellingborough
12/60	15B	Kettering: 15C 9/63
11/63	2E	Saltley
5/66	6C	Croes Newydd

12/66	12A	Kingmoor: *Wdn 12/67*		8/66	6C	Croes Newydd
92126	15A	Wellingborough: 15B		12/66	12A	Kingmoor: *Wdn 9/67*
		9/63		**92138**	21A	Saltley: 2E 9/63
2/64	15C	Kettering		8/66	8C	Speke Jct: *Wdn 7/67*
3/65	8B	Warrington: *Wdn 8/67*		**92139**	21A	Saltley: 2E 9/63
92127	15A	Wellingborough		12/66	8C	Speke Jct
7/63	17C	Rowsley: 16J 9/63		8/67	12A	Kingmoor: *Wdn 9/67*
4/64	16E	Kirkby-in-Ashfield		**92140**	34E	New England
10/64	8C	Speke Jct		1/65	41J	Langwith: *Wdn 4/65*
1/65	8H	Birkenhead: *Wdn 8/67*		**92141**	34E	New England
92128	15C	Leicester (Midland)		9/62	36A	Doncaster
6/62	21A	Saltley: 2E 9/63		3/63	34E	New England
7/64	2D	Banbury		1/65	41J	Langwith
9/66	2E	Saltley		11/65	40E	Colwick: *Wdn 12/65*
11/66	10A	Carnforth: *Wdn 11/67*		**92142**	34E	New England: *Wdn 2/65*
92129	18A	Toton		**92143**	34E	New England: *Wdn 2/65*
8/59	15B	Kettering		**92144**	34E	New England
2/60	18A	Toton		9/62	40B	Immingham
5/60	14A	Cricklewood		3/63	34E	New England
10/61	16D	Annesley		1/65	41J	Langwith
12/61	21A	Saltley: 2E 9/63		11/65	40E	Colwick: *Wdn 12/65*
7/64	2D	Banbury		**92145**	34E	New England
9/66	12A	Kingmoor: *Wdn 7/67*		1/65	41J	Langwith
92130	18A	Toton: 16A 9/63		11/65	40E	Colwick
5/64	12A	Kingmoor: *Wdn 5/66*		12/65	40B	Immingham: *Wdn 2/66*
92131	18A	Toton		**92146**	34E	New England
1/60	18B	Westhouses: 16G 9/63		1/65	41J	Langwith
12/64	8C	Speke Jct		11/65	40E	Colwick
5/65	8H	Birkenhead: *Wdn 9/67*		12/65	36A	Doncaster: *Wdn 4/66*
92132	15A	Wellingborough: 15B		**92147**	34E	New England
		9/63		3/63	40B	Immingham: *Wdn 4/65*
2/64	15C	Kettering		**92148**	34E	New England
3/64	16B	Annesley		6/60	40B	Immingham
6/65	2D	Banbury		9/61	34E	New England
8/65	1H	Northampton		3/63	36A	Doncaster
9/65	2D	Banbury		6/63	40E	Colwick
8/66	8B	Warrington		9/64	41E	Barrow Hill
10/67	12A	Kingmoor: *Wdn 10/67*		1/65	41J	Langwith
92133	15A	Wellingborough: 15B		11/65	40E	Colwick: *Wdn 12/65*
		9/63		**92149**	34E	New England
2/64	15A	Leicester (Midland)		1/65	41J	Langwith: *Wdn 6/65*
4/65	8H	Birkenhead: *Wdn 7/67*		**92150**	21A	Saltley: 2E 9/63
92134	15A	Wellingborough: 15B		5/64	2A	Tyseley
		9/63		6/64	2E	Saltley
2/64	15A	Leicester (Midland)		10/66	56A	Wakefield: *Wdn 4/67*
4/65	8H	Birkenhead: *Wdn 12/66*		**92151**	21A	Saltley: 2E 9/63
92135	21A	Saltley: 2E 9/63		11/66	8H	Birkenhead: *Wdn 4/67*
5/66	6C	Croes Newydd		**92152**	21A	Saltley: 2E 9/63
10/66	56A	Wakefield: *Wdn 6/67*		11/66	8H	Birkenhead: *Wdn 11/67*
92136	21A	Saltley: 2E 9.63		**92153**	18A	Toton: 16A 9/63
	2E	Saltley: *Wdn 10/66*		10/63	16G	Westhouses
92137	21A	Saltley: 2E 9/63		6/65	8C	Speke Jct: *Wdn 1/68*

92154	15A	Wellingborough: 15B 9/63		12/62	6F	Bidston
2/64	16B	Annesley		2/63	6C	Birkenhead: 8H 9/63
7/65	16E	Kirkby-in-Ashfield		11/67	10A	Carnforth: *Wdn 6/68*
7/65	8C	Speke Jct: *Wdn 7/67*		**92168**	36A	Doncaster: *Wdn 6/65*
92155	21A	Saltley: 2E 9/63		**92169**	36A	Doncaster: *Wdn 5/64*
8/66	8C	Speke Jct: *Wdn 11/66*		**92170**	36A	Doncaster: *Wdn 5/64*
92156	18A	Toton: 16A 9/63		**92171**	36A	Doncaster
3/65	8B	Warrington: *Wdn 7/67*		11/63	34E	New England: *Wdn 5/64*
92157	21A	Saltley: 2E 9/63		**92172**	36A	Doncaster: *Wdn 4/66*
4/64	8H	Birkenhead: *Wdn 8/67*		**92173**	36A	Doncaster
92158	18A	Toton: 16A 9/63		6/65	41J	Langwith
10/63	16G	Westhouses		11/65	40E	Colwick
6/64	8C	Speke Jct: *Wdn 7/66*		12/65	36A	Doncaster: *Wdn 3/66*
92159	15A	Wellingborough: 15B 9/63		**92174**	36A	Doncaster: *Wdn 12/65*
				92175	36A	Doncaster: *Wdn 5/64*
2/64	16J	Rowsley		**92176**	36A	Doncaster
4/64	16E	Kirkby-in-Ashfield		11/63	34E	New England: *Wdn 5/64*
9/64	9D	Newton Heath		**92177**	36A	Doncaster: *Wdn 5/64*
5/65	8H	Birkenhead: *Wdn 7/67*		**92178**	34E	New England
92160	15B	Kettering: 15C 9/63		1/65	41J	Langwith: *Wdn 10/65*
3/65	8B	Warrington		**92179**	34E	New England
2/66	8H	Birkenhead		1/65	41J	Langwith
11/67	8C	Speke Jct		11/65	40E	Colwick: *Wdn 11/65*
5/68	10A	Carnforth: *Wdn 6/68*		**92180**	34E	New England
92161	26A	Newton Heath: 9D 9/63		1/65	41J	Langwith: *Wdn 4/65*
5/65	12A	Kingmoor: *Wdn 12/66*		**92181**	34E	New England: *Wdn 2/65*
92162	26A	Newton Heath: 9D 9/63		**92182**	34E	New England
5/65	8H	Birkenhead: *Wdn 11/67*		1/65	41J	Langwith
92163	15B	Kettering		11/65	40E	Colwick
6/59	15C	Leicester (Midland)		12/65	36A	Doncaster: *Wdn 4/66*
11/59	15B	Kettering: 15C 9/63		**92183**	34E	New England
3/65	8B	Warrington		6/63	40E	Colwick
6/65	8H	Birkenhead: *Wdn 11/67*		1/65	36A	Doncaster: *Wdn 3/66*
92164	15B	Kettering		**92184**	34E	New England
6/62	21A	Saltley: 2E 9/63: *Wdn 7/66*		1/59	36C	Frodingham
				6/59	34E	New England
92165	21A	Saltley		6/63	40E	Colwick
6/62	6F	Bidston		11/63	34E	New England
2/63	6C	Birkenhead: 8H 9/63		1/64	40B	Immingham: *Wdn 2/65*
11/67	8C	Speke Jct: *Wdn 3/68*		**92185**	34E	New England
92166	RTS	Rugby Testing Station		6/63	40E	Colwick
5/59	21A	Saltley		11/63	34E	New England
8/59	86C	Canton		1/64	40B	Immingham: *Wdn 2/65*
9/59	86A	Newport (Ebbw Jct)		**92186**	34E	New England
2/60	21A	Saltley		6/63	40E	Colwick
6/62	6F	Bidston		1/65	36A	Doncaster
2/63	6C	Birkenhead: 8H 9/63		6/65	41J	Langwith: *Wdn 8/65*
	8H	Birkenhead: *Wdn 11/67*		**92187**	34E	New England
92167	21A	Saltley		6/63	40E	Colwick: *Wdn 2/65*
5/62	52H	Tyne Dock		**92188**	34E	New England
10/62	21A	Saltley		6/63	40E	Colwick: *Wdn 2/65*
				92189	36A	Doncaster

1/59	36C	Frodingham
4/59	36A	Doncaster
9/63	40E	Colwick
1/65	41J	Langwith
11/65	40E	Colwick: *Wdn 12/65*
92190	36A	Doncaster
1/59	36C	Frodingham
4/59	36A	Doncaster
9/63	40E	Colwick
6/64	36A	Doncaster: *Wdn 10/65*
92191	36A	Doncaster
9/63	40E	Colwick
1/65	41J	Langwith
11/65	40E	Colwick: *Wdn 12/65*
92192	36A	Doncaster
9/63	40E	Colwick
11/63	36C	Frodingham: *Wdn 2/65*
92193	36A	Doncaster
2/59	40B	Immingham: *Wdn 6/65*
92194	36A	Doncaster
2/59	40B	Immingham: *Wdn 12/65*
92195	36A	Doncaster
2/59	40B	Immingham
6/64	34E	New England
1/65	41J	Langwith: *Wdn 5/65*
92196	36A	Doncaster
2/59	40B	Immingham: *Wdn 12/64*
92197	36A	Doncaster
2/59	36C	Frodingham
4/59	36A	Doncaster
9/60	40B	Immingham: *Wdn 9/65*
92198	36A	Doncaster
2/59	36C	Frodingham
6/59	36A	Doncaster
9/63	40E	Colwick
11/63	36C	Frodingham: *Wdn 8/64*
92199	36A	Doncaster
9/63	40E	Colwick
11/63	36C	Frodingham: *Wdn 8/64*
92200	36A	Doncaster
9/63	40B	Immingham
6/64	36A	Doncaster
6/65	41J	Langwith: *Wdn 10/65*
92201	36A	Doncaster
9/63	40B	Immingham
6/64	36A	Doncaster: *Wdn 3/66*
92202	36A	Doncaster
4/59	40B	Immingham: *Wdn 12/65*
92203		*(New 4/59)*
	82B	St Phillips Marsh
10/60	81A	Old Oak Common
3/63	84C	Banbury: 2D 9/63

9/66	8H	Birkenhead: *Wdn 11/67*
92204		*(New 4/59)*
	82B	St Phillips Marsh
10/60	81C	Southall
11/60	81A	Old Oak Common
3/63	84C	Banbury: 2D 9/63
10/63	2A	Tyseley
8/66	8C	Speke Jct: *Wdn 12/67*
92205		*(New 5/59)*
	82B	St Phillips Marsh
10/60	82D	Westbury
1/61	71A	Eastleigh
6/63	70B	Feltham
9/63	50A	York
10/66	56A	Wakefield: *Wdn 6/67*
92206		*(New 5/59)*
	82B	St Phillips Marsh
10/60	82D	Westbury
1/61	71A	Eastleigh
6/63	70B	Feltham
9/63	50A	York
10/66	56A	Wakefield: *Wdn 5/67*
92207		*(New 6/59)*
	82B	St Phillips Marsh
2/60	81C	Southall
11/64	86B	Newport (Ebbw Jct): *Wdn 12/64*
92208		*(New 6/59)*
	83D	Laira (Plymouth)
3/60	81C	Southall
11/61	88A	Canton
9/62	88L	Cardiff East Dock: 88A 9/63
10/63	9D	Newton Heath
6/64	12A	Kingmoor: *Wdn 10/67*
92209		*(New 6/59)*
	83D	Laira (Plymouth)
8/59	86C	Canton: 88A 10/60
5/61	86A	Newport (Ebbw Jct): 86B 9/63
10/63	88A	Cardiff East Dock
6/65	81C	Southall
7/65	88A	Cardiff East Dock
10/65	82E	Bristol (Barrow Rd)
11/65	82F	Bath (Green Park): *Wdn 12/65*
92210		*(New 8/59)*
	86C	Canton
9/60	82E	Bristol (Barrow Rd)
7/62	82F	Bath (Green Park)
8/62	88A	Canton

9/62	88L	Cardiff East Dock: 88A
		9/63
12/63	81C	Southall
6/64	86B	Newport (Ebbw Jct):
		Wdn 11/64
92211	*(New 9/59)*	
	81A	Old Oak Common
6/61	82D	Westbury
8/61	71A	Eastleigh
6/63	70B	Feltham
9/63	50A	York
10/66	56A	Wakefield: *Wdn 5/67*
92212	*(New 9/59)*	
	84C	Banbury
6/61	82F	Bath (Green Park)
9/61	86A	Newport (Ebbw Jct)
7/62	84E	Tyseley: 2A 9/63
11/66	10A	Carnforth: *Wdn 1/68*
92213	*(New 10/59)*	
	82B	St Phillips Marsh
12/59	84C	Banbury: 2D 9/63
10/66	12A	Kingmoor: *Wdn 11/66*
92214	*(New 10/59)*	
	86C	Canton
11/59	84C	Banbury
11/61	86A	Newport (Ebbw Jct):
		86B 9/63
5/64	82F	Bath (Green Park)
6/64	86B	Newport (Ebbw Jct)
7/64	86E	Severn Tunnel Jct: *Wdn*
		9/65
92215	*(New 11/59)*	
	84C	Banbury: 2D 9/63
10/63	2A	Tyseley
10/66	56A	Wakefield: *Wdn 6/67*
92216	*(New 12/59)*	
	86C	Canton: 88A 10/60
9/62	88L	Cardiff East Dock: 88A
		9/63
10/63	87A	Neath
9/64	81C	Southall
9/65	86E	Severn Tunnel Jct: *Wdn*
		10/65
92217	*(New 12/59)*	
	86C	Canton
1/60	82B	St Phillips Marsh
3/63	84C	Banbury: 2D 9/63
10/63	2A	Tyseley: *Wdn 7/66*
92218	*(New 1/60)*	
	82B	St Phillips Marsh
3/63	84C	Banbury: 2D 9/63
10/66	8B	Warrington

3/67	8C	Speke Jct
8/67	12A	Kingmoor
1/68	8C	Speke Jct: *Wdn 5/68*
92219	*(New 1/60)*	
	82B	St Phillips Marsh
2/60	86C	Canton: 88A 10/60
9/62	88L	Cardiff East Dock: 88A
		9/63: *Wdn 9/65*
92220	*(New 3/60)*	
	86C	Canton: 88A 10/60
8/62	82F	Bath (Green Park)
10/62	81A	Old Oak Common
11/62	81F	Oxford
8/63	82F	Bath (Green Park)
10/63	88A	Cardiff East Dock: *Wdn*
		3/65
92221	84C	Banbury
6/59	83D	Laira (Plymouth)
3/60	84C	Banbury
6/60	83D	Laira (Plymouth)
9/60	82D	Westbury
10/60	84C	Banbury
11/60	82E	Bristol (Barrow Rd)
9/63	50A	York: *Wdn 5/65*
92222	84C	Banbury
6/59	83D	Laira (Plymouth)
3/59	84C	Banbury
6/60	83D	Laira (Plymouth)
10/60	86A	Newport (Ebbw Jct):
		86B 9/63
11/63	87A	Neath
9/64	81C	Southall: *Wdn 3/65*
92223	84C	Banbury
6/59	83D	Laira (Plymouth)
3/60	84C	Banbury
6/60	83D	Laira (Plymouth)
9/60	82D	Westbury
3/61	86A	Newport (Ebbw Jct):
		86B 9/63
10/63	85D	Bromsgrove
3/64	2A	Tyseley
11/66	2E	Saltley
12/66	12A	Kingmoor
1/68	10A	Carnforth: *Wdn 4/68*
92224	84C	Banbury
6/59	83D	Laira (Plymouth)
7/60	81C	Southall
11/62	81F	Oxford
9/63	82E	Bristol (Barrow Rd)
10/63	88A	Cardiff East Dock
11/64	2D	Banbury
8/66	8B	Warrington: *Wdn 9/67*

92225	84C	Banbury
6/59	83D	Laira (Plymouth)
3/60	86A	Newport (Ebbw Jct):
		86B 9/63
10/63	87A	Neath
6/64	86B	Newport (Ebbw Jct):
		Wdn 7/65
92226	84C	Banbury
7/60	81C	Southall
10/60	86A	Newport (Ebbw Jct)
10/61	81A	Old Oak Common
11/62	86A	Newport (Ebbw Jct):
		86B 9/63
5/64	82F	Bath (Green Park)
6/64	86B	Newport (Ebbw Jct)
7/64	86E	Severn Tunnel Jct
11/64	86B	Newport (Ebbw Jct)
6/65	86E	Severn Tunnel Jct: *Wdn*
		9/65
92227	84C	Banbury
1/61	88A	Canton
8/62	84C	Banbury: 2D 9/63
10/66	8B	Warrington
3/67	8C	Speke Jct: *Wdn 11/67*
92228	84C	Banbury: 2D 9/63
10/66	8C	Speke Jct: *Wdn 1/67*
92229	81A	Old Oak Common
1/60	86A	Newport (Ebbw Jct):
		86A 9/63
11/63	81C	Southall
6/64	86B	Newport (Ebbw Jct):
		Wdn 11/64
92230	81A	Old Oak Common
1/60	86A	Newport (Ebbw Jct)
9/62	81A	Old Oak Common
10/62	86A	Newport (Ebbw Jct):
		86B 9/63
1/64	85D	Bromsgrove
7/64	86B	Newport (Ebbw Jct)
10/65	85B	Gloucester (Horton Rd):
		Wdn 12/65
92231	86G	Pontypool Rd
1/59	86E	Severn Tunnel Jct
2/59	86C	Canton
10/59	86A	Newport (Ebbw Jct)
2/60	86C	Canton
10/60	82E	Bristol (Barrow Rd)
1/61	71A	Eastleigh
6/63	70B	Feltham
9/63	50A	York: *Wdn 11/66*
92232	86G	Pontypool Rd
1/59	86E	Severn Tunnel Jct

2/59	86C	Canton
9/59	84C	Banbury
9/62	88L	Cardiff East Dock: 88A
		9/63: *Wdn 12/64*
92233	86G	Pontypool Rd
1/59	86E	Severn Tunnel Jct
2/59	86C	Canton
9/59	84C	Banbury
1/61	88A	Canton
7/62	82F	Bath (Green Park)
9/62	86A	Newport (Ebbw Jct):
		86B 9/63
10/63	9D	Newton Heath
6/64	12A	Kingmoor
1/68	8C	Speke Jct: *Wdn 2/68*
92234	86G	Pontypool Rd
1/59	86E	Severn Tunnel Jct
2/59	86C	Canton
9/59	84C	Banbury
9/61	85D	Bromsgrove
11/61	84C	Banbury
8/62	84E	Tyseley: 2A 9/63
9/64	2D	Banbury
10/66	2E	Saltley
12/66	8H	Birkenhead: *Wdn 11/67*
92235	86G	Pontypool Rd
1/59	86E	Severn Tunnel Jct
2/59	86C	Canton
9/59	86A	Newport (Ebbw Jct):
		86B 9/63
10/65	82E	Bristol (Barrow Rd):
		Wdn 11/65
92236	86C	Canton: 88A 10/60
9/62	88L	Cardiff East Dock: 88A
		9/63
11/64	86E	Severn Tunnel Jct: *Wdn*
		3/65
92237	86C	Canton: 88A 10/60
9/62	88L	Cardiff East Dock: 88A
		9/63
11/64	86E	Severn Tunnel Jct
2/65	86B	Newport (Ebbw Jct):
		Wdn 9/65
92238	81A	Old Oak Common
9/60	81C	Southall
12/61	86A	Newport (Ebbw Jct):
		86B 9/63
10/63	82E	Bristol (Barrow Rd)
2/65	85B	Gloucester (Horton Rd)
7/65	86E	Severn Tunnel Jct: *Wdn*
		9/65
92239	81A	Old Oak Common

Above:
BR Standard Class 9 2-10-0 No 92012 (12A) runs onto the turntable at Holbeck past 'B1' 4-6-0 No 61306 (56F) on 23 September 1967.
J. A. M. Vaughan

9/60	81C	Southall
7/61	82D	Westbury
8/61	71A	Eastleigh
6/63	70B	Feltham
9/63	50A	York: *Wdn 11/66*
92240	81A	Old Oak Common
9/60	81C	Southall: *Wdn 9/65*
92241	81A	Old Oak Common
10/60	86C	Canton: 88A 10/60
9/62	88L	Cardiff East Dock: 88A 9/63
11/63	81C	Southall: *Wdn 7/65*
92242	86A	Newport (Ebbw Jct): 86B 9/63
11/64	86E	Severn Tunnel Jct: *Wdn 6/65*
92243	86A	Newport (Ebbw Jct)
11/62	81A	Old Oak Common
9/63	88A	Cardiff East Dock
11/64	86E	Severn Tunnel Jct
1/65	88A	Cardiff East Dock
7/65	86B	Newport (Ebbw Jct)
10/65	82E	Bristol (Barrow Rd)
11/65	82F	Bath (Green Park): *Wdn 12/65*
92244	81A	Old Oak Common
10/60	86C	Canton: 88A 10/60
9/62	88L	Cardiff East Dock
10/62	81F	Oxford
11/62	88L	Cardiff East Dock 9/63
7/65	86B	Newport (Ebbw Jct)
10/65	85B	Gloucester (Horton Rd): *Wdn 12/65*
92245	81A	Old Oak Common
10/60	86C	Canton: 88A 10/60

6/62	82F	Bath (Green Park)
9/62	81F	Oxford
10/62	81C	Southall: *Wdn 12/64*
92246	81A	Old Oak Common
10/60	86C	Canton: 88A 10/60
9/62	88L	Cardiff East Dock: 88A 9/63
11/63	81C	Southall
9/65	86E	Severn Tunnel Jct
10/65	85B	Gloucester (Horton Rd): *Wdn 12/65*
92247	81A	Old Oak Common
2/62	88A	Canton
8/62	84C	Banbury: 2D 9/63
9/66	9D	Newton Heath: *Wdn 10/66*
92248	86A	Newport (Ebbw Jct)
9/59	21A	Saltley
9/60	82E	Bristol (Barrow Rd)
1/65	88A	Cardiff East Dock: *Wdn 6/65*
92249	86A	Newport (Ebbw Jct)
6/60	83D	Laira (Plymouth)
10/60	86A	Newport (Ebbw Jct): 86B 9/63
10/63	9D	Newton Heath
6/64	12A	Kingmoor
1/68	8C	Speke Jct: *Wdn 5/68*
92250	84C	Banbury
11/59	86A	Newport (Ebbw Jct): 86B 9/63
11/63	81C	Southall
6/64	86B	Newport (Ebbw Jct)
7/64	86E	Severn Tunnel Jct
10/65	85B	Gloucester (Horton Rd): *Wdn 12/65*

Demise of the BR Standard Class 9 ▬▬▬▬▬▬▬▬ 2-10-0s
Withdrawals
5/64: 92034, 92169/70/71/75/76/77
8/64: 92198/99
11/64: 92210/29
12/64: 92036, 92196, 92207/32/45
2/65: 92037, 92142/43/81/84/85/87/88/92
3/65: 92003, 92220/22/36
4/65: 9238/44, 92140/47/80
5/65: 92066, 92195, 92221

```
 6/65:  92149/68/93, 92242/48
 7/65:  92000, 92225/41
 8/65:  92005/40/41, 92186
 9/65:  92033, 92197,
        92214/19/26/37/38/40
10/65:  92039/57, 92178/90, 92200/16
11/65:  92179, 92235
12/65:  92007/42,
        92141/44/48/74/89/91/94,
        92202/09/30/43/44/46/50
 1/66:  92068/72
 2/66:  92035/53/81, 92115/45
 3/66:  92173/83, 92201
 4/66:  92010, 92146/72/82
 5/66:  92130
 6/66:  92062
 7/66:  92043/98, 92158/64, 92217
 9/66:  92059/61/75/99
10/66:  92013/28/60/92/95/97, 92136,
92247
11/66:  92063/64/67, 92116/55,
        92213/31/39
12/66:  92085, 92124/34/61
 1/67:  92001/31, 92105, 92228
 2/67:  92030/76/83/87/89/96, 92104/07
 4/67:  92006/15/18/32/65/74, 92150/51
 5/67:  92078/80/90, 92100/03, 92206/11
 6/67:  92019, 92135, 92205/15
 7/67:  92106/14/20/21/29/33/38/54/56/59
 8/67:  92027/52, 92126/27/57
 9/67:  92045/48/50/93, 92119/31/37/39,
        92224
10/67:  92008/12/14/16/20/46/51,
        92101/11/13/23/32, 92208
11/67:  92002/11/21/22/23/24/25/26/29/47/49/56/58/70/71/73/79/82/
        84/86,
        92102/08/09/12/22/28/52/62/63/66,
        92203/27/34
12/67:  92017/55, 92110/17/25, 92204
 1/68:  92153, 92212
 2/68:  92233
 3/68:  92004/09, 92165
 4/68:  92088, 92223
 5/68:  92054/69/91/94, 92118, 92218/49
 6/68:  92077, 92160/67
```

British Railways Regional Withdrawals

For the periods

Western Region:	January 1959 to March 1966
Eastern Region:	January 1959 to April 1966
Scottish Region:	January 1959 to May 1967
Southern Region:	January 1959 to July 1967
North Eastern Region:	January 1959 to November 1967
London Midland Region:	January 1959 to August 1968

Withdrawals

Class	Total WR	Total ER	Total ScR	Total SR	Total NER	Total LMR	Total Withdrawals
4-6-2 Cl 8:	–	–	–	–	–	1	1
4-6-2 Cl 7:	–	–	–	–	–	55	55
4-6-2 Cl 6:	–	–	5	–	–	5	10
4-6-0 Cl 5:	21	–	48	40	–	63	172
4-6-0 Cl 4:	10	–	–	12	–	58	80
2-6-0 Cl 4:	–	–	38	42	–	35	115
2-6-0 Cl 3:	–	–	10	1	8	1	20
2-6-0 Cl 2:	6	–	12	–	1	46	65
2-6-4T Cl 4:	12	1	70	52	–	20	155
2-6-2T Cl 3:	16	–	–	23	–	6	45
2-6-2T Cl 2:	–	–	–	–	–	30	30
2-8-0 Cl 8:	8	293	58	–	222	152	733
2-10-0 Cl 8:	–	–	24	–	–	1	25
2-10-0 Cl 9:	29	55	–	–	23	144	251
Regional totals	102	349	265	170	254	617	1,757

Packed with steam, 5B Crewe South on 23 April 1967. Facing (left to right) Class 9 2-10-0 No 92110 and Class 7 4-6-2 Nos 70022 *Tornado* and 70013 *Oliver Cromwell* all of Carlisle Kingmoor awaiting their return north. *D. L. Percival*

Above:
**Class 5MT No 73140 noses out of Patricroft MPD
on 8 June 1967**. *J. A. M. Vaughan*